WITHOUT
REGRET

WITHOUT REGRET

An intriguing insight into life below decks

Leonard Harris

First published by Chatty Goose Publishing

© 2021

Every effort has been made to trace copyright. Any oversight will be rectified in future editions at the earliest opportunity by the publisher.

All rights reserved. No part of this book may be reproduced, sold or utilised in any form or transmitted in any form or by any means, electronic or mechanical, including photocopying, recording or by any information storage and retrieval system, without prior permission in writing from the Publisher.

A CIP catalogue record is available for this book from the British Library.

ISBN 978-1-9162994-4-3

Cover design and typesetting by Lorraine Inglis

Acknowledgements
Shotley postcards included from Royal Navy photographs from 1910 to 1920 (within public domain).

Front Cover: Wikimedia 1937 by Alan C. Green (image is in State Livrary of Victoria).

CONTENTS

PART I: A WAY OF LIFE

1. The New Entry 11
2. Training Begins. 24
3. High days and Holidays 39
4. The Culinary Art 48
5. Jack's Ashore 57
6. Body and Soul 70
7. Crime and Punishment 77
8. Spit, Polish and Flannel. 89
9. Fun and Games. 95
10. Jack at Work 102
11. All God's Creatures. 108
12. The Demon Drink 115
13. Perks and Fiddles 119

PART II: SHIPS & SHIPMATES

14. *Ganges*, *Viscount* and *Marlborough* 129
15. *Pembroke*, *Tetrarch* and *Victory* 148
16. *Pembroke* and *Ramillies* 159
17. *Pembroke*, *Curlew* and *Cyclops*. 177
18. *Pembroke* and *Daring* 187
19. *Pembroke* and *Skipjack* 203
20. *Pembroke* and *Emerald* 210
21. *Pembroke*, *Eskimo*, *Pembroke* and *Vernon* 224
22. *Pembroke* and *Harvester*. 231
23. *Pembroke* and *Aster* 251
24. *Danae*, *Pembroke* and *Cowdray* 271
25. *Pembroke* to Civvy Street 277

Epilogue. 282
Postscript 285
Ships on which Leonard Harris served or was closely associated 288

AUTHOR'S NOTE

The second son of a very strict father, my punishment for a boyhood misdemeanour was the choice of joining either the Army or the Navy. I chose the Navy, and in naming these, my memoirs, *Without Regret*, I leave you the reader, to judge, and form your own opinion, as to whether it was without regret, as a young lad of sixteen that I went off to join the Royal Navy as a boy seaman, or twenty-four years later, as a chief petty officer, that I accepted my discharge.

April 1973,
Cheshunt, Hertfordshire

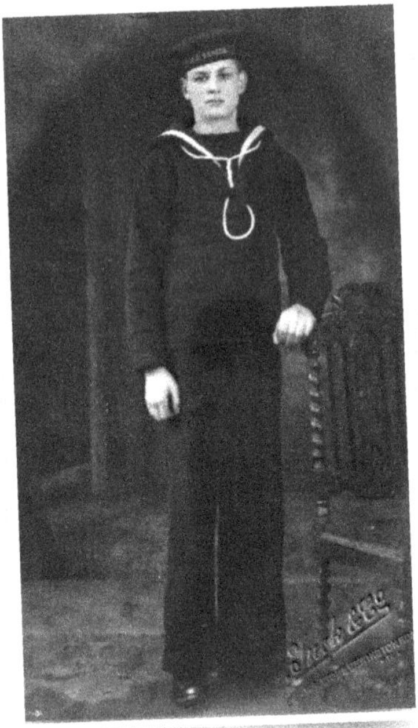

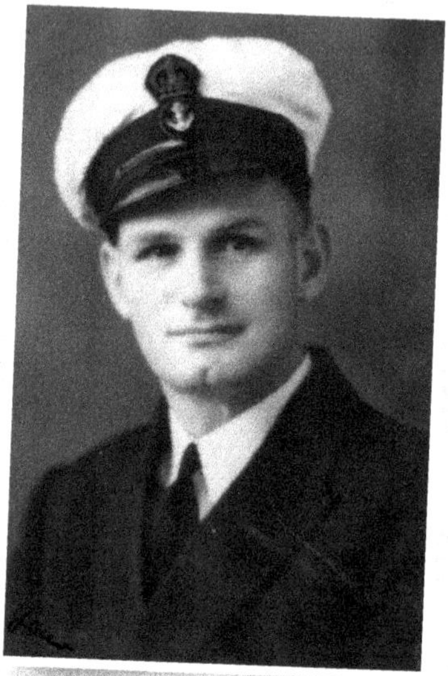

PART I

A WAY OF LIFE

Chapter 1

The New Entry

THE EIGHTH of November nineteen twenty-three, was a typical day for the time of year; damp and cheerless, but to me, everything seemed rosy, for here I was, at the age of sixteen, about to embark upon a new way of life.

A postcard, received a few days earlier, had given me instructions to report at the Admiralty recruiting office at 9 a.m. and now, here I was taking fond farewell of all my family.

First my sister Florrie; dear chubby Florrie. Now twenty-three years of age, for the past six years having had very little life to call her own, she being taken away from service at the age of seventeen to look after the remainder of us when our mother died, seemingly of a broken heart, over the loss of our baby sister.

Then my elder brother; the studious one. Not over strong, he had been a problem to rear in his infancy, and now twenty, went daily to the city, where he was something in insurance. Christened Edwin, our father had never called him anything but Son, and so he became known to us all as Sonny.

To my other sister, Dorothy, I suppose that I was closer than to any of the others. Although she was two and a half years my senior, we were kindred spirits, and if any of the family were on the painful end of a cane, more likely than not it would be one of us two. Only when she became interested in boys as boys did I turn to the company of my younger brother Albert, four years junior to me, he had often tried to emulate my escapades, and for my last three years at home it was we two boys who had contrived to get into scrapes together.

There was also a stepmother and had been for a little over three years, she being the fifth of my father's lady friends in his efforts to bring an end to his widowhood.

Father himself had not been included in my farewells, for he was to accompany me. This was not my wish, but he had been adamant. Whether it was to ensure that I reached my destination, or whether he was regretting his decision, and wished to enjoy my company for as long as possible he did not say; neither did he give any clue to his feelings.

It was a matter of an hour's bus ride to our destination, and on arrival, my father took his leave of me and went over to speak to the recruiting officer, although his reason for doing so did not become apparent until much later in the day.

I was shown into a room very much like a doctor's or dentist's waiting room, and although one usually has to wait for quite some time in either of these, such waits could not possibly compare with the one we had to endure on that day. You will have noticed that I have said had to endure, for there were five others in the room, I, the sixth, being the last of that day's intake.

The preliminaries had all been gone through at an earlier visit, educational test, medical etc., mine having been done at this same establishment, but the others, not living in London, had carried out these tests at recruiting offices nearer to their homes.

Except for leaving, one at a time, to undergo a further medical, and going to the dining room for a mid-day meal, we spent the next seven hours in that room. Our home towns, which were as far apart as Brighton and Newcastle, and the merits of their respective football teams, were the main topics of conversation, and although we found plenty to talk about, not one of us mentioned that which must have been uppermost in our minds, namely, what might the coming weeks hold in store for us.

It was nearing 5 p.m. when a female clerk appeared and paid each of us the sum of four shillings and eight pence for which we had to sign. This formality over, she then demanded that we each return to her two shillings and sixpence, this apparently being payment for the lunch and a bag meal which was to be provided for the journey; the four shillings and eight pence we gathered, being one day's pay and one day's victualling money. Bag meals issued; we were next visited by a resplendent being whom I later learned was chief yeoman of signals. It was he who was about to escort us to our final destination, which only then did we learn, was to be the Royal Naval Training Establishment at Shotley, better known as HMS *Ganges*.

On arrival at Liverpool Street station, where we were to join the Harwich train, I realised why my father had been speaking to the recruiting officer, for he and my step-mother were there to see us off, with a parting gift of cakes, sweets and fruit sufficient for the whole party. Such largesse, and so unexpected.

The train journey was uneventful, our escort leaving us to our own devices, but when nearing Harwich he came to our compartment and warned us that it was an offence for boy ratings to smoke, or even to be in possession of smoking materials, the penalty for not conforming to this regulation being six cuts with the cane for a first offender and twelve cuts for any subsequent offence. This did not bother me as I was not addicted to smoking, but one or two of my newfound friends lit a last cigarette and presented the remainder to the chief.

Our journey to Harwich completed, we were hurried to a naval trot boat which was lying at the jetty, and here, for the journey across the river to Shotley Pier, we were left in the charge of the boat's coxswain. It was but a short distance, and very soon we had reached our final destination.

At Shotley Pier, a petty officer, who turned out to be the new entries duty instructor, marched us at double time to what us land lubbers thought was just a stretch of road in front of an office block, but which we learned later, was that most holy of holies, the Quarter Deck.

Here we were reported to the Officer of the Day, and this over, a regulating petty officer emerged from one of the offices and said his piece. Any: cash over two shillings which we had in our possession was to be given up. This would be taken care of until we proceeded on our first leave. No boy was allowed to have more than two shillings whilst in the establishment. We were again warned about the penalties for smoking and asked if we had any smoking materials to surrender, but the chief yeoman had beaten him to it.

These formalities over, the new entries instructor marched us off to the bath, and that was the end of our privacy. This bathing routine was the regular thing for all boys coming into the establishment, whether as new entries or returning from leave.

The boy would strip and bathe under a shower: after drying off, he would present himself for inspection by the petty officer in charge of the parade, but this was not just a cursory one to make sure that the boy was clean, for with the aid of an inspection lamp would come the most minute inspection of the more hirsute parts of his anatomy.

You can well imagine my feelings then, when I, who for some years, had been seen in a naked state only by a doctor, had to strip and bathe in front of these other boys and then parade before this petty officer who, but a short time before, had been a complete stranger to me. However, it was something which I soon had to get used to, for these bathing parades were a twice weekly feature of life at HMS *Ganges*.

Bathing and inspection over, we were given a uniform of sorts; all second-hand cast-offs, so a near fit was all that could be expected. When dressed we looked anything but smart: this however, was to be our only wardrobe for the next ten days.

Next, we were marched to the new entries block, and after parcelling up our civilian clothing for sending home, we were given supper.

My first supper in the navy was one which I will never forget; pea soup and bread. There was nothing wrong with the quality or the quantity, but in this instance the soup was only lukewarm, and although in other circumstances it might have been an enjoyable meal, on this occasion it did little to whet my appetite.

So to bed; but as I walked into the new entries dormitory I wondered what I had let myself in for: one long room, with beds on either side, and on nearly every pillow rested one semi – bald head, for these boys, intakes of earlier days, had already paid their first visit to the royal marine barber.

The instructor had issued each of us with a night-shirt, and these we had to put on before turning in. They were real flannel night-shirts, just like those worn by grandfather in bygone days, and these were part of the regulation kit issued to all boys at new entry training establishments. When the boys had turned in for the night, it was part of the instructor's duty to go round and make sure that each boy was wearing his night-shirt and had not gone to bed in the uniform flannel which he had been wearing all day.

Whilst I was undergoing training at Shotley, someone must have had a brain wave, for the issue of night-shirts was discontinued, and two extra uniform flannels were issued instead. This extra issue had the words NIGHT SHIRT printed across the front in one inch block capitals, the idea being that they would do duty as such during the time that the boy was under training, but by the time he was ready for sea the print would have worn off, so leaving him with two extra uniform shirts. At a later date, all new entries were issued with two pairs of pyjamas. Such progress!

However, to get back to my own story: the instructor had allotted us beds and these we had to make up, for the bedding was still rolled up in the day position. This bedding consisted of one horsehair mattress, two blankets and two pillows; sheets apparently were unheard of. Our beds made, we then turned in. The instructor made his way towards the door. Only the police lights were on, so lights out was not necessary. As he reached the door he turned and spoke – "First thing in the morning you will be doing swimming tests." Then he was gone, leaving us alone with our thoughts.

I must have slept well, for I remembered very little until I was awakened by the lights being switched on and a raucous voice bellowing – "'Rise and shine, come along then, rise and shine the morning's fine, the sun's scorching your eyes out." It was of course the instructor, returning to awaken us for the start of another day, and as he came further into the dormitory, he continued, – Make a move, make a move, come along then, show a leg." The time was 5.45 a.m. It was quite dark outside, but despite this the dormitory was all activity, boys dressing, folding up their bedding, and then proceeding, stripped to the waist, to a washroom at the end of the building. It was to this washroom that the instructor then came, and woe betides any boy who tried to get away with a lick and a promise.

At this period of time, many of the instructors still carried a stoniky – the rope's end of sailing ship days, and believe me, they were not averse to using it if they thought that the offence warranted their doing so, and it was the washroom where only cold water was provided, that this stoniky was put to good use, especially in the colder weather.

Our ablutions over, the instructor went off and left us in the charge of two sub-instructor boys, and perhaps, at this stage of my story, a few words of explanation about the latter might not come amiss.

Boys joining Shotley were not put into classes immediately, and the dormitory which I had joined the night previously was known as the New Entries Block, this being set apart from the dormitory blocks of the boys already classed up for training.

Each such class numbered sixteen boys, and there were two classes in a dormitory. Approximately ninety classes were in various stages of their training, and as each two completed the course and were drafted, two new ones were formed from the boys in the New Entries Block.

THE NEW ENTRY

After a few weeks of preliminary training, it was usual for one of the boys to be appointed class leader, and as training progressed, he would be promoted to sub – instructor boy, a badge to denote the rating.

It was not usual for these boys to be drafted with the remainder of their class, one possible reason perhaps, being to prevent bloodshed, for the rating had to be relinquished on going to sea and it would hardly have been wise for them to be drafted with the boys over whom they had held some position of authority: this however, is entirely my own opinion, only given for want of a better one.

I feel that I have transgressed somewhat from my story, but this was only to explain how two such sub-instructor boys were available to take charge of us new entries, for this was the kind of job they would be given after parting company from their own class.

The washing and dressing had taken about fifteen minutes, and now we had a further fifteen minutes to partake of cocoa and biscuits. This consisted of a basin of cocoa and two ships biscuits which the boys detailed for cook duties had been to fetch from the galley. This cocoa, which was of the ship's variety, might have been enjoyable were it not for the fact that the basins were made of enamel, and so became too hot to put to one's mouth: by the time this could be done, one no longer had a hot drink.

Basins were a regular issue as drinking utensils at this time, but whereas those issued to the boys were made of enamel, the men had an issue which were made of china; a much better proposition.

Cups and saucers did not become a general issue until nineteen twenty-seven, but even so, old habits die hard, and the men, preferring to drink their beverages from a basin, would, for quite an appreciable time, go ashore to buy their own.

The cocoa and biscuits finished; we had a few moments to ourselves before the instructor returned. It was during this time that I learned of a black market in cigarettes among the boys, we six newcomers being thought of as a possible source of supply. I suppose that we could have been, for there had been no search the previous evening and although we did not then realise it, we were not yet subject to the Naval Discipline Act, the dotted line still having to be signed.

There was no business done on this occasion, but we did learn that the black-market price was usually fourpence for a full-sized cigarette and threepence for the smaller Woodbine or Weight.

This may not seem much by present day standards, but it must be remembered that in those days cigarettes were ten for only sixpence, whilst the smaller varieties were packed in fives for two pence.

With the return of the instructor we had all fallen in, the majority of the boys being detailed for cleaning duties, whilst I and the other five new boys were marched off to the swimming bath: the time was 6.15 a.m.

Fortunately for me I was a fairly able swimmer and so had no fear of the water, but the next half-hour probably made one or two of the others wish that they had never left home.

The routine was the same for all six of us: without asking whether or not we could swim, we were ordered up onto the high diving board from whence we were expected to jump into the water. This presented no difficulty for four of us, but the other two were non swimmers. There was no turning back; however, a plea of – "Please sir I can't swim" – only bringing the reply "Well now's your chance to learn – jump!" So, in fear and trepidation they jumped, it being small consolation to them that a P.T. instructor was standing at the edge of the baths with a long pole for them to clutch at when they surfaced.

This ordeal over, those of us who had been able to make our own way to the side of the baths then had to attempt the standard swimming test, whilst the others had to practice with leg and arm movements both in and out of the water.

For the standard test we each had to put on a white duck suit, dive in at the shallow end, swim three lengths of the baths, and then remain afloat for three minutes. For me, the worst part of this was putting on a cold, wet duck suit over my warm body, but it so happened that it was something which I never had to do again, being successful with the test at my first attempt.

During training there were regular periods of swimming instruction, and once the standard tests had been passed, one could aspire to greater heights by practising for the Royal Life Saving Society's awards.

The morning's activities had given me quite an appetite, and as we were marched back to our dormitory-cum-messroom, I felt more than ready for my breakfast.

We saw, on arrival, that the remainder of the boys were fallen in outside; knife, fork and spoon in hand, and after hanging up our towels we joined them.

The only ones not having to wait outside were those who had been detailed for cook duty. They had been to the galley to collect our rations, and under the supervision of the instructor, were now in the process of serving them out in equal portions.

Meanwhile, one of the sub-instructor boys was instructing the remainder of us in the art of forming fours, this being the correct marching formation of that time.

Before long the cooks came out and joined up with the remainder of us after which we were all marched into the messroom and round the tables on which our breakfasts had been laid out; but when the tables had been circumnavigated a couple of times , the instructor gave the order – "Halt! Toward the tables, right or left turn!" and there we were, each boy with a breakfast in front of him. This procedure was fairly general at all mealtimes, it being an idea to deter the cooks from putting out larger portions for themselves, not knowing where they would eventually settle.

I have written earlier that the swimming had given me an appetite, but this first morning's menu somewhat blunted it, for what confronted me was bacon and tomatoes, bread and margarine, with tea for a beverage; the bacon was of the streaky kind, and the tomatoes tinned. This gastronomic luxury became better known to the boys as

Train Smash, because of its similarity to torn flesh and the gore which would result there from.

The meals were never hot, for they had to be carried several blocks in open dishes and then served up on cold enamel plates; bread was never sliced, but cut up into large chunks, for if a loaf was the ration for sixteen boys, then it would be cut into sixteen equal portions.

Imagine then, this half cold dish, a large chunk of bread thinly spread with margarine, and a basin two-thirds full of lukewarm tea, small wonder that my appetite had gone, but the other boys set too with a will, and in the days that followed, like them, ate everything put before me, and then looked round for more.

Breakfast over and the clearing up done, the earlier arrivals were left to their own devices, but we newcomers had a full morning ahead of us. First a visit to the sick bay for a final medical examination, then to the dental officer for his inspection, after which it was the school room, and the educational test once again.

One of our party experienced some difficulty with this last, and I overheard the schoolmaster – an instructor lieutenant – asking whether he had received any help with his earlier test at the recruiting centre. This could have been the case I suppose; either that, or he wanted no further part in the navy, for he had been one of the non-swimmers.

The educational test was a while you wait affair, and it was only then, after the results had been made known, that we signed for enrolment. The engagement was as Boy 2nd Class, for a period of twelve years from the age of eighteen, with an option, of re-engaging at a later date for a further ten years in order to complete time for pension.

One boy thought that he would like to sign on for the full twenty-two years, but his offer received the following reply: "If I were you son, I should try twelve first; even that might prove too much" – and how right that could have been, for quite often, attempts were made to run away, none of them successful, the escapee being brought back within a couple of days, or even less, to face a punishment which included twelve cuts with the cane.

This caning was always carried out by a master at arms, in the presence of an officer, the recipient – or should I say victim – wearing nothing on his buttocks but a pair of white duck trousers, which became skin tight when he was strapped across the caning horse.

None of us however, had any thoughts of running away at this stage of the proceedings, but we had one more call to make before dinner; this was to the Royal Marine barber. One did not have to decide whether a short back and sides or a trim was required; the decision had already been made. A close crop with a front fringe was what we came out with, but I am glad to say, that on future visits, our hair was not treated quite so severely. We did not have to pay for this first haircut, but on future visits we were expected to hand over three pence, This was later shown up as a racket, and the two barbers put on a charge – for robbing the boys apparently – the cost of the hair cuts being charged against boys' credits and the threepences going into the pockets of the barbers.

By the time that the barbers had finished with us, we were beginning to feel hungry, and were glad to be marched back to the mess-room for dinner. The midday meal was always called dinner, never lunch; only the officers had mid-day lunch and evening dinner.

Arriving at the new entries block, we saw that the remainder of the boys were again fallen in outside, but there was no forming fours on this occasion, for it was mail time. This was the only time of day at which mail was issued, and then only post-cards and letters which were above suspicion. Chits were issued for the more bulky letters and parcels, these having to be exchanged at the mail office, where the regulating petty officer in charge would open up the package, ostensibly to search for cigarettes, which if found he would confiscate, but he would not be averse to also helping himself to any other tasty morsel which might take his fancy.

Dinner over, we were free to do as we liked within our own area but were not allowed to visit other parts of the establishment.

Because of this restriction, there now began ten of the most boring days of my existence. Except for Meal parades and a few fatigues, we were left entirely to our own devices. True we had a football pitch on which scratch games could be organised, but having no sports kit, had to play in our bell-bottomed trousers, and to aid recognition, one side would play without wearing their jumpers. There would be no referee of course, so you may well imagine the arguments that ensued.

There was however one day's relief from this monotony. Wednesday was a red-letter day, for this was the day on which we attended pay parade, and in the evening, a cinema performance in the gymnasium.

First the pay parade. The pay of a Boy 2nd Class was one shilling per day plus clothing allowance, but all that he received on pay day was one shilling and sixpence, the remainder being placed to his credit. This meant that it was compulsorily saved for him until he received his first pay as an ordinary seaman.

The parade always followed a set pattern, boys lining up in fours according to their ship's book numbers. When this had been accomplished, they would slowly move towards the pay table at the head of their section. As each boy's turn came, the paymaster's writer would call out his name, whereupon the boy concerned would step up to the table, remove his cap and hold it in front of him, at the same time stating his ship's book number. The paymaster would then place one shilling and sixpence on the cap, the boy would remove it with his left hand, and replacing cap on head, turnabout and double smartly away.

After twelve weeks preliminary training, boys were rated 1st class, their pay was raised to one shilling and ninepence per day, and they then received two shillings at each pay parade.

This was the procedure right throughout the service, men and boys alike, except that chief and petty officers did not remove their caps, but saluted before receiving their pay, and then left the table at quick, instead of double time.

Weekly pay parades were only for boys under training, the general rule being that home service personnel were paid fortnightly, whilst those on foreign service received theirs only once a month.

One other point worth mentioning, is that pay parades were compulsory, and even if a man knew, that because of a pay stoppage for some misdemeanour he had nothing to come, he still had to attend in order to be told that he was *not entitled,* when he stepped up to the table.

Further mention of the cinema show will come later in my story, so I will say nothing more about it now, except that it was a welcome break in the monotony of those first ten days.

Chapter 2

Training Begins

AT LAST the day came which I, and many others, had been waiting for: we were to leave the new entries block in order to be classed up for preliminary training.

Two classes were formed, each of sixteen boys. Not all had become new entries from civvy street, for numbered among them were boys from the training ships *Arethusa, Warspite* and *Mercury* Known as *Stodger Boys* – a term the origin of which was never made clear – they thought that they knew all the answers, having been through it all before.

From their conversation, it seemed that whilst aboard their respective training ships, they had completely lost their identity, being known by a number, and referring to their ex ship-mates in the following manner "Do you remember when 2685 fell overboard and finished up on the ship astern?" or, "How about poor old 2972 being awarded six cuts for messing himself." These apparently were boys who had gone before, but how my new classmates remembered the numbered ex-shipmates, and could bring recognition to others, solely by quoting a number, was always beyond my powers of reasoning.

The classes formed; we were then moved to a group of huts outside the main establishment. Everything here was self-contained, for it had been a kite balloon station during World War I, and here we were to be domiciled for the next four weeks.

Both classes shared a hut, and also two instructors, one of whom would be taking us for gunnery instruction, and the other in seamanship.

Our first day was spent in *kitting* – first came a large Canvas kit-bag, and then the remainder of our kit in two, three or single items, the supplies assistants being quite adept at sizing us up, for few, if any, had to return for a change of size.

Also, at this time, we were issued with our own horsehair mattress, which was to last me for the whole twenty-four years of my service.

With this mattress were also issued two loose covers, together with several single items, not clothing, but items which were all part of one's kit. These included a jack-knife, cap-box, ditty – box and a half inch name tape, this last, I suppose, having been in the process of preparation whilst we were still in the new entries block.

This kit issue, and another supplementary issue before leaving the establishment for sea service, were the only free issues of standard kit; any replacement due to wear and tear, loss, damage or theft, had to be paid for, as did boot repairs; not from one's weekly pay however, but charged against credit. During men's service of course, one did have to pay cash, for the men were always paid every penny of their entitlement, and so had no credit on which to draw.

The kit issue completed, we returned to our hut, and now began the marking of everything which had been issued to us; with the half-inch tape, white clothing was marked with black paint, white paint being used on our blue uniform suite. We also had a length of white tape stamped with our name in black paint, and this had to be cut up into name tabs for sewing on to our socks, stockings, muffler and collars. All other items of kit, such as boots, shoes etc., which were not easily marked with paint, now had to have a name punched into them with steel type, and then we thought that all was finished. But no; as a spare time occupation we were told, all the names had to be sewn over, so that eventually every item of clothing would have a sewn in name, right down to the last sock.

Although it was a regulation throughout the service, that all articles of clothing should be properly marked with one's name, it was only in the training establishment that the names had to be sewn in, and how glad I was that I only had eight letters to contend with, for the task had to be completed in time for a kit inspection at the end of the four weeks preliminaries.

We could now divest ourselves of the loan clothing and put on something which fitted us and we were able to call our own.

Things had not been quite so bad for the *stodger boys*, as they had joined the establishment in the uniform of their respective training ships, and these they had been allowed to wear whilst awaiting kitting up. Now the cast-offs were bundled up and; taken away, that being the last we saw of them, except perhaps, on the backs of new entries in a later intake.

Training now began in earnest, one class being taken by the gunnery instructor, the other in seamanship, changing round according to the syllabus, but first of all, there was our introduction to the Shotley mast.

Situated on the parade ground, it was one hundred and forty-three feet in height: there were three yards-arms, one about a third of the way up, another at halfway, whilst the third was some forty feet from the truck (button). The actual layout of the rigging does not affect my story, so long as the reader has some idea of what a mast and yardarms look like and can so draw on their imagination. This then, was the ascent we had to make at our first attempt; going up one side and descending the other. Perfectly straightforward I can imagine you saying, but there was one snag: to reach the fighting top – a platform situated about half way between the two lower yards – there were two means of access; one by means of the *lubbers hole,* a square hole cut into the platform itself, thus giving a fairly straightforward entry, or by way of the *futtock shrouds* or *devil's elbow,* and this was the way we were expected to take.

These futtock shrouds went up to the outside of the fighting top, and to negotiate them, one had to lean backwards at an angle of some forty-five degrees, continuing to climb whilst in this position. Although it was only a short distance, bearing in mind that there was a lot of give in the ratlines (rope rungs), it was a tricky proposition for us first timers, and many, like myself, were stuck there, and took the easy way out, until becoming more accustomed to the climb. The mast was always available during recreation times, and boys could be seen climbing just for the fun of it, even to sitting on the truck, which meant shinning up the last twenty feet or so.

Besides gunnery and seamanship classes, we also had to attend school, for educational tests had to be passed even to attainable seaman status. Visits were also made to the laundry so that we could acquire the know-how of washing our own clothes, but it was not just a case of standing up at the wash-tub; we had to strip off and then spread our washing out on the stone floor, kneeling to the job the whole class completely naked.

Washing completed, it would be placed in a large spin dryer, and then in a drying oven, where it would remain until the next day.

Instruction was always in the mornings and early evenings, the afternoons being left free for recreational purposes, but I'm afraid that I have rather got ahead of myself here, for during the four weeks of preliminaries, we did not have to conform to the routine of the main establishment, and stay out of doors during the afternoons.

This helped us to get on with our kit preparations, for not only did we have to get over the sewing in of our names, but also become quite expert at rolling each article of clothing to a uniform size, and then tying it with two clothes stops, these also having to be uniform in their spacing.

The gauge for this was a seamanship manual: each article had to be as wide as the manual was long, and the width of the manual decided the spacing of the clothes stops. This then, was our ultimate aim; a complete kit laid out in two parallel lines, each article of clothing with the owner's name showing and of uniform width, with all the clothes stops as straight as a set of railway lines.

At this stage of our training, gunnery instruction consisted mainly of rifle drill and marching, whilst for seamanship we concentrated on boat pulling, bends and hitches, and of course, several visits to the mast.

During this period, the instructors promoted me to *acting leading boy*, purely an honorary rank, with not much to do as yet, but a promise perhaps, of a further promotion to come.

After three weeks had elapsed, the instructors sprang a surprise kit inspection on us, mainly to see how we were progressing with our name sewing etc., and because of this, it came about that I had to surrender my newly won promotion.

I had become friendly with a boy who was not very adept with a needle, and I had been giving him a helping hand. Although my own sewing was not completed, I was confident that it would be by the time the kit inspection came up after four weeks, but I was not ready for this surprise one. I was not alone in this, but the instructors were of the opinion that as an acting leading boy I should have set an example, and so I was demoted. Whether this was detrimental to me will always be a debatable point, for although petty officer and sub-instructor boys were allowed extra pocket money, their daily rate of pay was no higher; the extra meant that they had less money accruing for their first pay day as ordinary seamen.

After another week had passed, and with the main kit inspection safely behind us, we were on the move again, this time back to the main establishment. Here we were to be domiciled in one of the mess-rooms which were situated on both sides of a long, covered way which led from the quarterdeck.

There were thirty-four of these mess-rooms, and together with another eight situated in a shorter covered way leading from the parade ground, they provided the full accommodation for all the boys who were being trained as seamen. The boy seamen were divided into five divisions, each under its own divisional officer: a sixth division was made up of boys training as signalmen or telegraphists, but they were accommodated in a block set apart from the remainder. Whether it was because of this segregation that they considered themselves a race apart, I don't know, but they always seemed to think themselves a cut above the boys of the seaman branch.

There was never much variation in our routine. We were called at 5.45 a.m., although, having been instructed in the twenty-four hour clock, it was now known to us as 0545: cocoa and wash then followed, after which certain chores had to be carried out until 0700, or one day perhaps, it might be the turn of my class to attend a bathing parade, these parades taking place at all times of the day according to a very strict time-table.

Breakfast was at 0700, and it was during our breakfast hour that we would change into a white duck suit, this being the normal daily rig, winter and summer alike.

After breakfast it would be a continuation of chores, or perhaps short classes on varying subjects, these bringing us up to 0845 and the main parade of the day; *Divisions*.

For this we were paraded and inspected, first by one of our instructors, and then by the divisional officer: Mondays and Thursdays were the worst, as they were clean suit days, and a not so clean one could result in a punishment of extra work or extra drill.

Divisions over, instructions became the order of the day, seamanship, gunnery or schoolwork according to the syllabus.

As each seamanship or gunnery subject was completed, there would be an examination, but failure would not prevent the next subject being taken; such failures would become members of the backward classes mentioned a little further on.

At 1145 it would be "Cooks to the Galley," which meant that boys detailed for cook duties were to muster at the galley in the long-covered way in order to collect dinner for their respective messes. The procedure at mealtimes is already known to readers, so it is sufficient for me to say that there was also a rota for washing up duties, so that everyone did their share.

Dinner and the chores arising there from completed, it would be nearing 1315, and time for another parade, this, in order to set the boys about their afternoon endeavours.

At this parade, the commander (or his deputy) would fallout the backward seamanship and gunnery classes, and also the back-ward swimmers: these were the poor unfortunates who had failed various of their intermediate examinations, or in the case of the backward swimmers, those who had not yet been able to pass the standard swimming test, and were therefore obliged to attend extra classes in their spare time.

Voluntary classes would also be fallen out; these consisted of boys who wished to become proficient in the use of a bosun's pipe, and others who wished to become buglers.

Once these classes had been taken care of, the remainder of the parade would be dismissed.

On a Wednesday, there would be one mad rush for the canteen, everyone having money, only that morning having been in receipt of their weekly pay. At the canteen one could get a bar of chocolate, a cream doughnut, and a bottle of pop for sixpence, and this was the most popular buy, although a bar of Sharp's Kreemy Toffee for three halfpence was another favourite.

The canteen had a steady trade on other days also, for not only could one buy stamps, they were also accepted as legal tender for other purchases, so that many a doting parent must have thought that their son was keeping up a large correspondence because of the amount of stamps they were sending him when he was in fact, passing them over the counter in payment for items of tuck.

Boys were not allowed in their mess-rooms during the afternoons; they either had to take part in, or be a spectator to, the various sporting activities which would be taking place; but many a game of halfpenny pontoon, I and others have played, crouched under a bed at the far end of our dormitory, because we did not fancy the open air on that particular afternoon.

Discovery would have meant a different ending, for we would have been on the carpet. Discipline had to be maintained of course, but we used to think that the Royal Marine sentries and regulating petty officers delighted to see a boy in trouble, and we hated them for it. I never heard of a boy being caught smoking and given another chance. Usually it would be a group of boys caught, for cigarettes being in short supply, one would always be shared, being passed round for a couple of draws each, and then stubbed out and tucked away for a future session. One cigarette would usually last for three such sessions, being smoked down to the last by impaling it on a pin.

Matches were never used, for being in possession of matches was being in possession of smoking materials. In my own class, a boy returning from Shotley leave was found to be in possession of one red-topped match. It was found in his oilskin pocket, and he avowed that it must have been left there when he returned from home leave, but it availed him nothing; he was awarded six cuts just the same, his punishment for being in. possession of smoking materials.

Lights were obtained in a much more technical manner. First, the top of an electric light switch would be removed: then two pencils would be produced, each sharpened at both ends. Two of the pencil points would be touched on the bared leads in the switch, and the other two brought together in order to make an electric arc. A piece of cotton waste, preferably impregnated with metal polish would be used for tinder, and so a light would be obtained.

Most of these smoking sessions took part in the heads (toilet) and if any boy happened to go into the heads on legitimate business when one of these sessions were taking place, it was up to him to get out quick and do his business elsewhere, for in the event of discovery, all in the heads, innocent and guilty alike, would be changed with the offence and punished.

Sport participation was always encouraged, athletics, cricket and swimming in the summer months, and soccer, rugger and boxing during the winter.

For soccer and rugger, the season was divided. During the first part, only soccer would be played, after which, the pitches would be taken over for rugger; an idea which could well be copied by those rugger only schools, where a boy must spend the whole season playing rugger, when he would have preferred to take part in a game of soccer.

The main sporting activities were run on a divisional basis, competition being very keen. Various trophies were awarded for these divisional competitions, but not every boy could represent his division, and inter-mess tournaments were also organised.

So much then, for a brief outline of the afternoons' endeavours: at 1545 it would be – "Cooks to the Galley" – which would be followed by – "Hands to Tea and shift into Night Clothing" – meaning, that following tea, which usually consisted of bread, margarine and jam, all boys would have to change into a blue serge suit for the remainder of the evening.

On Mondays, Tuesdays and Thursdays, there would be another parade at 1700, after which we were marched off to further instructions which lasted until 1900, when it would be – "Hands to Supper."

This evening parade also took place on Wednesdays, but this would be followed by a cinema show in the gymnasium.

The show was usually preceded by a singsong and the showing of cartoon slides, mostly humorous, and depicting various happenings of the week passed.

After supper the next two hours were free, unless one happened to be on duty, or under punishment. A recreation room was at our disposal, equipped with miniature billiard tables which were always fully occupied, even on a Wednesday, some of the boys preferring this form of entertainment rather than that provided by the cinema show.

One evening each week, the Royal Marine band played dance music in the gymnasium, but of course, there were no partners of the opposite sex, two boys having to dance together, a form of relaxation which never appealed to me, which may have some bearing on the fact that I never did learn to dance.

TRAINING BEGINS

Evening rounds were at 2100, and all boys had to be turned in by this time, the duty instructor of each mess reporting that this was so to the officer carrying out the rounds.

Saturday mornings were spent in giving the establishment that extra bit of spit and polish; working parties being detailed for this purpose. After dinner, the remainder of the day was free, but the afternoon, as with other days, had to be spent out of doors.

Sunday would allow for still more free time, but first, Sunday Divisions had to be attended, followed by a church service according to one's denomination. The Church of England service was held in the gymnasium, but there were several chapels in the establishment for the use of boys belonging to other faiths.

Shotley leave was allowed on Sunday afternoon. This was of three hours duration and gave the boys a chance to stretch their legs outside the establishment, and if they had any cigarettes, an opportunity to have a smoke without fear of being caught.

Readers may be beginning to wonder how, with such strict precautions being taken, boys were able to obtain cigarettes at all. I being a non-smoker, and therefore never in the market, cannot throw much light on the subject, but tobacco barons did operate, and I know that their source of supply was not through the main gate after Shotley leave, for the tobacconist would not serve any boy with cigarettes.

Training now became more advanced, incorporating six-inch gun drill, together with fire control procedures, whilst the seamanship instructor, with the aid of his stoniky, tried in earnest to make seamen out of us.

We were also taught to be tidy and put things away when they were finished with; personal belongings not so put away (left sculling about), being put into the scrap-bag, from which they could only be recovered by the giving up of one inch of soap for each article.

After seven weeks had elapsed, it was time to proceed on Christmas leave: packing had to be done the evening before, a very early start having to be made in the morning. A blue bundle handkerchief had to duty as a suitcase: attaché cases came into use much later in my service, a break with tradition, for seafaring men had, in all probability, carried their belongings in bundle handkerchiefs even before Nelson's day.

Seasonal leave from Shotley was given on the basis of those having the furthest to go would be the first to leave and the last to return, and I, being in the London group was one of the last away.

The school and recreation rooms were used as mustering points; but eventually, as time for the departure drew nearer, we were moved on to the gymnasium, and here issued with a return railway ticket to our destination, together with fifteen shillings spending money from our credit, and a post office draft made out to our next of kin for two weeks victualling money.

A short march to Shotley pier embarkation for the trip to Harwich, and joining a special train, our leave had begun. Being a special train, there were no scheduled stops, but arrangements had been made for a break to be made in the journey at Witham, this to allow refreshment to be taken. It was here that the first of our spending money changed hands, for a large assortment of foodstuffs had been laid out on the station platform, and our needs were ministered to by a bevy of women, probably from some local organisation. Breakfast having been so early, they did a good trade during the twenty minutes or so we remained at the station, and then we were off once more, Liverpool Street next stop.

Within half an hour of reaching Liverpool Street, I was home on my first leave, the family all there to welcome a sailor into their midst, and a sailor I had to remain for the whole fourteen days, the Navy certainly having done something to me in seven weeks, for my civilian clothing was too small for me to wear ever again.

* * *

Fourteen days passed all too quickly, although not without a certain amount of ennui, for my erstwhile civilian friends had not been available during the day-time, and even when we did meet, there did not seem to be so much in common as had been the case when I was also a civilian.

In a way, I was not sorry to be catching the train for the return trip to Harwich. As the train left at 0900, my brother was there to see me off, his place of business being quite close to the station.

Once again making a refreshment stop at Witham, it was not over-long before we arrived at Harwich, the instructors waiting to welcome us, and not exactly with open arms, at least with a certain amount of friendliness.

More amenable to discipline than I had been nine weeks earlier, it was not so hard for me to hand over my surplus cash, or to muster through the bath, but as there were such large numbers returning from leave, the laundry rooms had to be brought into use to help out with this communal bathing.

Whereas on the day of joining my civilian clothing had been parcelled up for sending home, on this occasion, every article of clothing which had been worn to, or taken on leave, was now destined to the calorifier for heat treatment, this, in order to make absolutely certain, that all unwanted vermin went with us to the dormitories.

Three more seasonal leaves came my way whilst I was under training, and in every instance the procedure was the same, but I am happy to say, that once free of the training establishment, de – bugging was discontinued, although it was always routine, both ashore and afloat, for boys to be mustered through the bath.

* * *

After a further five weeks training, I was rated Boy 1st Class and at the same time because of my schoolwork, I was put into the Advanced Class. This meant moving on to another mess room, where the newly formed class was to be domiciled, and although the seamanship and gunnery course was to be the same as for other classes, schoolwork now took in science, navigation and more advanced maths. This meant that members of an advanced class, if they had the mind to, could become warrant officer material, or even attain commissioned rank, and it was made known to us that at that particular time, there was a serving admiral who had started his career as a Boy 2nd Class.

So, the days passed; instructions, fatigues, leisure, religious instruction, and plenty of sporting activities.

The art of sailing, together with the names of every part which went into the making of a boat and its equipment, were instilled into our minds: anchor and cable work, together with a certain amount of expertise in knots and splices, were all part of the seamanship training, and on the gunnery side, we were acquiring enough know – how to become efficient members of at gun crew, or ammunition supply party, and, of course, expert square bashers, all this, I might add, still with the aid of a stoniky.

Training lasted for fifteen months, but actually, three of these were duplicated, as, having become advanced class at twelve weeks, the whole of the gunnery and seamanship syllabus, had to be started again from the beginning.

Having almost completed the course, my class now had to carry out sea training, which consisted of one day at sea aboard HMS *Tring*, a coal-burning minesweeper of World War I vintage.

The dry land training of earlier weeks was now put to practical use afloat: for instance, we had learned to steer on an electrically operated steering model in the seamanship room, but the real thing proved somewhat different, for the model had not been able to simulate pitch and roll, or allow for currents, so now, these being with us, HMS *Tring* steered some very erratic courses during that day.

One day at sea may not seem much for sea training, but there were a number of things we had learned ashore, which did not need a final polishing up aboard ship: for example, one could become proficient at knots and splices, bends and hitches, or signals, either ashore or afloat, and so our day at sea only took into account those things which needed a deck beneath one's feet in order that a little more know-how might be achieved.

One thing learned on this occasion, due to the experience of a few, was, that nothing should be thrown over the windward side, and one Dusty Miller, destined to one day become a master at arms, demonstrated this only too well, when, feeling under the weather because of the ship's movement, he dashed to the windward guardrail in order to be sick, and got his own back with a vengeance.

My class was fortunate in that it never seemed to have anyone attending backward classes. Whether this was because our instructors were exceptionally good at putting things across, or whether we were lucky in always being asked the right questions, I should not like to hazard a guess. Suffice it to say, we all completed our examinations successfully, and after being issued with our sea kit, were placed in the awaiting draft category.

The awaiting draft period varied according to the demand, and would be anything between a few days and several weeks, but first, each boy was sent on ten days draft leave, which could well be his last leave for two and a half years, depending on whether his first ship was on a home or foreign station.

During the waiting period, boys were employed on various duties in, and about, the establishment, and it so happened that I, together with several of my classmates, were detailed as Captains House party.

The house was situated about a mile from the establishment, and every morning after breakfast, Saturdays and Sundays excepting, our party would report at the galley and collect a hamper which contained our mid-day meal. This we had to carry – Shank's Pony being the only transport allowed – and on arrival at the house, we became domestic servants unpaid. Various household chores had to be carried out under the direction of a maid, a real slave driver, who really kept us going.

Our meal had to be eaten in the stables, and in spite of our unpaid labours, we were never so much as offered a single cup of tea or another beverage.

One thing which I have forgotten to mention, and must now do, is that during our last few weeks, we were given our draft numbers and allocated a port division, which could be Chatham, Portsmouth or Devonport.

This was really the beginning of the parting of our ways, for in those days it was the practice for a ship to be commission with a crew all from the same port division, which meant that there could never be the remotest possibility of my serving afloat with those class-mates who had been allocated to Portsmouth or Devonport.

Although I had been on my ten days draft leave, the demand for boys to join sea-going units seemed to have fallen off somewhat, and it seemed that I might be fortunate enough to get home for Easter leave and my sister Dorothy's wedding, but it was not to be, for it so happened, that I, with eleven others, all having been allocated to Chatham port division, were the first to part company, for we learned that we were to join HMS *Marlborough*, a coal fired battleship, serving with the Mediterranean Fleet and based at Malta.

As the ship was already on station, it meant that passage would have to be taken, and for this purpose we were dispatched to Portland, there to join two destroyers, six boys to each, and so, as a fully fledged Boy 1st Class, I embarked aboard HMS *Viscount*.

Of the five who had been with me on that November morning at the recruiting office, only one remained, and, H.M.S *Marlborough* was to be the only ship on which we served together.

In the following pages, my story continues, not in chronological order I'm afraid, but in such a way as to give the uninitiated an insight into the trials and tribulations besetting the seafaring fraternity of that particular time, and perhaps, bringing nostalgic memories to those who also served.

Chapter 3

High days and Holidays

NO MATTER how long the duration of a foreign commission, even if it lasted for the full two and a half years, there would never be a full day off for the ship's company. Bank holidays didn't mean a thing – and even Christmas day had its limitations.

The day would start by the hands being fallen in at 0615 they would then be called to attention by the Chief Bosun's Mate and reported to the Commander, the continuation of the dialogue being as follows – "Thank you Chief" in a louder voice "A Merry Christmas" – "Scrub and wash the upper deck." He would then return to his cabin, leaving the men to carry out the normal daily routine of scrubbing decks until "Hands to breakfast" at 0700.

Breakfast over; the mess-decks would be decorated in the traditional manner, although a certain amount of improvisation had to be called upon; spare flags from the signals department being brought into use, and also, surprisingly, a certain amount of crepe paper appearing as if from nowhere.

Not like home of course, but it all helped to brighten things up, and although nothing could compensate for the absence of family life, many photographs would be on display.

Decorating over, the Captain would then carry out his rounds: accompanied by a retinue of officers, and the youngest member of the ship's company masquerading as a master at arms – a tradition of some obscure origin – he would make his way through the mess-decks, wishing a "Merry Christmas" to all, remarking on the decorations and perhaps some of the photographs, and then, with his followers, departing to his own Merry Christmas, with a few duty free gins to help make it so.

Although the lower deck was supposed to be dry, except that is, for the daily rum ration and although liberty-men returning aboard were always searched for illicit liquor, there always seemed to be something to drink and help along the festivities, may be part of a rum ration would have been saved for a few days, to brighten things absence of family life or perhaps an obliging ward room wine steward, adept at giving short measure, might have a few bottles to spare; and on the rare occasion, improvisation, for I was one offered a drink which I thought-was rum, but turned out to be cold tea and methylated spirit, which was of course refused, for one would have to be in dire need to partake of such a concoction.

Although I hate to have to record it, one did come upon the occasional meths drinker, with no money and a craving for alcohol, so improvising in the manner which I have already mentioned.

Christmas dinner was usually of the traditional kind, with mince pies, pudding etc., sometimes augmented with the contents of parcels from home; but the meal over, festivities came more or less to an end.

Leave would be piped, but being the twenty-fifth of the month, money would be scarce, and so an afternoon's head down would be more in the pattern of things.

Tea would be available for those who wanted it, with perhaps a few more liberty-men going ashore afterwards, and then, at 2030, would come the pipe – "Clear up the mess-decks and flats for rounds" – the duty watch would be fallen in, down would come all the decorations, the duty officer would do his rounds, and Christmas would be over for another year.

There were other occasions when an appreciable amount of free time was available; the most notable of these, in my opinion, being regatta day.

Preparation for this would have commenced some two or three months earlier, volunteer boats crews going into training, getting both themselves and the boats into racing trim.

First the crews; for until they were in the peak of condition, it was not possible for them to hold races against one another in order to establish which were the best boats.

Once this had been decided, they would not be used again for training purposes, but hoisted inboard to see whether any improvements could be made. All excess paint would be removed; new planks fitted if the existing ones showed any signs of being waterlogged, and anywhere that an ounce or two could be shaved off this would be done.

Great care had to be taken not to overdo this however, as a few days before the regatta, a race committee would inspect all boats, and if they did not conform to the requirements of a ship's lifeboat, they would be disqualified.

The crews never spared themselves during training, and it was nothing unusual for a man to rub sore patches on his back side, there being no sliding seats fitted, the only sliding therefore, was' the oarsman's bottom on the thwarts.

There was no breaking of training because of these sore patches; however, a few dabs of methylated spirit, and the man would consider that he was as good as new.

Battleship Squadrons, Cruiser Squadrons and Destroyer Flotillas each: held their own regattas, but that of the battleship squadron took pride of place, the winner becoming the *Cock of the Fleet*.

All branches of the service would take part in such a regatta, and I have no doubt that it will be of interest to the reader if I give the makeup of such a programme.

1. Racing Cutters	3 miles	2. Seamen's Cutters	3 miles
3. Stokers Cutters	3 miles	4. Young seamen's Cutters	2 miles
5. Petty Officers Cutters	2 miles	6. Racing Whalers	2 miles
7. Seamen's Whalers	2 miles	8. Stokers' Whalers	2 miles
9. Boys Cutters	1 mile	10. Young Seamen's Whalers	1½ miles
11. Seamen's Gigs	1 mile	12. Miscellaneous Gigs	1 mile
13. Communications Gigs	1 mile	14. C.P.O.s' Gigs	1 mile
15. Wardroom Gigs	1 mile	16. Warrant Officers' Gigs	1 mile
17. Gun Room Gigs	1 mile	18. Skiffs (2 oars pr sculls)	½ mile
19. Skiffs (double skulls)	½ mile	20. Skiffs (single sculls)	1 mile
21. Veterans Skiffs	½ mile	22. All Comers	3 miles

From 1927 onwards, the three-mile cutter races were reduced to two, and the two-mile whaler races to one and a half miles. With regards to the veterans' skiffs, this did not mean that the boats were manned by old greybeards that were nearly past it; in all naval sporting activities, anyone over the age of thirty-five was classed as a veteran.

Prior to the day of the regatta, the squadrons would have anchored in line ahead in two columns, and the course was between these, the finishing line being on a compass bearing from the flagship's bridge, the start having been made between two buoys which had been laid out on the same bearing.

Boats not needed for racing were manned by chucking up parties in varying arrays of fancy dress, and although the occupants usually had a preference for the crews of their own ship, there was sometimes a cheer for one of the opponents, especially if they had been backed on the tote to win. This totalisator would be in operation for all races, and in the weeks beforehand, form was studied in the hope of being able to get on to a good thing.

Before the advent of the tote, some enterprising rating might open up a book on the results; but it was more usual for a crew and their supporters to lay a wager with another crew in their race: not backing themselves to win, but to beat the crew with whom they had laid the wager.

The Racing Whaler and Racing Cutters' crews were always reckoned to be the best of their class, be they manned by seamen, stokers, or any other branch, but occasionally something would go wrong with the form book, and a red hot favourite would lose money for the supporters.

This happened in 1931, when the stoker's Whaler of HMS *Curlew* was far and away the best whalers crew in the ship, and so had the honour of being the representative crew in the Racing Whalers, which they duly won.

On paper, this made them the best whalers' crew in the squadron, and a certainty for the Stoker's Whalers due to be raced the next day. Came the day; and the tote made them the hottest favourites ever, but alas; they could do no better than finish in third place: another turn up for the book.

The last race on the programme was always the All Comers, and a fitting climax to the proceedings.

As the name implies, it was in effect, a free for all: the cutters, instead of a twelve man crew, had twenty-four, each oar being double-banked: gigs became centipede, a six man crew being increased to sixteen, each wielding a smaller scull usually associated with a skiff; hence the name centipede, the similarity in appearance being so pronounced. For this race, launches and pinnaces would also take part, having, over the previous two days, been used solely for the purpose of carrying chucking up parties.

The pinnace, forty feet long, had fourteen oars, each one triple banked, whilst the launch, ten feet longer, and also triple banked, with the crew usually in fancy dress, had, to complete the picture, a passenger in the stern sheets beating out the stroke on a big drum.

There would also be six oared skiffs and double banked whalers, none of them really in with a chance, but all helping to make it quite a spectacle, and in any event, all the boats scored points for their ship according to their order of finishing.

The race was usually won by a centipede gig, occasionally by a double banked cutter, but rarely did any of the other classes finish in the first half dozen, although I well remember, that in 1928, to everyone's surprise, the launch of HMS *Ramillies* finished in third place.

Each race scored points, the ship finishing with the highest aggregate becoming the *Cock of the Fleet,* a title greatly cherished by the holders.

A number of races also carried a trophy, but it was possible for a ship to become cock of the fleet without carrying off a single one of these, and in the Mediterranean fleet regatta of 1929, this is precisely what did happen.

HMS *Royal Oak* had almost swept the board as far as trophy races were concerned but had fared none too well in the remainder.

On the other hand, HMS *Queen Elizabeth,* the flagship, had been consistent in finishing well placed, so winning the cock, after two days racing by only one and a half points.

A win for the flagship for – some unaccountable reason was never very popular, and the sending of the following signal, after the win which I have just mentioned, does, I think, illustrate this rather well.

> To: *Queen Elizabeth*
> From: *Royal Oak*
> Congratulations on winning the cock, but we have all the feathers.

There was a similar occurrence in 1933, when HMS *Daring* became Cock of the First Destroyer Flotilla without winning a single race, finishing either second or third in all but two.

Regattas would be brought to a close on the final day by the overall winners doing a lap of honour round the squadron or flotilla, being greeted with cheers or invective according to the popularity of their victory.

The holiday spirit so prevailed during the day on which a *Crossing the Line* ceremony was taking place. This would only be when a ship crossed the equator for the first time during a commission and it did in effect, start the evening before this latitude was reached, when a member of the ship's company, suitably attired as a member of King Neptune's Court, would be slung, on staging, over the bow of the ship, where he would remain until eight bells was struck, at which he would hail the ship, supposedly from the sea, calling up n the captain to stop.

"Ahoy there!" – "In the name of His Oceanic Majesty *Neptunus Rex*, I call upon you to stop your ship, that I, a herald from his court, might board you and deliver a message to as many of your company as it may concern." The captain would make some suitable reply and give the order, "Stop both engines". The herald would then appear over the bows, and after being asked by the captain to state his business, would reply; "I bring you greetings from His Majesty" and warn you that none shall enter his domain until they have paid, court to him and his beautiful daughters. – "There being many among you who have yet to pay their respects, take warning that at nine of the clock in the forenoon, of tomorrow, His Majesty, together with his beautiful daughters and his retinue, will come aboard to hold court and decide what penalties and forfeits are payable for your misdeeds." – "Until tomorrow, I bid you farewell." He would then disappear over the bows" and the ship would resume course.

Next morning, a large canvas bath would be rigged and filled with seawater in readiness for the ceremony. A canvas screen would also be rigged in. the bow of the ship, for it would not be possible for the complete court to do as the herald had done the evening before, and come up over the bows: the screen would hide them from view until the ceremony commenced. The court consisted of crewmembers who had crossed the line on a previous occasion, and so were conversant with the initiation procedure. Besides Neptune and his daughters, there would be the Heralds, Clerk of the Court, a Doctor, with his foul-tasting medicine and soap pills, the Barber, with his oversized wooden razor and bucket of whitewash, and also many Policemen and Bears.

So, at two bells in the forenoon watch, the Herald would once again hail the ship, which would again be stopped, but this time, the captain would be waiting on the foc'sle to welcome King Neptune and his court, conducting them to the ceremonial dais situated by the side of the bath.

Everything would now be ready for the initiations to commence, and the bears taking to the bath, the clerk of the court would carry on with the proceedings.

From a prepared list, he would read out a real, or trumped up charge against one of the uninitiated, and he the barber then sat upon his stool, commencing to shave him. King Neptune, sometimes in consultation, with his daughters, pronounced sentence – *so* many soap pills, with; number of duckings – the doctor administered the pills together with a swig from his bottle, and the barber tipping the stool, our victim would find himself in the bath with the bears pouncing upon him in order to carry out the prescribed number of duckings.

In the event of there being no answer to the clerk's call, the policemen would be sent to search the person out. Few, if any, escaped, and on one occasion, an unwilling candidate was lowered from the spotting top by means of being strapped into a Neil Robinson's stretcher.

The initiations over Neptune would make a short speech, and then give *Carte Blanche* for the tables to be turned and a ducking given to the members of the court, after which the ship would again be stopped in order to allow the royal visitors to depart.

The wording of certificates given to commemorate having taken part in such a ceremony vary from ship to ship, but the purport is the same, and I give overleaf, the text of one presented to me whilst serving aboard HMS *Emerald* on the East Indies station, but these events are of course quite rare, and I, during my twenty-four and a half years service, took part in only two, first as one, of the uninitiated, and later as the doctor in King Neptune's Court.

> DOMAIN OF NEPTUNUS REX
>
> HIS BRITTANIC MAJESTY'S SHIP EMERALD, HAVING THIS DAY VISITED OUR ROYAL DOMAIN" THE UNDERMENTIONED PERSON HAS RECEIVED OUR ANCIENT REQUISITE INITIATION AND CERTIFICATE TO BECOME ONE OF OUR LOYAL SUBJECTS. WE DO SIGNIFY TO ALL WHOM IT MAY CONCERN THAT IT IS OUR ROYAL WILL AND PLEASURE TO CONFER UPON HIM THE FREEDOM OF THE SEAS AND TO EXEMPT HIM FROM FURTHER HOMAGE AND SHOULD HE FALL OVERBOARD ALL SHARKS, DOLPHINS WHALES, CRABS AND OTHER DWELLERS OF THE DEEP ARE TO ABSTAIN FROM MALTREATING HIS PERSON.
>
> L.A. HARRIS.
>
> GIVEN AT OUR COURT ON THE EQUATOR LONGITUDE 69°E THIS FIFTH DAY OF MAY NINETEEN HUNDRED AND THIRTY-EIGHT. HIGH CLERK…………………………NEPTUNUS REX…..……………..

Chapter 4

The Culinary Art

THERE WERE several different methods of messing in the service, these varying according to the size of the ship or establishment.

Battleships and larger cruisers, together with the major shore establishments, were usually on what was known as *General Messing*, a method which meant that the cook ratings prepared and cooked all dishes, the cooks of the messes only going to the galley in order to receive the end product.

Cooks of the mess worked in pairs as detailed by the leading hands in charge of their respective messes, this usually being arranged so that a junior in order to gain experience, was paired off with one of the more staid members of the mess.

The term used for two men working together was opposite numbers, but this was usually shortened to oppo's, and so, in this instance, they would become cooking oppo's.

The chief and petty officers however, had staid able seamen or stokers to carry out this cook of the mess duty for them: they were known as chief and petty officers mess-men, being paid a small gratuity by the chief and petty officer, besides which, they were excused most other duties'

Cooking oppo's were usually in opposite watches so that there was always one available, their spell of duty lasting for twenty-four hours,

THE CULINARY ART

commencing with the washing up after dinner. From then on they were responsible for everything to do with the cleanliness of the mess in which they were domiciled, bringing meals from the galley and the serving of such meals, together with, the washing up afterwards., They would also be responsible for the scrubbing out of their mess after breakfast, standing fast from "Both watches for exercise" in order to do so.

As I have already mentioned, aboard general messing ships, little would have to be done by the cooking oppo's in the way of preparing food, but with smaller ships, *Canteen messing*, was the method most likely to be adopted.

Canteen messing ships carried a much smaller complement of cook ratings, sometimes only one petty officer or leading cook, it being their job to tend to the cooking of the various dishes brought up to the galley, the 'cooks of the mess having done the preparing beforehand.

Whereas aboard general messing ships a paymaster commander had to balance the budget; with canteen messing, it fell to the lot of each mess to balance their own.

A general issue was made of all staple foods: meat, bread and potatoes daily; tea, sugar, tinned milk and flour etc., once or twice each week. A cash allowance was also made to allow for the purchase of other incidentals, and it was then up to the leading hand of the mess, or some other member who had been appointed caterer, to arrange menus that would keep within the limits of this allowance. Extra tea, sugar and milk could be obtained on repayment, but other items of food had to be obtained by chit from the N.A.A.F.I. canteen.

Once a month, the cost of such items would be balanced against the cash allowance, and if there was a credit balance, it would be paid to the mess concerned as mess savings. On the other hand, a debit balance would result in a mess bill having to be paid by each member of the mess, amidst much grumbling, and the possible appointment of a new caterer.

Mess savings were usually shared out amongst the individual members of the messes so entitled, but occasionally, a farsighted leading hand would keep them against the possibility of a debit balance the following month.

It is because of these varying messing arrangements that I have decided to devote a chapter to the *Culinary Art,* for the art of cooking is surely in the preparation, and it is this preparation that has caused many a pitfall for the uninitiated.

Preparation of the mid-day meal did not allow for a great deal of time if everything was left until morning, for it had to be in the galley by 0830, so allowing the cook rating to know just what he had to contend with. For this reason, where possible some of the chores, such as the preparing of vegetables, were often done the evening before, whilst other dishes might be partly prepared in the morning, and then finished off at "Stand Easy," which was usually at 1015.

Meat Pie was one such dish; the meat having been brought back to the mess in order to have an awning (pie crust) put on.

Sometimes, to save the trouble of bringing the meat back to have a crust added, a *Steamed Pie* might be decided on. For this, a dough would be made using suet instead of margarine or lard: which after being rolled out, would be placed over the raw meat, covered over with greaseproof paper, and then taken to the galley for steaming: it could then be forgotten about until dinner time.

One evening, a young ordinary seaman aboard HMS *Curlew,* his oppo having gone ashore on night leave, decided that the next day's dinner would be one of these steamed pies, and to get ahead for the next morning, he made the dough overnight. This would have been alright were it not for the fact that the daily meat ration was never issued until morning, so it was never really possible to decide beforehand, just how the meat should be used.

Next morning, at the pipe "Hands of the mess for meat," our young friend returned to his mess with that rarity of rarities, a roasting joint that would really roast; a leg of mutton.

This did not deter him however, his mind had been made up the night before: out came the knife, the joint was cut up into small pieces, and had been cooked, a new dish had arrived. *Leg of Mutton Steamed Pie.*

From the foregoing, it will be seen that cooks of messes were not really able to decide what the main course was to be until they had first collected the joint.

Anything that looked as if it would roast became a *Straight Rush;* this deriving from the fact that it could be laid on a dish of potatoes and rushed straight up to the galley.

Heat pie and steamed pie I have already mentioned., but then there was the *Oosh*, which was in effect, a pie without a lid: it consisted of pie meat cooked with onion and the usual thickening, but any cook of the mess who produced only an *oosh* for dinner, was usually pronounced a lazy bastard, I especially as it could be so easily improved upon by the addition of a layer of sliced potatoes, this also changing the name of the dish to *Water Lilies.*

A popular cold weather dish was a *Pot Mess*, and as the name implies, it really was a mess of pottage: into a large iron pot went the meat, carrots, onions, beans and anything else available which would be likely to add to its flavour. About half an hour before dinner a little thickening and dumplings would be added. And you can no doubt imagine, the gravy from such a concoction would be most tasty, but the reception given by his messmates to another youngster, when he arrived in his mess with a pot mess minus gravy, having strained it off "Like mother does potatoes," would, I have no doubt, be beyond the imagination of most readers.

Some messes did not always appoint a caterer, and the cooks of such a mess would do their own catering. This often led to quite big mess bills, the inclination being for them to arrange meals which took the least preparation, these of course, more often than not, also being the most expensive.

This practice did however lead to one amusing incident; amusing that is, to members of nearby messes. The senior of the two oppo's was about to go ashore on night leave, and his junior partner asked what he should lay on for breakfast next morning. More interested in his shore going than in the next day's breakfast, the following was the reply: "Why not give them a packet of Woodbines and a bar of chocolate." Sure enough, when the men came to their breakfast next morning, they found twenty packets of five Woodbines laid out, together with one bar of chocolate apiece.

It was mainly for breakfast and supper that a caterer had to decide on the menu, for as you have already learned from what I have written previously, the joint issued was the deciding factor on the main dinner course, only the choice of vegetables being left to him.

This last would create quite a problem in the galley if every mess left two or three pots of vegetables for Cookie to look after, so nets were provided for this purpose. Boiled potatoes, cabbage, peas and beans were all cooked in this manner, the nets, each marked with a wooden tally, being placed in a large copper.

The tallies themselves, denoting the mess to which the net belonged, sometimes caused a problem if, being insecure, they happened to come off, and on occasion, a mess might forget to put any tally on at all, which again did not help identification. Another happening, fortunately rare, would occur when someone had been stupid enough to mark a net tally with indelible pencil, for this would guarantee the potatoes being a – very pale shade of blue.

Custard with everything, or nearly everything, was the route so far as sweets were concerned, but this was always taken care of by cookie, a container and ingredients being given to him in the morning, and the end product being collected with the rest of the dinner.

It was an unwritten law that rice pudding should not be on the menu when the ship was at sea, the movement of the ship being likely to cause somewhat of a mess as the rice slopped about during the earlier stages of its cooking.

In the initial stage, only rice grains covered with water were taken to the galley for part cooking, the other ingredients being added later. One grain of rice swells to about six times its original size, as housewives and cooks would know.

A rating concerned with my story was not aware of this. He had eaten many rice puddings no doubt but had never been particularly interested in their make up; not, that is, until it fell to his lot to prepare one for his mess-mate's dinner. The outcome was that cookie, opening his oven door, discovered a dish of rice well and truly overflowing, for our friend, not knowing the quantity of rice required, and not wishing to appear ignorant, had guessed none too well, enough having been put into the dish for puddings far in excess of the one required.

On another occasion, an able seaman said to his young oppo, "I won't be able to get to the mess at Stand easy to see to the rice pudding; you'll have to do it. "O.K" said the youngster, ``what do I have to do?" "Bring it back from the galley" said his oppo, "put the milk and sugar in, also some nutmeg which you will have to get from the canteen, and then take it back to the galley."

Came dinner time, and this young ordinary seaman, very pleased with himself, brought the dish into his mess saying, "Here's your rice pudding lads, but go easy on the nutmegs, they only run to one each" Twenty men in the mess, and he had put in twenty whole nutmegs" just like dumplings into a pot mess.

Some messes, especially if the caterer had an eye to mess savings, did not bother with a cooked breakfast, making do with bread and marmalade or a few cereals, not much considering that the men had already done an hour's work and it was another five hours to dinner. Sometimes on such occasions, a disgruntled mess mate, perhaps having a few coppers to spare, might buy something from the canteen and prevail upon Cookie to cook it for him, then sitting down to his own private breakfast.

Usually however, breakfast consisted of such items as bacon, tinned sausages, tinned tomatoes dried eggs; sometimes a Welsh rarebit, and if available – kippers. These last were not always grilled, for I have eaten them when the only means of cooking was a mess kettle full of boiling water. One would come into the mess, place a pair of kippers in the receptacle, cut some bread and spread it with margarine, pour tea, and by this time, the kippers were considered to be ready for eating. Very tasty too.

Porridge; better known to the men as *Burgoo*, was always cooked in a big iron pot, and although it produced a tasty dish, the washing of this pot was one of the most irksome jobs one could get during a twenty-four hours duty as cook of the mess. Sticking like glue to the inside of the pot, and with only limited washing up facilities, sometimes as much as half an hour would be spent in removing the residue.

A mess kettle of hot water had to suffice for washing up after a meal; plates, cups, saucers, utensils and knives forks and spoons all going through the same water, for hot water was always at a premium.

When finished with, the dirty water had to be taken to the upper deck and thrown down a chute, sometimes an eating implement or two also being ditched, having been inadvertently left in the kettle, the first intimation of this being the clatter in the chute:

Tinkle tinkle little spoon knife and fork will follow soon.

Nearing the end of a quarter, because of these losses, knives forks and spoons were at a premium, so that to eat their meals, one man might have only a fork, another a spoon, whilst another, last to enter the mess perhaps, might come up with the adage "Ah well! Fingers were made before forks" – and tuck in.

Knives forks and spoons could be obtained on repayment, but the majority of messes preferred to wait for the quarterly muster; when a member of the paymaster's staff would muster all the mess equipment, shortages having to be replaced and paid for.

Getting back to menus; supper dishes more often than not, consisted of canteen items, but these being rather expensive, there would sometimes be fish cakes made with tinned salmon or rissoles made with, corned beef, both of these items being available quite cheaply on repayment from the paymaster's stores.

THE CULINARY ART

Cottage pie, also using corned beef, was another possibility and sometimes this would be laid on for dinner, with the meat ration being kept for supper, especially if it had the remotest resemblance to steak; for given enough bashing, it could usually be made tender enough for steak and chips to be served, providing of course that it was the turn of your mess to have chips, these only being allowed on a rota basis; otherwise the cook would not be able to get everything cooked in time for supper.

Supper swapping was quite commonplace between members of the various messes, for with canteen messing, if one did not care for his own caterers choice, it was usually possible to find someone in another mess who had the same opinion about their menu, and a swap would be made. With general messing it was a case of take it or leave it, and if leaving it, then at one's own expense, the canteen could provide an alternative.

The following story, related to me by a chief engine room artificer with whom I once served, is worth repeating because of its humorous side.

This chief belonged to Chatham port division but was on loan to a Devonport ship. The majority of his messmates, including the mess-man had gone ashore on night leave, but there were three remaining for supper, himself and two regular members of the mess. When supper was brought down, it turned out to be a large *tiddy-oggi* (Cornish pasty). One of the two regular members turned to this chief and asked, "Do you care for the ends?" "Not particularly" he replied: whereupon the *oggi* was cut in two and the regulars took half each. The laugh was on them however; for a visit to the canteen produced a meal which was eventually charged up to their mess.

The caterer always made it his business to find out how many of his messmates would be ashore at supper time so that he could cut down on the amount of food ordered. This of course, helped towards mess savings and also prevented wastage, for all leftover food had to be disposed of.

Known as *Gash,* in Malta anyway, these leftovers helped the canteen funds, as a contractor from ashore, known as a *Gashing King,* would pay for the privilege of being allowed to come aboard at meal times to collect it, which same would later be seen on sale outside the dockyard gates at one penny a handful, such a handful being the mid-day meal of the purchaser.

It was generally accepted by naval personnel that the foregoing could be the reason why seagulls were never to be seen in Malta's harbours, for being scavengers by nature, and having been outdone by the gashing kings, they moved on to regions more in keeping with their habits.

A few more words about the cook ratings before closing the chapter. Many a time they would be accused of producing a burnt offering because the end product was perhaps a little overdone, and as the following may show, they were often called anything but Christian.

The ship's company had fallen in, and the executive officer addressed them. "I have received a complaint," he said: "Who was it that called the cook a bastard?" Came the reply *sotto voce* "Who called the bastard a cook?"

From the foregoing it will be seen that the men responsible for putting' the food through its final stages were often the recipients of a few brickbats: bouquets rarely came their way, although they were often deserving of them, for neither Mrs. Beaton or any Cordon Bleu ever had to produce a meal whilst their kitchens were rolling through thirty degrees or more, but these were the conditions that cookie in the small ships navy, quite often had to contend with.

Whether the menus would have met with the approval of anyone who was making a study of dietetics is open to debate, but one thing is certain, and that is that wind was most prevalent on the mess-decks; not always pleasant in such confined spaces, although sometimes quite musical.

Chapter 5

Jack's Ashore

I SUPPOSE that the three most popular pipes one would hear aboard ship were – "Hands muster for payment" – "Up spirits" and "Liberty-men fall in."

Whenever a ship dropped anchor, tied up to a buoy, or secured alongside; providing there were sufficient facilities, some kind of leave would usually be given.

In the larger ports and coastal towns, it would-be all-night leave: this would expire at 0730 for chief and petty officers, but other ratings had to return aboard by 0700. Men underage however, would not be allowed to remain ashore all night, they had to return aboard by 2300.

There was a certain amount of ambiguity about the under age category; for it applied to men under twenty years of age; but if a man was of able seaman status, or it's equivalent in other branches, he was allowed the privilege of all night leave even though he might not have attained his twentieth birthday.

In my own case I was rated able seaman at the age of eighteen years and nine months, and was in effect, underage with over age privileges for a period of fifteen months. Leave for boy ratings however was only given during the afternoons of Wednesdays, Saturdays and Sundays, and then only if they were watch ashore.

Whilst at sea, a ship's company would normally be in three watches; Red, White and Blue, but on returning to harbour there would be a change to Port and Starboard. As both these watches were in two parts, leave would be given to one watch and part of the other, thus allowing three quarters of the ship's company to proceed ashore.

Not everyone took advantage of this, lack of funds being one reason although of course there were others, such as being under punishment, on the sick list, or perhaps, saving up for some specific reason, and there were the odd few, the tight fisted type who, if they had nineteen shillings and sixpence, would try and borrow sixpence so that they could put a pound in the ship's bank.

Once ashore, one's pursuits varied according to taste and the amenities offered, but you can discount the tales which you may have heard about a sailor having a girl in every port, for that is as much a fairy tale as little red riding hood.

It is true that attachments were sometimes formed, but *give a dog a bad name*; the self-respecting girl usually gave us seafaring gentlemen a wide berth, and the not-so self-respecting, setting themselves on a collision course as it were, left it to us to take avoiding action.

At Malta, which in the earlier days of my story was the base for quite a large Mediterranean fleet, it was possible, with only five shillings in one's pocket, to visit a cinema, have two bottles of beer, supper, and a bed for the night, yet still have a small amount of change in the morning. Our finances would usually restrict us to this kind of a run ashore towards the end of the month, but when we were a little more affluent, then perhaps, we might pay a visit to the *Gut*, or to give it a proper name, Strada Strata.

This was a street of steps, with practically every building being a pub, lodging house or cabaret type dance hall, starting with the *Victoria* and *Happy Return* at the top end, and finishing with the *John Bull* and *Morning Star* at the bottom. A few of the pubs were named after ships of the fleet, but this did not mean that the company of that particular ship would frequent it.

The attraction of the larger places was the atmosphere, with the music, the girls, and the cabaret. This cabaret was usually third rate, all the girls of diverse nationalities, quite a number of them claiming to be Russian princesses, the period being not so long after the revolution.

The girls would give one the pleasure of their company if they were treated to a drink, seating themselves expectantly at one's table, but if no drink was forthcoming, they would soon move hopefully to another table. These drinks were not at all potent, being mostly coloured lemonade, the girls augmenting their income in this manner, being given a token with every phoney drink.

The smaller bars, not having these attractions, usually had someone outside touting for business, with vague promises of change upstairs or some other such inducement. One of these, the *Sussex*, was said to have a proprietress who did fantastic things, best left to the imagination, with various empty bottles. As this bar was out of bounds to service men more often than not, I can only assume that the suppositions were correct.

Lodging houses also used to tout for business, but it was usual for the men to find a good one and stick to it for the whole of the commission. One such was the *Wembley*, where Charlie, the proprietor, would put his regulars up on tick when "it was nearly the end of the month, besides which, he would lend a few bob to these same regulars at a slight rate of interest.

The Gut was not the only area such as this: Sliema also had its beer and dance halls; mostly along the waterfront and frequented more by the destroyer men, the destroyer, flotillas mooring in Sliema Creek, whilst the remainder of the fleet, apart from a few auxiliaries s, securing to buoys in the Grand Harbour, Bighi Bay or French Creek.

Valetta also had it's waterfront bars, one of these being" aptly named the *First Last,* it being just that, the first one on getting ashore and the last before returning aboard.

Tombola played quite a big part in the providing of entertainment, two servicemen's clubs, the *Vernon* and the *White Ensign,* producing fairly substantial houses for the lucky winners.

On occasion, visits to what have now become tourist attractions would be arranged: bathing parties to St Julian's Bay, the ancient walled city of Mdina, the Catacombs, and many ancient monuments and temples, but in the main, these last were much too highbrow for jack ashore, and shore-going in Malta was mostly confined to Valetta, Sliema, and other towns adjacent to the harbours.

It sometimes happened that a rating would fall for one of the lovelies from the *Gut* or it's environments and request permission to marry. Was it coincidence I wonder, that such a request was, all too often, followed by a U.K. draft before any wedding arrangements could be made.

Leave granted to watchkeepers was more flexible than that granted to the remainder of the ship's company. These watchkeepers were men that worked watch and watch, four hours on and four hours off for twenty-four hours, then having twenty-four hours off. They were signalmen, telegraphists, engine room auxiliary watch keepers and seamen who were employed as quartermasters or bosun's mates. This watch entitled them to the privilege of remaining ashore until four hours before their next watch, so that an afternoon watchman would not have to return aboard until 0830, whilst a dog watchman could remain ashore until 1130.

Although it was usual for ships' boats to take liberty men ashore, in Malta one made use of *Dghaisas* (pronounced disohs) which plied for hire. These were similar in shape to, but smaller than the Venetian gondola, and they gave one the advantage of being able to return to the ship at any time instead of having to wait for the next liberty boat, there always being an abundance of these dghaisas available.

Having mentioned these two facts, I now come to the story which they have been leading up to. It concerns a watchkeeping signalman returning aboard three quarters of an hour absent over leave through oversleeping. His leave should have expired at 0830, and when taken before the "Officer of the Day" he gave the following excuse for his lateness. "Well sir, it's like this. I left shore in plenty of time, early in fact; but before I could get back to the ship it was eight o'clock and *Colours*. I told the dghaisa man to lay on his oars (a salute given by ships' boats at such a time) but he refused, so I made him pull round the fleet for punishment: and that sir, is why I am late.

A good excuse, and worthy of a better fate than the one day's pay and leave stopped which was meted out to him, the story being disbelieved by both the Officer of the Day and the Captain.

If a man's wish was just to drink beer at a slightly reduced cost but in less pleasant surroundings, he would proceed on Canteen Leave to one of the naval canteens, leave being from 1930 until 2200 for this purpose, with ships' boats being used and no dressing up required. There were two of these canteens; one at Corrodino for ships in the Grand Harbour and another at Manoel Island for the destroyermen.

Being aboard a unit of the Mediterranean fleet did not mean that one remained permanently at Malta: The Spring Cruise took us in the direction of Gibraltar and combined exercises with the Home fleet.

The two fleets would become known as the red and blue fleets respectively, and after they had done battle to the satisfaction of the many admirals present, the might of Britain's navy would make their way into Gibraltar, and what a gathering that would be.

During the 1920 to 1939 period, the Mediterranean fleet consisted of two battle squadrons (8, ships), two cruiser squadrons (8 ships), four destroyer flotillas (36 ships), and when aircraft carriers became operational, these would also be in company. In addition, there would be submarines in varying numbers, together with the many auxiliary vessels necessary for the fleets' operations. Take a like number for the Home fleet and it was indeed a show of strength, but in those days, Britain really did *rule the waves*.

With the combined fleets being berthed at Gibraltar, no all night leave was given, accommodation being not nearly enough to sleep the number of men who would require it.

I suppose that for entertainment value, the highlight of the Spring Cruise was the Home fleet versus Med fleet soccer match. Far more partisan than Celtic versus Rangers or Arsenal versus Spurs, no matter what the result, it was always taken in good part, and the match over, both spectators and players would proceed to the canteen and play the match all over again, using their pint pots to illustrate the various moves.

Another competitive event was the sailing for the Gibraltar Cup; a spectacular indeed, with hundreds of boats of all classes taking part, the crews of each and everyone hoping to have the honour of winning the cup for their own respective fleet.

It was at Gibraltar that the Crown and Anchor boards came into their own. Illegal; as were all forms of gambling, it was also big business. Bribes to keep away would be offered to the petty officers in charge of the naval patrols, and if they would not cooperate, then lookouts would be posted so that the operator could be given the tip off when a patrol was approaching, the board then being quickly gathered up.

If an operator thought that he had an intruder encroaching on his territory, he would sometimes pack up his own game and try to break the interloper. I once watched such a happening, but in that instance, it was the intruder who came off best.

Double up and you can't lose is a generally accepted tenet in the gambling world, but it is equally true that to do so one must have enough capital to continue betting.

For the uninitiated I must explain that the game of Crown and Anchor is played by means of a board marked off in six sections and each being marked with a symbol, these being a crown, anchor, heart, club, diamond and spade; there are also three dice which have the same symbols. To play, the mugs would back their fancy; the operator would roll the dice, and then pay out on the three symbols which were showing. Take for example the diamond; one showing would pay even money, two would pay two to one, and all three up would pay three to one.

In the instance in which I am writing, the operator out to break his rival stuck to the diamond, starting with a five-shilling stake. At first he more than held his own, but then the diamond began to have a bad run, and having stayed down for ten consecutive throws, with our operator having doubled up at each throw, he had to pull out, having lost £128 on the last throw and a total of £255-15-0 altogether. Of course, if three diamonds had come up on the last throw he would have collected £384 plus his stake; but continuing to watch the game, I have to confess that diamonds stayed down for twenty nine consecutive times, and then only one came up for an even money chance. Perhaps you can now understand why I said earlier that the *Mugs* back their fancy, for in the long run it is only the operators who are on the winning side, hence the bribes and lookouts.

On sailing from Gibraltar, the Home fleet would return to their home ports and Easter leave, but the Mediterranean fleet would split up in order that many of the Algerian, Moroccan and Tunisian ports might be visited.

I well remember a visit to Sousse, long before it was a holiday resort, tying up to leeward of a load of camel dung which was awaiting shipment, so that although we were afloat, it meant taking a trip ashore for a breath of fresh air.

A visit to Algiers comes to mind because of a rather expensive essay into night club life; expensive that is by my standards, for at the time I was an able seaman with a total income of five shillings per day, my companions being in like circumstances. *Le Chat Noir* as the nightclub was called, served drinks to the customers, but one was only presented with the bill when about to leave. It therefore came as quite a shock to us when we found that a drink which could be obtained in any ordinary bar for sixpence, had here been charged at three shillings a time, and to make matters worse, there being no all night leave, we had to be back aboard by 2300, and so had been too early for the cabaret.

The spring cruise was sometimes extended into the Atlantic so that a visit could be made to Madeira; alright for some, but only those in the higher hierarchy, leave being given to chief and petty officers, and I had not, at the time of my visit, reached such an exalted position. It was, however, an entertainment in itself watching the bum boats trying to do business alongside; fresh fruit found a ready sale especially when we were able to translate the words of the boatmen. "Changey for Changey," they kept calling out, meaning that they were willing to barter their wares against any articles of clothing that were going spare.

Many of the boats were piled high with basket chairs and the like, and I have no doubt that plenty of business might have been done were we a cruise liner, but with H.M ships space was at a premium.

After a cruise, the return of the fleet to Malta was somewhat of a red-letter day for the inhabitants of the island. The Barracca Gardens, which overlooked the Grand Harbour, would be crowded with people, the majority of them Maltese watching the return of their bread and butter, but there would also be a few naval wives numbered among them.

On the first night ashore after a cruise, the *Gut* would be well patronised; the pubs would be still touting for business, perhaps with a new cry – "Come inside Jack; new girl while you've been away" In some instances it might have been true, a new face having come to the island, but more often than not it meant that a girl from one of the other bars had transferred her allegiance.

Two months at Malta, With the exception of short absences in order to carry out gunnery and torpedo exercises, would give the inhabitants nice time to replenish their coffers; at least insofar as the contributions from jolly jack were concerned, and then it would be time for the fleet to proceed on the First Summer Cruise.

The fleet's summer absence from the island was always in two parts; the first taking in ports and resorts in France and Italy, and then, after a few weeks of renewed acquaintance with Malta, the second part would take us more into the areas of the Aegean and Adriatic Seas, with visits to the Grecian, Yugoslavian and sometimes Turkish resorts. It was during this second cruise that the regatta took place, the fleet coming together in such places as Navarino Bay or Argostoli, where a great expanse of fairly sheltered water was available.

In all I spent eight years with the Mediterranean fleet, and if all the places visited were mentioned, it would be like reading from an oversize travel brochure, so I will con-fine myself to mention just a few.

The south of France had a fair share of visits, Cannes, Nice, Juan les Pins and most other resorts on and around the French Riviera. At this time, these watering places were the playgrounds of the well to do British so that although both the ships and the officers were welcome, no one had much time for the ratings; not that it mattered a great deal, for the average matelot was quite adept at creating his own amusements.

Posh the resorts may have been, but they still had their brothels, which we used to visit, more for, to use a present-day idiom, a giggle, rather than to sample the end product, although of course, some did succumb.

In conversation with a girl in one of these places, I gleaned the information that she was not a regular, but a shop assistant on holiday, hoping soon to be married and using her leisure to give pleasure, at the same time making money towards her nuptials.

Some of these houses also had a small cinema, showing the most erotic of films; not merely for the entertainment of the visiting crews, for the elite, male and female alike, were the main audiences.

The rate of exchange in those days was very favourable, and with, champagne at five shillings a bottle – not vintage, but quite palatable – we were able to make merry at a reasonable cost; but Oh, the hangover!

On occasion, when anchored off Juan les Pins and given all-night leave, the liberty-men would mostly proceed to Nice by train, a better choice of cafes being available in the larger town. These visits however, sometimes finished with one having to sleep rough on the railway station at Nice, waiting for the early morning train.

Accommodation was available, but many of the hotels within our means must have had some sort of arrangement with the street walking sorority, would be guests having to be accompanied by a member of the opposite sex.

Whilst writing of Nice, I must mention a most pleasing journey from there to the scent factories at Grasse, an exhilarating drive by a crack-brained French coach driver only adding to the enjoyment. Visits to the Italian resorts were very much the same, the only difference being the language and the currency, but being unable to speak in foreign tongues anyway, it only left us with the various currencies to contend with. Naples merits a mention however, as visiting there gave us an opportunity to take part in an excursion to see Pompeii with its erotica, which I believe, is now shown only to male tourists, the females meanwhile, having to visit the kitchens and find out more about the erotica from their men folk.

Fiume, on the Adriatic coast, I visited on several occasions, and I was always struck by the friendliness of the people. One can only suppose that this was because the majority of the inhabitants were not true Italian, the town belonging to Austria Hungary before World War I. It cannot be found on present day maps though, for after the second world war it was ceded to Yugoslavia and is now known as Rijeka.

Unfortunately for the junior ratings, there were many places in the Mediterranean, where, like Madera in the Atlantic, leave was restricted to chief and petty officers, whilst at others, a ship would come to an anchorage and there would be no facilities ashore whatsoever. As I have mentioned before, adept at creating their own amusement, the men would, in these circumstances organise picnic parties on the deserted beaches.

Requests for permission to use one of the ships' boats would go to the boat officer, but as in all probability he would have more requests than there were boats available, a rota system might have to be operated.

I have myself played beach cricket among other games, on beaches absolutely deserted except for our own party, beaches which later became a. holiday maker's paradise, and have now become so overcrowded, that such games are practically impossible.

Seine net fishing was another popular pastime, there being ample room to run out the net in a large semi-circle from the shore, both ends then being manned and pulled in hand over hand, hoping for a large catch, and sometimes getting absolutely nothing but a few sea-cucumbers.

These expeditions would be mostly under sail: a whip round would be made among the participants to offset the cost of food from the canteen, and then they would be away. Sunday was the most popular day for these jaunts, the party being able to leave immediately after divine service, thus being assured of a nice long day.

Whilst abroad, a record was always kept of leave taken, and where it was found that a man had not set foot ashore for three months – and this did sometimes happen – he would be compelled to take part in some form of recreational leave.

Although this leave record was also kept aboard ships serving in home waters, this service had so many advantages, that compulsory leave never had to be resorted to for apart from the three seasonal leaves at Easter, Summer and Christmas, there was always the opportunity for the odd week-end or two when berthed in one's home port.

There were also courtesy visits to be paid to many British watering places, together with showing the flag cruises to Scandinavian and other western European countries, but having myself spent very little time aboard a fashionable unit of the home fleet, most of the knowledge I have of such visits is only hearsay.

Never having served on the China or West Indies stations, I have no first hand knowledge about either of them, but I do know that ships serving in the West Indies were manned almost entirely by volunteer crews, and I volunteered for such service myself, but without success.

Life afloat in far eastern waters was not very different to Mediterranean service, or so I have been led to believe. Plenty of sporting activities, bars with dancing girls, spending Chinese dollars, Hong Kong dollars or Japanese yen instead of francs, lira or drachmas, using sampans instead of dghaisas to go ashore in; what's the difference?

The East Indies station was different however. Most of the shore going was confined to having a few lukewarm beers in the canteen at Trincomalee, visiting a cinema at Colombo, and to gratefully accepting the hospitality of the garrison sergeants' messes, they also appeared to be extremely glad to see us. Believe me, there were very few volunteers for service, on this station, and I do not intend to write more about it now, as my one East Indies commission is being dealt with more fully in a later chapter.

During the war years there was no set pattern for granting leave to men afloat. When in harbour night leave might be granted, but more often than not the ship would be under sailing orders, so this would be restricted.

In home waters boiler cleaning usually meant a leave, as did refitting; but when operating in the South Atlantic, Indian or Pacific Oceans, home was a long way off.

Fortunately for the men serving, the civilian population of South Africa and Ceylon were most kind, and there was an abundance of offers for the spending of a few days in their homes. Of a few days spent on a tea plantation at Telewakele in Ceylon, and a week in the South African fruit growing district of Paarl I still have vivid memories, and when undergoing a war time refit at East London, it was practically open house for the whole ship's company.

The reader will not I hope, come to the mistaken conclusion that we were having a whale of a time, for the above, to me were but a few pleasant interludes during the two years and nine months that my ship was operating in these waters, and this period will also be dealt with more fully in a later chapter.

Chapter 6

Body and Soul

NO ONE can expect to go through life without suffering from some ailment or other, no matter how small, and members of the Royal Navy being no exception, there was always some provision to alleviate their suffering, be it the well equipped sick bay of the larger ship or the medical chest carried by even the smallest unit.

There was never any sick parade as such: certain times were set aside for fresh cases to report to the sick bay, and it had to be serious indeed if one wished to see the medical officer at any other time.

A rating feeling under the weather would, in the larger ships, report to the duty sick berth attendant. Better known to the men as poultice walloper, he, after taking down all particulars, made arrangements for the sufferer to see the medical officer, who would place the patient in one of the following categories.

Attending List. Fit for duty, attending sickbay only to receive treatment as prescribed by the M. O.

Light Duty List. As above, but duties to be of a sedentary nature only.

Sick List. Excused all duties. Leave and rum ration stopped.

Hospital Case. Patient in need of nursing care. To be transferred to hospital or hospital ship.

Men placed on the attending or light duty lists would have to attend the sick bay, probably three times a day, in order to have wounds dressed or receive medicines, but would otherwise carry out normal ship-board duties. Although ratings on the sick list were excused from these duties, more often than not they would spend the working day keeping the sick bay clean.

On occasion, when there was no hospital or hospital ship within reasonable distance, cots in the sick bay had to be brought into use to accommodate ratings in need of hospital treatment, the sick berth attendants then having to carry out nursing duties. Smaller ships rarely included a medical officer in their complement, and members of such ships' companies had to throw themselves upon the mercy of the coxswain.

Qualified in first aid, he would be able to take care of minor casualties, or prescribe and. administer a dose of opening medicine, but for more advanced ailments, the patient would have to be sent to some other ship in company which carried a medical officer.

Towards the latter part of my service, as a coxswain, apart from dressing a few boils and minor cuts, together with prescribing the occasional number nine or aspirin, the only other need of my limited medical knowledge, was when called upon to assist with the setting of a broken leg.

There was another category of sickness which, although it did not render a man unfit for duty, did cause his rum ration and his leave to be stopped.

Call it what you will, be it Ladies Fever or Penal Catarrh, it was officially known as C.D.A. (caught disease ashore). Not for these unfortunates the secrecy one sees offered to a civilian in similar circumstances: segregated, irrespective of rating, they would be messed apart from the remainder of the ship's company, probably screened off; and as one hard case was heard to remark – "We don't have to ring a bell and call out 'Unclean', for everyone already knows it." Such segregation was not possible aboard the smaller ships, neither would the necessary treatment be available, and in these circumstances, transfer would have to be arranged to a ship which did have such facilities.

The medical officers with whom we usually came into contact were of lieutenant or lieutenant commander rank, but I once had a surgeon rear admiral intercede on my behalf, and in doing so he probably saved my life.

At the time I was in the Royal Naval Barracks at Chatham undergoing treatment for gunfire deafness, and because of this I was classified as unfit for sea service. Such a classification should have caused my name to be removed from the drafting roster, but for some unknown reason I was posted for the corvette *Zinnia*.

To appeal against this draft I had to appear before a surgeon commander, but it was of no avail: in his considered opinion, the only treatment I required was to sniff a little salt water up my nose and I was therefore perfectly fit.

Fortunately for me, I had time to keep one more appointment with the E.N.T. specialist, but when I told him that I would not be coming again, and the reason for it, he, although only of lieutenant commander rank, must have got busy, for the outcome was that a signal from the surgeon rear admiral stopped my drafting. A few weeks later *Zinnia* was lost with all hands.

Another medical officer, a surgeon lieutenant, must be remembered by many a boy undergoing training at Shotley at the same time as I was there. No matter what the ailments, be they concerned with parts of the anatomy as far apart as a sore throat or a bruised toe, the boy was always required to pull his foreskin back so that a thorough inspection could be made of the penis.

Known to us all as *Foreskin Freddie*, the reason I think being obvious, he, under the slightest pretext, would prescribe a dose of the foulest tasting medicine, not because of medical attributes, but rather as a punishment. For such things perhaps, as feet a little unclean, not reporting sick earlier, or even speaking overloud, whilst awaiting one's turn, would almost certainly mean a dosage; and boys feeling unwell, quite often, when learning that *Foreskin Freddie* was duty, preferred to suffer a little longer rather than' face the possibility of a *F/F* special.

In times of peace, death aboard ship was very rare, due no doubt to the fact that the very sick were, where possible, transferred to hospital; most to recover, but some unfortunately to end their days, often in places far removed from their native land.

So, in the event of the medical staff being unable to do more for an. ailing man, so that he passed on, passed over, or just died, it would fall to the lot of the chaplain to say a few words over the mortal remains of such a man before commending his soul – to God.

It was the chaplain who ministered to the men's spiritual needs, but unlike the medical officer, who except for an emergency could only be seen at specified times, the chaplain, or *sin bosun* as he was more commonly called, usually let it be known that he was available at any time.

All the larger ships carried a chaplain and in most instances he would be representative of the Church of England, although there were, also Roman Catholic chaplains, and others representing the Non Conformist bodies.

Church on Sunday was compulsory, the Church of England service being held on the quarter deck. Seating arrangements consisting of planks laid across capstan bars, which in turn were raised from the deck by being placed on wooden buckets, somewhere along the line caused the opening lines of the hymn, The church's one foundation Is Jesus Christ our Lord, being parodied as follows:

The church's one foundation. Is capstan bars and buckets.

But seating for officers at these services was on chairs brought up from the wardroom by the officer's stewards, assisted by seamen of the duty watch.

If the fleet was in company, one of the ships would hold a Roman Catholic service which Catholics from other ships would have to attend. This might also be possible for other denominations, but if facilities existed, they would be allowed to proceed ashore for their service.

I never came across a Salvationist chaplain, and to this day I do not know whether such a person exists; but no matter where a ship happened to be, there nearly always seemed to be ample provision for members of this order.

A man could request to change his religion, and although this did not happen very often, the new religion was most likely to be that of Salvationist, but whether it was the doctrines of their General Booth, or the possibility of some buckshee runs ashore that made them change, one can only hazard a guess.

Holy Communion and Mass were always held for the more devout, and even aboard ships which did not carry a chaplain, the men, were never refused permission to attend such services aboard other ships.

Aboard ships without chaplains the Sunday service was still compulsory, the commanding officer assuming responsibility for the conducting of it, unless of course he was a catholic, in which case the next officer in the chain of command would take over. It would be the same with morning prayers, although these were often waived aboard small ships, the routine being much more flexible.

These officers, and likewise the chaplains, were only doing their jobs, but life afloat sometimes brought one into contact with men suffering from a religious mania, these being known on the lower deck as *Holy Joes*.

During my service I came into contact with only two, both officers. The first, a commissioned gunner, had a thing about swearing, and he would give a bible quotation to any man who he overheard letting it rip. Why he should be so concerned about it is beyond me, for a one-time Bishop of London was once heard to remark that a deaf ear should be turned to the swearing of a sailor, as it was part of his everyday language.

The second was an engineer officer, and besides being a bible thumper he was a rabid teetotaller. This being the case, it came as quite a shock to a certain stoker petty officer, when having worked late to finish off a job, he was asked by this officer if he would care to come to the wardroom for a drink.

This was a fairly general practice throughout the Royal Navy, anyone doing something out of the ordinary to help an officer being asked down to the wardroom pantry for a drink; very much appreciated bearing in mind that in the days which I am writing of, the lower deck was dry.

But to get back to my story – the drink offered in this instance was the choice of either a mineral water or an orange squash, and the petty officer told Holy Joe in as many words, that he could *stuff* it.

It was rather gratifying, a few days later, to hear that this particular Holy Joe had been made to look rather small by none other than the chaplain.

The wardroom officers gave a party. These sometimes get rather hectic, and on this occasion, the chaplain had joined in with a will, the result being that he became decidedly merry. The next day our holy friend decided to take the chaplain to task for his part in the festivities, the following conversation taking place.

Said H.J., "I cannot understand how you, a man of God, could disgrace your cloth by taking part in last night's exhibition."

The chaplain's reply was quite short and left him speechless. "If you can show me anywhere in the bible you are so fond of quoting from," he said, "Where it states that our Lord drank nothing else but cocoa, then I will become a teetotaller."

Chaplains themselves though, did not attempt to push religion down one's throat. They would discuss it with anyone who had a mind to, just as they would hold confirmation classes for those wishing to attend, but they could equally well join in a discussion about the more mundane things of life.

Whilst the chaplains looked after our spiritual needs, there were many religious bodies ashore that made themselves responsible for those of a more down to earth nature.

Missions to Seamen are to be found in all parts of the world, as are the Salvation Army; there to help with a bed or a meal at very down to earth prices, and I doubt if there are many naval ratings who, at some time or another, have not had cause to be thankful for Agnes Weston.

Having religion and a little money, she put the latter to good use by opening up hostels in both Portsmouth and Plymouth, and at these one was able to get a bed for a shilling and a meal for very little more.

I myself have spent many a night at Aggie Weston's as it was called, and no one ever asked me if I was Christian, Jewish, or even an atheist for that matter. This surely, is true religion, doing good without Bible punching. Was it some kind of endearment I wonder, that when the ship was launched and named HMS *Weston Super Mare*, it immediately became known as *Aggie on Horseback*.

To end this chapter, I would like to pose a question, although I doubt if I will ever know the answer. If there is a hereafter, who will be most likely to make the grade, the Aggie Westons or the Holy Joes.

Chapter 7

Crime and Punishment

MANY AND varied were the punishments metered out to the wrongdoer and to my sorrow the information which I gained about them was mostly at first hand.

From the rope's end of the new entries instructor, to a spell in the detention block I still have vivid memories, but whilst in my service as a boy rating I managed to steer clear of caning, and in later years I was never to suffer the deprivation of good conduct badges or of disrating.

The Kings' Rules, Regulations and Admiralty Instructions was the guidebook to the awarding of punishments, and a quarterly record was kept by the master at arms, or aboard smaller ships the coxswain; these having to be sent to the Senior Officer of the squadron or flotilla. That he went through them I have no doubt, for they would sometimes be returned because a charge had been incorrectly worded, this too having to follow a set pattern – Did remain absent over leave – Was absent from place of duty – Did skulk on the mess-deck – Was in improper possession of etc.

Although illegal, minor punishments were sometimes given by a chief or petty officer, a junior rating preferring to do an hour's extra work rather than be put on a charge and taken before the officer of the watch.

This officer was not *allowed* to award more than two hours extra work, and if the offence warranted a more severe punishment the offender would have to be placed in the commander's or first lieutenants report. The commander and first lieutenant were also restricted in this respect, and in the event of *their* not being able to deal with the matter, it would have to be passed on to the commanding officer.

Punishments involving extra work were known as No. 16 and No. 11, the first mentioned consisting of two hours extra work each day for a specified number of days, the work usually being done between the hours of 1700 and 1900.

No. 11 punishment was rather more severe. Normal dinner time was from. 1200 until 1315, but a man under No. 11 punishment would only be allowed half an hour, the other three-quarters of an hour being spent on extra work. On make and mend days (a half day off, traditionally from the olden days, when men were given an afternoon off for the making and mending of clothes) the afternoon had also to be spent at work, and after tea, when the remainder of a ship's company had free time, the men under punishment would be working from 1700 until 1900 and again from 2000 until 2100. They would also be called half an hour before the remainder of the hands and start work that much earlier. No. 11 punishment also meant that a man so punished had his rum ration stopped, but this was sometimes got over by the mess caterer adding a tot of water to the mess issue.

The maximum period for this punishment was fourteen days. Sunday fortunately being a day of rest, no extra work: would have to be done, although it would be counted as a day of punishment.

Punishment for overstaying leave was stoppage of pay and leave, the scale being one day for every three hours absence up to forty-eight hours, and one day for every six hours absence thereafter.

Stoppage of leave did not affect seasonal leave – only night leave – and as the punishment had to run on consecutive days, time spent at sea would also count, so that it was possible for a man to have seven days leave stopped and yet be no worse off than the remainder of a ship's company, the ship having been at sea for the whole of the period.

Stoppage of pay could result in a man being placed in *crown* debt, and in this event, even though his stoppage of leave punishment might be finished, he would not be allowed to go ashore, for men in debt to the crown were also automatically under stoppage of leave.

One reason for crown debt could be a man's allotments to his next of kin, for being allowed to allot up to six days pay per day, this would continue to be paid even if he had suffered a forfeiture of pay for some misdemeanour.

I should have mentioned earlier perhaps, that leading rates and above were exempt from punishments which included extra work: they: could however have pay and leave forfeited, but any offence meriting a more severe punishment would be classed as a *warrant offence*, and this would be something that not even a commanding officer was empowered to' deal with.

Deprivations of good conduct badges and disrating were warrant punishments, as was cell punishment and detention. If an offence merited such a punishment, the offender would have progressed from the officer of the watch to *Captain's Report*. He would then appear before the captain who, being unable to deal summarily would order "Remanded for Warrant." The warrant would then have to be made out and sent to the Senior Officer for approval.

Should the offence have been committed by a junior rating, when the warrant had been approved and returned to the ship, lower deck would be cleared of all hands and the offender would stand, under escort and facing the remainder of the ship's company except the master at arms or coxswain, who would be standing behind him.

First 'the Article of War relevant to the offence would be read out, and then the warrant. These articles of war covered every possible offence punishable by naval discipline. They were always on display in the ship's company quarters and were also read-to them periodically. – Any person subject to this act, who shall show cowardice in the face of the enemy, shall suffer death, or such other punishment as may be hereinafter mentioned – Being in improper possession of –

Committing sodomy with man or beast – Remaining absent without leave – Striking a superior officer – etc. etc.

I suppose that the warrant arising from my own offence would be as good an example as any, the preamble going something like the following.

"Ship's Company – Off Caps". "That any person subject to this act, who shall remain absent over leave, shall be dismissed from His Majesty's service with disgrace or suffer such other punishment as is hereinafter mentioned." "Ships Company – On Caps."

"Whereas it has been brought to my notice, that on the twenty-eighth day of December 1926, Leonard Arthur Harris, "One pace forward March – off cap" "Did remain absent over leave 143 hours 27 minutes, namely from 0830 on the above mentioned date until 0803 on the third day of January 1927. Having heard the evidence of Lawrence Stride, Lieutenant Commander R.N. in support of the charge, and he calling no one on his behalf, I consider the charge to be substantiated against the said Leonard Arthur Harris and hereby sentence him to be detained in the Royal Naval Detention Quarters Portsmouth for a period of twenty-six days, together with the forfeiture of thirty two days pay and the stoppage of thirty-two days leave. Given under my hand this fifth day of January 1927, signed … Commodore R.N."

After this came the command. "On Cap – One pace back march – Prisoner and escort right turn – Double march," and I was on my way.

Chief and petty officers, leading rates, and men holding good conduct badges could not be sentenced to cell punishment or detention until they had first been deprived of their good conduct badges and disrated.

Occasionally, but happily very rarely, it had been known for a higher rating to commit an offence which led to his being disrated to able seaman and sentenced to a period of detention. Disrating did not mean that a man had to serve permanently in the lower grade,

CRIME AND PUNISHMENT

for after a probationary period of from six to twelve months he could apply to be reinstated.

With few exceptions, warrant punishment would disqualify a man from ever receiving the Long Service and Good Conduct Medal and the £20 gratuity that went with it, for such a punishment upset the period of Very Good character, which had to be continuous. The qualifying period for the award was fifteen years consecutively very good conduct, with the preceding years being not less than good. If however a man was able to obtain a character assessment of very good for eighteen consecutive years he could also qualify, providing he had no other assessment below fair, and I, having learned the error of my ways after a spell in detention at the age of eighteen, qualified for the award in this manner.

Of course it should really be said that the medal and gratuity were awarded for fifteen or eighteen years service with undetected crime, for many wear it who have transgressed, and the matelot is a great believer in the eleventh commandment – *Thou shalt not be found out*.

My spell of detention was not a very happy one, but as it was meant to be a deterrent one could not expect the detention quarters to be run like a holiday camp.

First came the journey from Chatham to Portsmouth, and for this there was an escort of one petty officer and two able seamen. For changing trains in London I was handcuffed to one of the escorts, and only after the train had left Waterloo station were these handcuffs removed.

At Portsmouth, we were met by a pick-up truck, which took us to the gates of the detention quarters, and from then on, except for Sundays, all movement was at double time.

The gates opened and a voice boomed out – "Prisoner – Double March." I entered the gates and the voice continued – "Right Turn." Still at the double I turned right and entered an office – "Halt," the voice commanded – "Right Turn." Obeying the order, I turned right, and only then did I see that the voice belonged to a

Royal Marine sergeant, he apparently being my one-man reception committee.

Everything of value was taken from me, the rules and regulations of the establishment were read out, and I was then informed that the chief and petty officers in the establishment, together with the Royal Marine sergeants, were always to be addressed as *Sir*. In the meantime, a petty officer had entered the office and he now took over. It was he who had opened the gates and given the escort a signature for my person. My kitbag and hammock were lying outside the office. "Pick up your kit-bag and hammock," the petty officer ordered. I did so. "Double march," he continued, and I was on my way to the cell block, being headed in the right direction by a "Right Incline".

As I was at the double and the petty officer was walking, there were several "About Turns" and "Double mark times" to, make certain that I did not get too far ahead, so that although the distance was only about sixty yards, I had in effect, travelled more like two hundred and fifty, at double time with the best part of one hundredweight on my back.

On arriving at the cell block I was required to bathe under supervision just as in the new entries, and after attiring myself in a white duck suit, I collected my toilet gear with the exception of my razor, after which I was locked up in my cell.

It did not take very long for the contents of my new surroundings to become imprinted on my memory, for apart from a table, stool and bedboard there was a polished metal bucket, a pot for emergency toilet use, a fork and spoon,(the meals turned out to be such that one never had to be in need of a knife) a Bible, and being a seaman there should have been a seamanship manual, but I found myself with a stoker's manual although I was able to change it later.

Before very long the cell door was opened, for it was tea time, and I was presented with a miniature loaf – probably about a quarter of a pound in weight, a small amount of margarine and a mug of tea, after which the cell door was once again locked.

Tea over, whilst the remainder of the inmates were locked in with their tasks, I had to go to the sick bay for a medical.

Before retiring for the night, all offenders had to pay a visit to the heads, again under supervision, for the heads had no doors and one's business had to be done in full view of the instructor.

Preparing for next morning our buckets had to be filled with cold water and taken back to our respective cells: when called, this was to be used, first for personal washing, and then for scrubbing the cell floor.

By the time this had been done the instructor would have been round opening the cell doors, thus allowing us to obey the call of nature and then collect razors in order to shave.

The length of time spent on these visits to the toilet was not decided by the requirements of nature, but by the instructor in charge: it was most excretion by numbers, for it was he who decided when we had finished, and even if the urge was not there, one still had to go through the motions.

Such visits were carried out five times a day; early morning, after breakfast, before dinner, before tea, and once again prior to being locked up for the night – Any urge after being locked up for the night meant that one had to use the pot provided, and if ever the need did arise for this eventuality, it would mean one added task to perform, for these pots had to be kept highly polished and the stains caused by excreta and urine took quite a lot of removing.

These of course were things which I learned as time went on, for I have really got no further than the first evening.

Everyone had to be turned in by 2100, bedding being laid out on the wooden bed board provided. Although I did not know it at the time, for reasons that will come to light later, this was the last I was to see of my bedding for several days.

Next morning, the washing, cell scrubbing, toilets and shaving over, it was time for the offenders to be locked up once again, leaving them free to continue with their task whilst awaiting breakfast.

As I had not yet been allotted such a task, I was able to look through the stoker's manual, which I had not, as yet, been able to change. For my sins, I also made good use of the bible, turning down the corners of twenty-five consecutive pages, each representing a further night of detention, one of which was to be straightened out each morning, a check on the number of days remaining.

Breakfast consisted of porridge seasoned with salt, bread and margarine, with tea as a beverage. There was never any variation from this, and as a matter of fact, all the meals were extremely uninteresting.

After breakfast it was time for the days out of cell activities to start. First a visit to the workshop to hand in the previous day's tasks and collect materials for those of the day just started, but I, as a new member of the club, did not go with the remainder on this first morning: instead, I was taken before the commander in charge of the detention block.

He told me that I would be allotted a task which could earn me so many points daily. My bedding would be taken away until sufficient points had been earned for its return; also, more points had to be earned before the receiving or writing of a letter would be allowed.

My task was to be the making of thrum mats, and this involved the punching of holes in a double thickness of canvas by means of a marline spike, thrums cut from a manila rope then being threaded through these holes. Thrums had to be a fixed amount to the row and the rows evenly spaced, the requirements being one and a half mats per day.

Out of cell activities consisted mainly of keeping the establishment clean, rifle drill with specially weighted rifles, six-inch gun loading drill – each projectile weighing one hundred pounds, and physical training with the accent on the physical.

After my interview with the commander I was taken to join up with a party of men who were scrubbing the floor of the gymnasium, and the method was typical of all cleaning jobs that were carried out by the prisoners.

The men were not left to get on with the job – In this instance they were lined up across the gymnasium floor in a kneeling position, each with a bucket of water, a scrubbing brush and a cloth.

Standing behind them was an instructor, and he gave his orders as follows.

"Wet the floor" – We did as ordered, carrying on until the next command.

"Scrub" – Scrubbing would continue for as long as the instructor thought fit; then came the next order.

"Rinse" – Wet cloths were applied.

"Dry Up" – We dried the patch which we – had scrubbed, sometimes – going through the motion as if one of the party was a bit slow and had not finished. The next command would be for us to "Move back," and then the cycle of events would be repeated until the whole of the gymnasium floor had been scrubbed.

One afternoon each week was given over to laundry and here one might almost have been back with the new entries, for nudity was the order of the day, and after clothes washing there would be bathing and inspection before returning to the cells for tea, a stop at the heads being made en route.

I set to at my task with a will, determined to win back my bedding as soon as possible; for sleeping on a wooden bed-board, with no bedding or coverings might have been alright in mid summer but this happened to be January.

My objective was reached in three days, but it had, I'm afraid, taken its toll. Two weeks leave, with another six days A.W.O.L had taken some of the toughness out of my hands, and in consequence the excessive use of the marline spike had made a large blister in the palm of my right hand.

The soreness of my hand had slowed me up somewhat, and I was now unable to complete my task. Because of this I was hauled up before the commander for punishment and sentenced to seven days deprivation of bedding, and so after only one night, it was back to the bed-board.

Having to continue with the mat making my hand became worse, and hoping to obtain some relief I requested to attend sick parade and hopefully showed my; hand to the medical officer: I need not have bothered, for after asking how it had happened, and listening to my; explanation, his only comment was – "Well, you'll have to use the other hand won't you"

Never having been ambidextrous, his suggestion did not help much; but I struggled painfully on and fortunately; although I was never able to complete a full day's task whilst under deprivation of bedding, I was not hauled up before the commander again, not that is until the last day of my punishment: it had all been saved, up for me.

This time I was sentenced to a three days punishment diet, which meant that the skilly which was served up for breakfast was also repeated at dinner time.

Because of this light diet I was excused from the strenuous exercises outside and was confined mostly to my cell, but unfortunately this meant that I was required to increase my mat making output.

To keep up with my task, my hand still being sore, I tried to work a fiddle by putting in less thrums per row, but did I get away with it? Unbeknown to me, the completed mats were checked by weight, and so I was in trouble once again, this time the punishment being three days close confinement.

This, I should imagine, was a punishment to end all punishments, three days being about as much as anyone could put up with.

Left to one's own devices, even the seamanship manual was taken away: the diet was bread and water, besides which I was deprived of both belt and shoes. This last I feel sure, was to prevent anyone with suicidal tendencies from using their shoelaces or belt for a successful conclusion by hanging, for one was at such a low ebb during this period.

On the first day of the three, the bread and water being issued at breakfast time it was quickly disposed of: after that there was nothing else to do but read the bible.

Hearing the rattle of plates at dinner time I waited hopefully by the door, hoping for some more bread at least, but nothing was forthcoming.

It was just the same at teatime, and by then I was ravenous and searched the floor of my cell for any crumbs which I might have dropped in the morning.

It was practically impossible for me to get to sleep that night, it was so cold and as I have mentioned before, it was January. I was also without bedding, my clothing hung loosely about me because I had no belt, and I had gone to bed on an empty stomach.

Next morning I. thankfully accepted my bread issue, but this time I did not eat it all, the lesson had been learned and I saved half of it until the evening.

One good thing did come of my close confinement however, for having no task to perform my hand had healed considerably, and as the day which followed was a Sunday and a day of rest, I was able to complete my spell of detention without falling foul of anyone again.

No tasks having to be performed on a Sunday it was almost a free day if you can call being locked up in one's cell free, but after returning from morning exercise (walking as it was a Sunday) and a service in, the dockyard church (compulsory) we were allowed to choose a book from the library and take it with us to our cell.

My punishments within the establishment would, in other circumstances, have affected any remission which I might have been able to earn on my sentence but having been awarded twenty-six days meant that I had to do the lot, for no remission could be earned on any sentence under twenty-eight days.

This could be better illustrated I imagine, if I give as an example a prisoner who started his sentence of twenty-eight days on the day after I commenced my twenty-six days. He was able to get three days remission on his sentence, and so only served twenty-five, which meant that we were both discharged on the same day.

I never did earn enough points to be allowed to write or receive a letter, but on the day that I was discharged three letters were handed to me, all of which had been opened for censorship.

Although there had been a few upsets during my period of incarceration, and although it had been hard labour unpaid, I must in all fairness say that at its conclusion I was at the peak of physical fitness.

Chapter 8

Spit, Polish and Flannel

BULL-SHIT BAFFLES Brains is a saying usually associated with the Army because of happenings such as whitewashing coal dumps in readiness for a V.I.P. visit. The Army is not alone in this respect however, and Jack had more than his fair share of flannel to contend with.

This flannel – much more polite than bull shit don't you think? – was instilled into naval personnel from the very beginning of their service, for as new entries their quarters were subjected to Captain's rounds on the Wednesday of each week, the cleanest mess in each division being awarded a cake.

To win this coveted award, which amounted to one slice for each boy in the mess, brightwork would be the order of the day, and although an article might look quite nice with a coat of paint on it, if polishing was likely to be an improvement, off came the paint and out came the metal polish.

This mania for spit and polish existed right throughout the peacetime navy, and although heavy weather at sea might play havoc with the upper deck bright work, as soon as an anchorage or mooring was reached, no time would be lost in getting the shine back once again.

Afloat, the captain would normally carry out his rounds in two parts; below decks on Saturday and the upper deck on Sunday.

Saturday was usually the only day of the week on which there were no divisions. Both watches for exercise would be fallen in after breakfast and then would be employed in the cleaning ship until 1100.

Below decks it would be what one might term organised chaos; watertight doors were kept shut to keep intruders from walking on the freshly scrubbed decks: not only would the doors be shut, but the dogs securing them being tied from the inside, anyone trying to gain entry would be told to "Go round the other way." What other way was open to them could be anybody's guess, all compartments being in the same state of *Getting ready for Captain's rounds.*

On the mess-decks men would sing away as they worked. Not the sea shanties of olden times, neither anything too modern, but some of the old favourites such as *Nellie Dean*, although before very long was almost certain to be rendered.

> She's a tiddley ship
> On the ocean she'll flit
> She's steaming by night and by day
> When she's in motion
> She's the pride of the ocean
> You can't see her arse 'ole for spray
> Side, side, *Curlew's** ship side
> Jimmy looks on it with pride
> He'd have a blue fit
> If he saw any shit
> On the side of the *Curlew's* ship side
> This is my story, this is my song,
> We've been in. commission too f-ing long
> Roll on the *Rodney, Nelson, Renown,*
> This two-funnelled bastard is getting us down

*or any other ship depending on which one the singers happened to be serving.

It only needed one man to start up, and the whole party would join in, not perhaps the best of male voice choirs, but it seemed to help with the scrubbing and polishing.

At 1100 the hands would be piped to – "Quarters clean guns" – more polishing of brightwork and burnishing of steel.

During this period the Captain, followed by a retinue of officers, together with the Master at Arms, Chief Bosun's Mate and various messengers would carry out his rounds below decks.

No cakes were awarded on these occasions, these being the prerogative of the new entry training establishments. There would however be a certain amount of buck passing, and I once saw a cartoon, which I will try to describe, depicting this rather well.

The Captain, finding something not quite to his liking, turned and tore the Commander off a strip, he in turn passed it on to the Divisional Officer, he to the Chief Bosun's Mate and so on down the line until it came to the poor little ordinary seaman who should have done the job, but he, having no one to get on to, without more ado turned round and kicked the ships cat.

Sometimes during these mess-deck rounds a mess, if not up to the required standard, would be ordered a re-scrub. This automatically stopped shore leave for all members of such a mess until there had been a complete dogwatch re-scrub and further inspection by the duty officer, and as you may well guess, those responsible for the original scrubbing would be sadly lacking in popularity for a time.

Saturday was not a regular day off, although if a ship was in harbour, leave would be piped for the watch ashore, the remainder of the hands being employed on last minute cleaning jobs on the upper deck in readiness for the next morning's rounds.

The hands would have a short lay in on Sunday morning, not being piped to "Fall in" until 0615. Because of this the scrub decks period would be of shorter duration; not that it mattered to any great extent, extra time having been spent on them, during Friday afternoon and Saturday morning, wooden decks being holystoned and steel decks polished. After breakfast there would be a short period for a final tidy up, and then it would be "Hands to clean" into either Number Ones or Number Sixes according to the station and time of the year. Ones being the best blue serge and Sixes the best whites.

Usually paint and brushes had to be returned to the paint shop by 1530 on a Saturday afternoon, but most captains of tops managed to have a pot and brush tucked away somewhere. These came in use for a last-minute touching after the hands had gone to clean, men being allowed, unofficially, to stand fast from divisions for this purpose. Known to all and sundry as the *Hook Rope Party*, it was their job, to carry out last minute touching up so that everything would be just so for the Captain. Because of this there was probably more cursing on a Sunday morning than at any other time of the week, for men could on returning to the upper deck after changing, brush against some paintwork that had been dry a short time before, only to find that they were now wearing a paint smeared suit, necessitating a hurried search for some turps in order to clean up. It always seemed nothing short of miraculous that inspecting officers could always be steered clear of these freshly painted areas, for I never knew or heard of one coming into contact with any.

In my opinion, the biggest load of flannel was reserved for the periodical Admiral's inspection. There was always plenty of warning given of these events, and events they were, for not only did the Admiral carry out an inspection of the ship for cleanliness, he also put all hands through their paces at *General Drill* and *Action Stations*.

On the morning of the inspection, all brooms, brushes, scrubbers, buckets and other equipment which had been used to clean ship for the occasion, together with any other unwanted paraphernalia, would be loaded into one of the ship's boats and towed away to remain out of sight until the admiral had departed. If any cleaning gear did happen to be on show it was all new and unused to help create a good impression. I would have dearly liked, just once, to hear an inspecting admiral say – "It's all very nice, but where is the cleaning gear in use at the moment."

General Drill was, more often than not, carried out in competition with other ships of the squadron, each of whom would break a pendant at the yard arm as an evolution was completed. It was also part of the drill for the yeoman of signals to interpret the signal hoist appertaining to each phase as soon as possible, – for as one evolution was completed another one would be under way.

For about two hours the before mentioned organised chaos would once again be in evidence, with men hurrying to their stations in response to such pipes as – "Prepare to tow For'ard" – or – "Collision at Number – - – Station" – and then perhaps – "Starboard Watch change over Lower Booms" – "Port Watch out Kedge Anchor."

"Clear Lower Deck, everybody aft" – would almost certainly be followed by – "Let go second anchor" – and this in turn meant that "Weigh second anchor by hand" – would be a natural in the train of events.

By the time that the drill was nearing completion, almost every wire, hemp or grass hawser in the ship would have been put to use, and this meant watching one's step for fear of a trip, but there would be a trip of a different nature still to come, for the last evolution was invariably – "Away all boat boats' crews, Pull round the Fleet." This was not necessarily the end of it however, for there was always the possibility that the boats might be ordered to carry out minor drills on their own, the signals being interpreted by means of a boat's signal book, with which the coxswains of boats were supposed to be conversant.

Completion at last, the admiral and his retinue would depart, the ships' officers in all probability making their way below to partake of a pre-lunch noggin, leaving Jack to restore order from chaos and make everything ship-shape once again.

A certain amount of flannel was of the men's own making, they vying with one another for that extra little bit of show. The coxswain of a boat might, at his own expense, buy a cotton rope and then, in his own time, make yoke order to improve the appearance of his boat.

Then there was the boat hook drill carried out by the bow man and stern sheet man of a power boat. The more movements in the drill the better it looked, but all really unnecessary; a boat hook being a means to an end, and either used for bearing off when leaving a ship's gangway or a jetty, or for holding on whilst the boat was alongside, and I can remember when boat hooks were used for just this purpose without the showmanship of the drill.

There are no longer any battleships in the Royal Navy, and consequently no longer are there any picquet boats with their polished brass funnels. A battleship had two of these craft, and known as the first and second picquet boats, the first had one brass band on its funnel, that of the second being graced with two.

If I remember correctly, it was HMS *Benbow* which first produced an all-brass funnel for her picquet boats: earlier these had been the prerogative of the Royal Yacht *Victoria and Albert's* boats. How many duty free gins it must have cost the *Benbow*'s commanding officer to have these funnels made only he and the dockyard official responsible would know, but this is only one of the many instances of one-upmanship that was, and probably still is, part of the way of life in the Royal Navy.

Chapter 9

Fun and Games

MEMBERS OF the lower deck were most adept at creating their own amusements; they had to be, for shore leave was not always possible, neither was the money for a run ashore available every time leave was piped. Card schools were very much in evidence, and as playing for money was taboo, scores would be surreptitiously kept on paper, settlement day coinciding with pay day.

Solo Whist and Nap schools were to be seen in operation almost every evening, and as these were made up of the same four or five men night after night, should one of the school want to go ashore, he would invariably have to get a stand-in for the game, and as scores were kept on paper such a stand in would not be responsible for any losses, neither would he gain any benefit from a winning streak.

Cribbage and Bezique were also very popular, and occasionally one would see Euchre being played, the stakes for these games probably being a sip of the next day's rum ration: Pontoon and Shoot were also played; but as money had to change hands at these games the men had to be most careful, for money changing hands over a game of cards could lead to dire consequences for the players if they were unlucky enough to be caught. Mahjong too was also quite popular, but I suppose that the most popular game of all was Uckers.

This Uckers was the parlour game of Ludo with a difference. Two dice were used, and an intricate system of barriers could be built up to give an advantage, for they could not be passed by an opposing player, although an opponent could send the counters in the barrier back to base :If he could get close up behind it and throw a specific number of double sixes.

The popularity of this game was such that ships had their own Ucker Leagues and Knockout Competitions, the finals of which would in all probability be played on the foc'sle, using a specially made board about six feet square, counters the size of dinner plates, a five gallon drum as a shaker, and dice proportionate in size.

There were also challenges issued to other ships in and a signal might be sent as follows:

To: Torpedomen HMS *Nonsuch*
From: Stokers HMS *Neverfloat*
We challenge you to an Uckers match our ground 1700 today

If the challenge was accepted, a suitable reply would be sent, and at the appointed time the visiting players, suitably attired in fancy dress, would repair aboard the host ship and battle would commence.

The larger sized board would be used for these encounters, and many 'comic interludes would occur, such as a team praying to Allah when a double six was badly needed.

I suppose that I should have mentioned Darts as another of the indoor pastimes which helped to while away a few hours whilst afloat, but I have no doubt that many of the pub – experts would lose some of their expertise if, like us, they had to take a ship's movement into account when making their throw.

So far I have only written about indoor pastimes, but on the large ships, Deck Hockey and Deck Cricket were played, and when at sea a 0.22 rifle range might be set up, with a Spoon Shoot to make matters more interesting.

Tombola, or Housey-Housey, was in vogue long before the advent of Bingo in England, and although played aboard most ships, it was only allowed at the commanding officer's discretion, so there might be the anomaly of perhaps three ships in a squadron being allowed to play, whilst the fourth, whose commanding officer was anti, would have to find some other form of amusement.

Many of the ships had their own concert parties, comparable with many Seaside Follies, and from time to time, ships of all classes, would organise impromptu talent competitions. Better known as *Sod's Operas*, the most noteworthy of these were, in my opinion, held on Thursday nights in the canteen of the Royal Naval Barracks at Chatham. Cash prizes were awarded on a popular vote, voting chits being distributed amongst the audience for this purpose.

Quite a varied programme would follow; ballads, monologues *a la* Bransby Williams, and sometimes smutty parodies of the same. Although smut when rendered, usually received a rousing reception, such items rarely figured on the prize list.

There had to be ten items on the programme before the full prize list could be effected, and there is a story which has been handed down, that on one occasion, when only nine participants had been forthcoming, the chairman gave out that unless another act came forward, the prize list would have to be restricted.

The consequence was, that an elderly stoker – elderly that is by R.N. standards – went up on to the stage and said; "Gentlemen I have enjoyed the acts, and it is hardly fair to them that through no fault of their own they should be penalised. "I now give you my act. I can't sing and I can't dance, but to make the number up I will show you my big, fat, hairy arse" and amidst thunderous applause he dropped his trousers and did just that.

There is probably more fiction than fact in the foregoing, but we did get the occasional stripper, hardly striptease, it being bread and bread, but the act always followed the same pattern, the stripper, starting with his cap, disrobing to the following ditty.

This old cap of mine
The inside is quite new
But the outside has seen some dirty weather
So, I cast my cap aside
For I mean to travel wide
As far across the world I'm going to wander

So it would go on, a verse for each article of clothing-right down to the last piece, and eventually the singer would be standing, full frontal, in full view of the audience, naked as the day he was born.

Another pastime, amusing to both participants and audience alike, was the children's parlour game *Priest of the Parish,* but the naval version was somewhat more hilarious. For the uninitiated, a few points about the game might be appreciated, and so I will do my best to make them as clear as possible.

A Priest of the Parish would be appointed, and he had a right-hand man known as Man John. The remainder of the court then named themselves as caps, but whereas in the children's version it was Red Cap, Blue Cap etc., naval participants named themselves Bunker Plate, Custard in a Pea Net, Swinging Tit, or some other such outlandish name. Started by the priest, the dialogue proceeded as follows:

The priest of the parish has lost his thinking cap. Some say this and some say that, but I say Bunker Plate!"

Bunker Plate: "Me sir? You lie sir"
Priest: "Who then sir?"
Bunker Plate: "Swinging Tit."
Swinging Tit: "Me sir? You lie sir"
Bunker Plate: "Who then" sir?"
Swinging Tit: "Man John."

It had to be remembered, that when talking to, or about the priest, a two handed salute had to be made, and for Man John a salute using only one hand, but it was definitely not done for any of the other caps to be saluted.

So the repartee went on; with quick fire question and answer until someone was put out of office for making a *Faux pas* of the drill or the dialogue. In this event, a court of inquiry would be held, and after punishment had been awarded and meted out, the priest would restart the game, providing all dues and debts are duly paid.

Probably my explanation does not make for very interesting reading, but I have known such a game to last for over three hours, with every minute of it being a laugh.

Participation in physical sport was always encouraged, and luckily the facilities for such participation were usually more than adequate.

There was an abundance of Soccer, Rugby and Hockey pitches at most naval ports, and in the warmer climates Water Polo could be played alongside one's own ship, the nets being suspended from spars. It was also possible for platforms to be rigged alongside so that other aquatic events might take place, these platforms being used for sprints, whilst competitors in long distance races were taken 'to the required distance by boat, and then swimming back to the ship.

Athletics also had their place in the sporting activities of naval personnel, individual ships having their own sport's day; this enabled a team to be selected to allow participation in their squadron or flotilla sports.

A canteen fund usually defrayed the cost of colours for the various teams, but as a general rule, all other items of sports kit were the personal belongings of the competitors. This canteen fund was administered by a committee elected by the ship's company, it being one of their functions to way up the pros and cons of a request for a grant before deciding for or against it. The funds main source of income was a percentage of the N.A.A.F.I. takings, and also, when tombola was played, there was a levy on these takings.

One did not have to be a member of a ship's team in order to get into a game of football; each part of ship had its own team, and there was an inter part league run by many of the larger ships. The honour of representing one's ship might also lead to the additional honour of being picked to play for the fleet, for representative matches were played against the Army and the Royal Air Force, and also Maltese teams such as Sliema Wanderers and Floriana. I also remember; in 1932 I believe, Tottenham Hotspurs visiting the island, the Royal Navy team being the only one that they were unable to get the better of.

Cross-country races over seven miles were also held at Malta, usually starting from the racecourse at Marsa. In my earlier days, the team representing a battleship numbered one hundred men, each of the two battle squadrons holding their own competition and the winners competing against each other on another day to decide who should hold the trophy. In later years, the teams were greatly reduced in numbers, each consisting of only twenty-five members, and both squadrons going in together.

Inter Services athletics also took place, and these have been the only occasions where I have been a spectator to, or taken, part in, a medley mile relay race. For this event teams consisted of four members, two running a 220 yards stint, one a quarter of a mile, and the anchorman running the last 880 yards. As I am writing of a time well before the introduction of staggered starts into athletics, you may well imagine the bumping and boring which happened at the first bend.

Another sporting event only seen during my service days was a Milling Competition. Teams for this comprised one at each weight in the boxing scale, two teams lining up at opposite corners of the ring. At the bell, the two lowest weights would climb into the ring and fight all out for one-minute flat. There would then be another bell, at which the first two contestants would leave the ring and the two at the next weight would climb in and have a go. The bouts would continue until every weight had been in opposition, the judges then deciding on the winning team by awarding points as in boxing;

the winners going on into the next round, the losers retiring to lick their wounds.

Six-inch gun loading drill also had a place in the competition world of the larger ships. This competition was not limited to the six inch gun crews: other departments also formed crews and. went into training for the event, so that there would be stokers, signalmen and miscellaneous ratings all competing for the honour of being the fastest crew to load twelve rounds, with perhaps a few bruised fingers and toes to show for it, bearing in mind that each projectile weighed one hundred pounds and that they did sometimes get dropped.

I have often thought that Tug of War could have a larger following in civvy street, even to being a three A's event at least, if not an event for the Olympic Games.

At one time, competition between the various branches of the Armed Services was very keen, and it was an event which was always included in the Royal Tournament, besides which, fleet athletic meetings also had a place in the programme for such a competition.

Teams would go into strict training, and although the event was decided on a knock-out basis, so that a team, after weeks of training, might have no further interest in the competition after the first two pulls, more than enough volunteers were forthcoming to go into these training sessions.

I hope that I have been able to give the reader some idea of how the men afloat might spend their leisure hours, but not all would take part in the indoor and outdoor activities which I. have mentioned.

Some there were who would spend such leisure time for profit: clothing and shoes sometimes needed repairing, and men with the necessary expertise would set themselves up in business, first appearing before the Captain in order to request permission to do so.

Apart from these two categories, there would be barbers requesting, the necessary permission and also men wishing to start up as a dhobeying firm, for not all men would do their own washing: some were always quite prepared to pay others to do it for them.

Chapter 10

Jack at Work

I DO not suppose for one minute that the term *Jack of All Trades* originated aboard ship, but it was true of the seaman branch in many respects.

The numerous chores that came their way during periods of cleaning ship would I think, be ideal qualifications for a housemaid; scrubbing decks, cleaning brass-work and washing paint-work coming into that category, whilst doing their own washing and ironing would no doubt, stand them in good stead if they wished to apply for a post as a laundry maid. Prowess in the culinary art has already been mentioned, but the aftermath of washing up plates, cutlery etc. and the cleaning of cooking utensils, left one fully trained for a post below stairs as a scullery maid.

There was also more to know about painting than which end of a paintbrush to use, but it did not always do to show too much prowess in this respect, for if there were any special jobs to be done, a special painting party would be detailed which would surely include the more adept, destined perhaps, to spend the working day below decks when the weather was more conducive to a job up in the fresh air.

When painting the ship's side, a certain amount of acrobatic know-how had to be acquired, whilst for painting or washing down aloft one had to be a bit of a trapeze artist.

For the high wire act there was the job of blacking down aloft. As the name implies, this meant the application of black bitumastic to all the standing rigging, and for such a job one certainly had to have a head for heights.

A more down to earth endeavour would be captain of the heads, ideal training for the position of public lavatory attendant, the only difference being the absence of rude words and obscene drawings on the walls.

Storing and provisioning ship was always carried out by the seaman branch, the latter task not without a certain amount of sarcasm, a favourite saying being, "Them as eats it ought to get it in," but it would avail nothing, and when going alongside a tanker to take on fuel, it would be the duty watch of seamen who would have to get the oil hoses aboard in order that the engine room department might take on food for their furnaces.

Occasionally a party of seamen would be detailed to help with the cleaning out of the double bottoms, a thankless task, with a naked candle flame for company to make sure that the surrounding air was fit to breathe. One had to scrap and chip away any rust, and then paint the bulkheads and deck heads with red oxide; not a very pleasant job in such a confined space. The only good thing about such a task was that while it lasted it paid an extra nine pence per day.

The day-to-day cleanliness of the ship's side was taken care of by a party of seamen, known as the *side party*, which party had a petty officer – known as captain of the side – in charge.

Having so many captains aboard a ship may be somewhat confusing to the layman so I will endeavour to clarify the situation. Although the rank of captain was denoted by the wearing of four gold rings, the commanding officer of any Royal Navy vessel would have the courtesy title of captain no matter what his rank, be it commander, lieutenant commander, or even lieutenant, such title being given by virtue of his, being in charge of the ship. So it was that any rating, being in charge of any specific part of that ship became known as captain of that part; captain of the foc'sle, captain of the quarter deck and captain of the side all being petty officers, whilst further down the scale there was the able seaman, employed in keeping the heads (toilets) clean, being known as captain of the heads.

This latter reminds me of a story concerning a doting mother who received a letter from her sailor son. She could not wait to get out and tell her neighbours the news. "I've just heard from my son Jimmy," she said. "He's getting on ever so well; they've made him a *Head Captain*." What he had written of course was that he had been given the job of captain of the heads.

But getting back to the side party, it was also one of their jobs to paint the cable between the hose pipe and the water line whenever a ship anchored or secured to a buoy, for it would never do for one of H.M. ships to have rusty cable in view: this had to be painted the same colour as the ship's side, and the task would be started upon almost before the order "Finished with Main Engines" had been passed from the bridge to the engine room.

A bosun's party would be responsible for the maintenance of the running rigging such as boats' falls and any other job where splicing expertise was necessary, the party being of the more staid, every finger a marline spike type.

All seamen were supposed to be proficient in the splicing of ropes and wires, but it did not come easy to many of the junior ratings, and although practice makes perfect, as most of the work was easily coped with by the bosun's party, opportunities for such practice rarely arose.

The majority of the torpedo party were torpedomen first and seamen afterwards, they being mainly employed on the maintenance of torpedoes and electrical installations, but they also had to conform to the early morning routine carried out by the remainder of the seaman branch.

Only the seamen, and where carried, the royal marines, were early risers: the remainder of the ship's company having the privilege of a lay in until "Guard and steerage" at 0615. There were of course a number of seamen employed on special duties such as quartermaster, bosun's mate, motorboat's crew etc. Known as quiet number men by the remainder, they too, when not on duty, were entitled to the privilege of this lay in, as were members of the duty watch who had been required to work after 2300 the previous night.

Even the men on the sick list had to be out of their hammocks by 0615, but this is likely to be more understandable when I say, that because of the lack of space, many hammocks would have to be slung over mess tables, and with the men coming down to breakfast at 0700, these hammocks just had to be out of the way.

Whilst at sea the daily routine did not alter overmuch. Cleaning ship still had to continue, but in addition, there were certain sea duties which had to be carried out.

Masthead and bridge lookouts, engine room telegraphs men who also acted as relief helmsmen in order to give the quartermaster a spell, and bridge messengers all came into this category; jobs, each in their small way, helping towards the running of a ship at sea. At dusk, a party, usually two in number, would be detailed to tend a set of oil burning navigation lights, these to be used in the event of an electrical breakdown. At least once during a watch the officer of the watch would pass the word for these emergency lights to be taken to the bridge, and woe betide a rating who had failed to keep his lamp properly trimmed. In time of war, when ships were completely blacked out, or *darkened* to use the proper term, the tending of oil navigation lights was one job which never had to be carried out.

Another seagoing job was that of life buoy sentry. He would be stationed in close proximity to a life buoy which would be complete with a flare working on an acetylene gas principle. The cry of "Man Overboard" would be the immediate signal for the release of this life buoy, the chain of events supposedly being that the seawater would activate the flare, the man overboard would see this and make for the buoy, whilst a boats' crew, also seeing the flare, would proceed in the same direction in order to effect a rescue.

When a ship was at sea, a boat's crew, known as the Sea Boat's Crew, would at all times remain in the vicinity of their boat so that it could be lowered and away without delay. If some unfortunate did happen to fall overboard however, the call would not be "Away Sea Boat's Crew," but "Away Lifeboat's Crew" thus bringing a greater sense of urgency into the proceedings.

A normal working day was reckoned to be from 0545 until 1600, with an hour for breakfast, a ten-minute break during the forenoon, an hour and a quarter for dinner, and another ten-minute break during the afternoon.

"Stand Easy," as the ten minute breaks were called, and the breakfast and dinner hours, were, officially, the only periods during the day when a man was allowed to smoke, but from time to time, one or another of the working party might steal away for a quick draw, first asking permission to go to the heads, for a man could not leave his place of duty in order to relieve himself without first asking permission from the petty officer or leading seaman in charge.

Permission granted, they would, on arrival at the heads, seat themselves and light up, a smoke being the only reason for wanting to visit the heads in the first place. These *dry idlers* as they were called, did leave themselves open to a charge of "Skulking in the Headroom," if such a charge could be proved, but who was to say whether a man, seated, with his trousers down, was in fact skulking, or really obeying the call of nature.

"Stand Easy" as a tea break was something that gradually developed, probably through the will of the majority, for in my earlier days it was just a ten-minute smoking break without any refreshment, but enterprising as always, a brewing up for the initiated began taking place in many odd cubby holes about the ship, and eventually the stand easy brew up became official even to the cooks of the mess being allowed time off to make the tea and then for washing up afterwards.

Any work outside normal working hours had to be accepted with good grace, and even the watch below would be called out if the occasion warranted it: all without extra pay of course, and men were often heard to say – "There are only twenty four hours in a day, but they expect you to work for twenty five."

Chapter 11
All God's Creatures

THE KEEPING of pets was always at the commanding officer's discretion, although it was not unusual for a man to bring the creature aboard and then request permission to keep it.

It was nothing out of the ordinary for a ship to have a cat or a dog for a pet; bears and lion cubs have also been known, and prior to a ship returning to the U.K. after a spell of foreign service, there would be numerous requests for the keeping of canaries, but not all would survive the change of climate, and they would be sadly depleted in numbers before reaching the home port.

Monkeys, mynah birds and parrots were also quite popular, and within reason, permission to keep such pets was usually given.

Requests were sometimes refused because the animal which had been brought aboard did not really come into the pet category, one such I remember being a mongoose, the owner being most disappointed when told that he would have to take it back ashore in order to return it from whence it came.

Chameleons sometimes found their way aboard; not because the owners wanted them as pets, but because they had been prevailed upon to buy them whilst they were in their cups. These creatures would become a source of amusement for a time; messmates of the owners catching flies and cockroaches to feed to them, this solely for the purpose of seeing their long tongues in action. They would also be a source of experiment of colour change, moving them quickly from one colour to another to see whether their colour would change likewise, chameleons supposedly being able to change colour according to the surroundings.

In my experience, the most amusing pets were the duck and drake of HMS *Emerald*. Donald and Dora, as they so obviously had to be called, did not join the ship together. One able seaman Polly Hopkins brought Donald aboard at Colombo after returning from camp at Diyatalawa. Originally bought to augment rations, Donald was allowed to live because the owner had not the heart to kill him, and neither would he allow any of his shipmates to do so. A request to keep him as a pet was to the surprise of everyone approved and he more or less had the run of the ship.

A wife for Donald was presented by some well-meaning civilian in Colombo, probably feeling sorry for him in his celibacy. It may have been the sea air, or perhaps they were getting the right kind of food, but whatever the reason Donald certainly made up far lost time, and mating occurred at frequent, and sometimes most inopportune, moments.

Probably the occasion which caused most laughter was when HMS *Emerald* played HMS *Norfolk* at Trincomalee for the squadron soccer cup. Gaily bedecked with emerald green ribbons about their necks, they were led onto the field, and then and there decided that it would be an ideal spot to carry out their amorous intentions, right at the feet of Rear Admiral and Lady Patricia Ramsey, who at that moment were about to have the players and officials presented to them. Often one would hear that either Donald or Dora had fallen overboard, and a boats' crew had been sent to carry out a rescue; but no, one seemed to mind, such was the popularity of the pair.

Dora produced only three eggs, and although the captain of the foc'sle, Petty Officer Shorty Matthews, tried to hatch them with an improvised incubator, it was without success.

When the ship eventually paid off, it was this same Shorty Matthews who took Donald and Dora home with him, where in the more natural surroundings of a rural back garden at Great Yarmouth, they were allowed to live out their lives in peace, *and* multiply.

A similar happening, which unfortunately did not have the same happy ending occurred whilst I was serving aboard HMS *Aster*, a flower class corvette. In this instance it was a chicken, which again had been bought to augment rations, and again the owner had not the heart to kill it. There was of course, no request to keep it as a pet; pet chickens were unheard of, but Stoker Petty Officer Fred Russell did become very much attached to the bird, too attached as it turned out, for one morning, looking aft from the bridge, the captain saw Fred lying in his hammock with the chicken for company. This was too much, and sending for me, the captain gave orders that the chicken must die.

Fred wanted no part in its demise and so it was left to me to carry out the execution and disposal, this disposal I might add, being a chicken supper for the chief and petty officers mess.

There was one exception from this repast – Fred – and the presentation of the wishbone neatly adorned with a black bow, did little to endear his mess mates to him, until the passing of time eventually healed the breach.

Aster had two other pets during my time aboard her, both of the canine species. The first was presented to one of the ratings by a girl at Cape Town. This girl was known to her many admirers as *Bubbles*, and so as *Bubbles*, the animal also became known. Unfortunately, her reign as ship's pet was short lived, as she went mad and jumped overboard somewhere in the Indian Ocean, no rescue attempt being made in the circumstances.

Bonzo was purchased ashore in Bombay as a puppy, and although he remained with us for longer than did *Bubbles*, he also went mad, but not being so accommodating as his predecessor he failed to jump overboard, so once again I had to act as an executioner and shoot him.

Many of the pets which found their way aboard ship would not have done so if the owners had been stone cold sober at the time of purchase, for it is a true saying that *when the beer is in, the wit is out,* and this; coupled with the expert salesmanship of some of the vendors; sometimes led to some quite amusing purchases.

One instance involved an able seaman at Alexandria. This A.B. was prevailed upon to buy a donkey at a give away price, but of course, as soon as; he arrived at the ship's gangway he had to release it, being told that donkeys as pets were not allowed. This would have been fairly obvious to anyone in their right mind, but our friend had been supping overmuch. The vendor of the animal, fully aware of what would happen – he had probably made a sale before – followed at a discreet distance, and when the animal was released he regained ownership, and I have no doubt, congratulated himself on a quite lucrative transaction.

Apart from the pets that were acquired from time to time, most ships had their quota of pests. One would become accustomed to rats, for they would often run along a fan shaft above a row of hammocks and I recall to mind a petty officer cook named Jackie Sharp setting snares for them as one would to a rabbit.

A dog watch pastime might be a rat hunt, where if a rat could be roused out from a coil of rope or some other hiding place, it would be chased all over the ship, eventually being done to death when cornered, or escaping perhaps to some inaccessible spot and living, perhaps to be hunted again at a later date.

There was always an abundance of cockroaches, especially in the warmer climates, and as these seemed to be found mainly where food was kept, I doubt if anyone who has served aboard one of H.M. ships can in all honesty say that he has never, at some time or another, swallowed a cockroach or two.

We did find a use for them as runners in a cockroach race occasionally, releasing them in the centre of a large circle, the winner being the first one to reach the perimeter.

Seagulls could also become pests of a kind, carrying out dive-bombing; without warning, such bombings not being at all conducive to our having their well-being at heart. In spite of this tit-bits would be fed to them, more I think, so that we could admire the artistry of their swoop, which would allow them to take such morsels from between a finger and thumb, without so much as harming either of these digits.

A favourite term for these birds was *Ruddy Great Chief Stokers,* not that anyone really believed that seagulls were are-incarnations of chief stokers who had gone before.

Although seagulls were rarely seen about the harbours of Malta, ashore there was no shortage of goats.

On hearing their cry one would know that the milkman was on his way, but not with milk float and bottles. He would have his herd of goats with him, milking as required into the customer's own container, and as each goat was milked dry, the goat herd would kick her backside and off she would trot, finding her own way home

When I first visited Malta, the summer headgear for the navy had not long been changed from straw hats to sun helmets, and the old timers tried to convince us newcomers that when this had happened, half the goats in Malta died of starvation, these straw hats having been their main source of food. Rather stretching it a bit, but they did seem to have a most varied diet, so perhaps a straw hat or two did figure in their menu of earlier days.

The last of God's creatures which I will mention in this chapter is the matelot himself.

Mickey Rooney once said in a television interview, that in his opinion, actors were like grown up children, and I suppose that in a way, without belittling his capabilities as a fighting man, the same was equally true of a sailor.

His love of dressing up on occasion, the ability to fall out with his best friend, and the making up after the black eyes and bleeding noses all being reminiscent of the school playground as was the bully who would sometimes appear on the scene.

One sometimes made good friends aboard ship, but more often than not the friendship would last only for the duration of the ship's commission. Such was the drafting procedure; it was certainly possible that two close friends, after a ship had paid off, might never serve together again. I will be dealing later with ships and shipmates, so will now bring this chapter to a close with a few details of what were probably the four most important pieces of paper which had any bearing on a man's career afloat

The first of these was a man's Service Certificate. As the name implies, this was a record of a man's service from the time he joined until the day of his discharge. On it would be recorded the names of all ships and establishments in which he had served, together with the dates of such service. Dates of passing for higher rating, the award or deprivation of good conduct badges, character at the 31st December each year, religion and next of kin were also recorded, together with many other items relevant to life in the Royal Navy.

A Conduct Sheet, which term is self explanatory, was a record of punishments, and did not have too great a bearing on a man's future service, for it was not kept as a long term record, but was renewed from ship to ship, the previous one being scrapped.

Form S507 was a form of recommendation for higher rating, and this was a quarterly return to a man's port division so that the advancement roster for that particular division could be updated.

The fact that each of the three port divisions had their own advancement roster, could perhaps have been a little unfair so far as advancement was concerned; as for example, a Chatham rating being passed for higher rating for a shorter time than a man from Devonport, but being advanced to the higher rating earlier because the Chatham roster happened to be less static.

It was most important to a man that his S507 was properly made out, for no recommendation meant that he would be passed by others, below him on the roster, but so recommended. A recommendation in black ink meant that a man would hold his place more or less, but better still, one in red ink would mean a gain in seniority by his being advanced still further up the roster.

The fourth piece of paper has, I believe, been discontinued in the present-day navy, and not before time. Known as form S264, it was a record of Commanding Officers' Personal Remarks, and once such remarks had been recorded, one might almost say that they were there for posterity, for they would go with a rating from ship to ship, each new commanding officer adding his own comments, and quite often allowing a previous entry to sway an indecision.

The rating himself had no access to this document: perhaps it was as well that he didn't; for, produced in a court of law, it could, in some instances I feel sure, have been irrefutable evidence in a libel action.

Chapter 12

The Demon Drink

WRITING AS I am in retrospect, it amazes me still, when I look back and think of what a few drinks could do to a man who, but a few hours before, had been in full possession of his faculties.

I can only suppose that taking a little too much after being on the wagon for days, or perhaps weeks, had a different effect on the stability of a man than it would have on someone who was a regular tippler. Some might be roaring drunk and wanting to fight, whilst with others it would be the exact opposite, they wanting to sleep it off just wherever they happened to be when the liquor took control.

When all night leave was given, the not so merry, more often than not, were able to get their less capable friends to a lodging house and into bed, thus avoiding the patrols.

Being apprehended by a patrol usually meant a night in cells and a return aboard next morning, under escort, to face charges which would include that of "Bringing disgrace on H.M. uniform."

In the event of there being no all night leave, but leave of a sufficient duration to allow of a man having a few too many, it would fall to the lot of his friends to stand on either side of him, giving a little support, in the hope that he would be able to get by the Officer of the Day's inspection without having to face a charge of, "Did return aboard drunk."

Anyone so charged, was booked for a night in the ship's cells, or in smaller ships which had no cells, a night in the cable locker flat, this meaning that someone from the duty watch would have to be detailed as cell sentry in order to keep an eye on him.

I hope that the reader will not get the impression that the majority of liberty men got themselves into this unhappy state. They were in fact, quite a small minority. But there were those, sober enough to escape the shore patrols, and equally able to get past an inspection by the Officer of the Day, but still not completely in command of their faculties. Men such as these – and I have known it to happen on many occasions – would bring his hammock and prepare it ready for turning in, but that would be about as much as he could manage, and he would spend the night sleeping on the hard deck underneath.. There would be others, not even capable of slinging a hammock, who would simply flake out (i.e. down) on the mess stool or table, spending a most uncomfortable night although they would not realise it until they awakened next morning, all aches and pains, a little sorry for themselves and longing for a *hair of the dog that bit them,* asking, "Has anyone got one in the bottle," meaning had anyone got a tot saved which they would be willing to lend.

Such was the *Esprit de Corps* of the lower deck however, that providing these unfortunates had returned aboard at a reasonable hour, every endeavour would be made to get them safely and properly turned in. Even so, a rating in a befuddled state, having been snugly turned in, might, as we all do at times, have to turn out again in order to obey the call of nature, and still being in a stupor there was no telling what he might do. Groping under his hammock, hoping to find a receptacle as one would, a chamber pot under a bed, but instead, and putting it to the same use, he might pick up his own or someone else's shoe.

Another time perhaps, having turned out, he might be facing in the wrong direction for the heads, but stepping out the approximate distance, and thinking in his subconscious mind that he had arrived,

THE DEMON DRINK

he would urinate just where he stood, be it up against the paint shop door or some other such spot.

Such happenings were fortunately rare, but they would never be allowed to go unpunished, and in the morning the offender would appear before the officer of the day charged with "Committing a minor nuisance in an improper place."

As opposed to "Did return aboard drunk," the charge of "Was drunk aboard ship, in a way, was much more serious, for it would mean an investigation into how the intoxicant had become available.

The daily rum ration could lead to such, a charge, for birthday usually meant that the rating celebrating a birthday would be offered *sippers* of his messmates' tots, and perhaps some from the adjoining messes also, and the inability to take it might lead to his wandering around a little incapable

In the mid 1930's this practice of giving sippers on birthdays led to tragedy when twin brothers, serving aboard the same ship, celebrated their twenty-first birthday. As can be imagined, sippers were offered from all directions, too many as it turned out; and too much for the constitution of one of the brothers, for he died.

This led to signals from Admiralty and the C in C, reminding all and sundry such practices were an offence against naval discipline, but in spite of this, the custom still continued.

Bottling one's tot was another way of obtaining illegal liquor; illegal because it should only have been drunk at the time of issue, but, a rating might drink only half his ration and bottle the remainder; even two water, the official mixing for a junior rating's issue, becoming quite potent when bottled with a few raisins; this being saved for a future binge.

Readers may have got the impression that it was only junior ratings that were subject to charges of drunkenness, but such charges applied equally well to chief petty officers, petty officers and leading rates, the difference being that they, having a position of some authority, would find the consequences of such a charge much more serious.

The punishment for drunkenness was usually the stoppage of one day's pay, providing it wasn't a repeated offence, and a junior rating would get away with just that. Higher ratings however, would probably have some stoppage of leave tacked on, with possibly the deprivation of a good conduct badge, or even disrating if it was a repeated offence.

The daily tot, besides being in the *demon* category when leading to drunkenness, could be classed as a *good fairy* also, this, because of the immense bargaining power that it had.

Doing another man's turn of duty, and even lending him the money for a run ashore would be a fair return for the next day's rum ration, and when it came to settling, payment in full would rarely be accepted, part of the ration being left for the original owner.

I have known of an instance when a shipwright made a fair sized wooden chest in return for a couple of tots and on another occasion, a good petty officer's messman was exempted from a drafting because the mess president was in a position to supply the drafting chief writer with a half quarter of rum.

Now that the rum issue has been discontinued, this is a bargaining, power which the lower deck no longer has, and I doubt very much if the offer of a can of beer would get the same response.

Chapter 13

Perks and Fiddles

THE DICTIONARY definition of *perks* is a slang word for perquisites, which in turn it states, are casual profits appertaining to one's trade or profession other than salary, and considered to be legitimate.

Perks find their way into many aspects of naval life, but to say that they are legitimate would be stretching things rather much.

Of course a tasty morsel left over after a meal had been served, could in all fairness be called *Cook's Perks,* and also perhaps, a small drop of rum, left after the mess issue and drunk by the member of the mess responsible for the issue, could just about be on the border line of legitimacy when know as *Rum Bosun's Perks*.

A few bottles of beer in exchange for a couple of gallons of paint may sound a fair deal, and perfectly legitimated, providing that the paint belonged to the recipient of the beer in the first place.

However, when the person doing the swap is a member of the side party, and the paint supposedly being used for touching up the ship's side, but going instead into a passing dghaisa in return for the beer, this could hardly be called legitimate casual profit, although it would be known to those concerned as *Side Party's Perks,* which, I think, proves my point. Such happenings were fairly widespread – still are I should think – and not only on the lower deck many officers also being partial to whatever perks might be going.

Duty free stores, such as wines and spirits for officers, and cigarettes for all ranks and ratings, were officially accepted perks providing certain restrictions on the landing of the same were adhered to.

The wines and spirits were only for consumption aboard ship, but cigarettes and tobacco were allowed to be taken ashore, the quantity allowed being one ounce of tobacco or twenty cigarettes for each night's leave, with a maximum of one pound of tobacco or two hundred cigarettes.

The matelot being what he was, he would of course, be more than pleased to share such perks with any friends or relations he may have had ashore, but this meant that quantities over and above those authorised would have to be smuggled.

Such items then became known as *rabbits*, a term of some obscure origin, but applying equally well to any naval stores, spirited from their rightful surroundings, eventually to find good use outside of the naval environment.

This rabbiting was accepted as being the perks of all naval personnel – providing that they could get away with it. I am not trying to say that it was condoned, for the ratings were always liable to search, but chances would be taken, for not every package taken through the dockyard gate was suspect, nor did time permit every libertyman being searched as he passed through. *Rabbits* was a colloquialism often to be heard called after a libertyman going ashore with a parcel under his arm, the inference I think, being fairly obvious.

The difficulty was not in getting the contraband off the ship: this arose only when proceeding through the dockyard gate. Not only would there sometimes be customs officers to contend with, but perhaps even worse, there were the dockyard police; ex royal marines mostly, who having served themselves, knew all the ropes and were not prepared to give an inch.

Even if a man had, at some time or another, served with one of these policemen it made no difference, for no favours would be given, or asked.

Many stories, concerning many things, are handed down in all walks of life, and the same being equally true of the navy, I repeat here a few concerning the battle of wits between authority and the would be rabbiters, but whether they come under the heading of tall stories one can only hazard a guess, but because of the ingenuity, there must I think, be an element of truth in them.

The first deals with a rating walking through the dockyard gate with a cat basket, who, when approached by a member of the dockyard police, stated that the basket contained the ship's cat, which, on his captain's instructions he was taking ashore to be put down. "Open it up," said the policeman; "Let's have a look inside."

"I can't do that" replied the rating, "It took me ages to catch, and if I open up it will only jump out and run back to the ship."

"I can't help that. Open up and let me have a look."

"Very well, "said the rating "If you insist," and opened up the basket, the cat then jumping out and haring back towards the ship.

"I told you so," said our friend, "Now I've got to go back and catch the ruddy thing again." and off he went.

The story continues some two hours later, when, complete with basket, the rating returns to the dockyard gate, and going up to the policeman, says, "A fine job you gave me, " and starting to open the basket he continued, "If it gets out this time it can be a dockyard stray for all I care." "O.K." said the policeman, "Don't bother to open it. "Carry on." Off went the rating, quite happy, with his basket, not full of cat, but duty-free cigarettes.

My second story also concerns a rating, a dockyard policeman, and duty-free cigarettes; but the rating in this instance knew the policeman, having once served with him.

Proceeding ashore on night leave he made a beeline for the policeman and said; "Being as we are old ships, how about letting me through with a thousand cigarettes tomorrow night."

"Sure," was the reply, "Come straight up to me on the way out."

Next evening, up came the rating as arranged, only to be told to go into the search room in order to be searched.

"Alright," said the rating, "But you are too late; I took them out last night."

During World War II it was compulsory for all ranks and ratings to carry gas masks when ashore in the U.K., but on many occasions this order was only partially complied with, the gas mask haversack being worn and containing, not a gas mask, but some other commodity which was in short supply ashore.

For the initiated, rabbiting took place on a far larger scale than most ratings would attempt, and it once fell to my lot to be in charge of a working party, detailed as it were, to de-rabbit the house of a warrant officer guilty of breaking the eleventh commandment – *Thou shalt not be found out.*

Fiddles were something a little different from the foregoing, and I suppose that the one most practised, especially during the war years, was that of fiddling the railways in order to get home a little more often when fortunate enough to have a spell in barracks.

For men proceeding on night leave it really wasn't much of a fiddle, as leave expired at 0700 and a workman's return could be obtained from London to Chatham for one shilling and sixpence.

The procedure was to buy a serviceman's single in the first instance, this enabling the man to get to London where he would be able to get a workman's return the following morning – all perfectly legal. The fiddle started when the purchaser, not being able to make use of the return half – perhaps because he was duty watch – would give it to someone who had been duty the night before so that there would be no break in the chain of travel. This, although being illegal – the ticket not being transferable – was usually accomplished without the least suspicion on the part of the ticket inspectors.

As it is with many good things, a spanner had to be thrown into the works, some of the travellers being over ambitious by purchasing two return workmen's' tickets in London so that a friend could make use of the second return half.

Eventually this was put to an end, the railway authorities somehow discovering what was happening and stopping the sale of workmen's tickets for the full London to Chatham journey.

Because of this, *Operation Bilking* came into being; not-practised by every rating, for it was still possible to book a workman's ticket to somewhere along the line, jump off the train whilst it was moving into the station, nip into the booking office a bit sharpish, book for the remainder of the journey and rejoin the train before it left. I somehow think that the guards must have been in sympathy with the men carrying out this manoeuvre, delaying the departure of the train in order to assist them.

Other men, not so energetic, or perhaps not in such good training, preferred the bilking operation, paying the fare for both ends of the journey, but travelling ticketless for the main part, hoping that a ticket inspector would not board the train. It really became a battle of wits between the bilkers and the inspectors, each trying to be one jump ahead of the other. Non-corridor carriages were favourite for the men, as with these there was no possibility of an inspector passing right through the train.

I think, on the whole, that the matelot came off best; but I will relate one incident where the ticket inspector did have the last laugh.

This concerned four ratings travelling together, only one of whom was in possession of a ticket. Hearing an inspector asking for tickets further along the corridor, they all made for the toilet and locked themselves in. On seeing the locked toilet, the inspector knocked on the door and called "Tickets Please," whereupon the door opened slightly, a ticket was pushed through, which the inspector clipped before passing on, continuing with his call of "Tickets Please."

The four came out, but to their surprise found the inspector waiting for them. "Now I'll have the other three," he said, and the three ticketless ones had to pay up. Whether some sixth sense had told him that there was more than one in the toilet is anybody's guess, but he had of course doubled back and stood waiting to collect. It must have made his day.

Not everyone fiddled the railway, for the forces did have a concession on fares, and many were prepared to pay; but bearing in mind that leave was allowed on three nights out of four, pay was poor by civilian standards, and that four workmen's tickets could be obtained for the price of one services ticket, I suppose that the Southern Railway were really to blame for the starting of the fiddle against themselves, when they made it so much harder for a workmen's ticket to be obtained.

What other fiddles were there? A great many, but as I have no doubt that most of these are still being practised, who am I to reveal them to the uninitiated?

However, as service pay is now much improved, I will lose no sleep for having mentioned the railway fiddles, the men now being able, if not willing, to pay their just dues.

Before ending this chapter, I will however, give mention to a few schemes, not actually fiddles, although they would sometimes be referred to as such by other ratings – a little jealous perhaps – because they had not got in first, or alternatively, had not the necessary know-how.

Most ships had someone conversant enough with a pair of scissors to consider that he was capable of carrying out the job of ship's barber; be he only able to give what one might term a four-penny gnaw off, or perhaps, something a little more professional which would be well worth the standard charge of sixpence.

These men carried out their normal shipboard duties during the day and were only available for the cutting of hair during the dog watches, setting themselves up in some corner to await custom.

More expertise was necessary before one could start up as a *Jewing Firm,* but in the larger ships there would certainly be two or three of these in operation: experts with a tape measure and a sewing machine, who could make a bell bottomed suit to order in the shortest possible time; in an emergency, almost while one waited.

But alas, big business began to move in, shore based tailors inducing the men to make an allotment to them and then allowing six months credit, thus getting most of the business, which unfortunately, caused many of the one man jewing firms to fade from the scene.

I say unfortunately, for this jewing was one of the few traditions which had passed down from the old time navy, when the pipe "Hands to make and mend clothes," meant just that, the men having been given an afternoon off to mend their clothes or to make new ones.

Boot and shoe repairs were just as necessary aboard ship as they were ashore, and many ships had their *Snobbing Firm,* but I suppose that of all the dog watch endeavours to earn a few extra shillings, that of *Dhobeying* was the one where the money was the hardest earned.

Washing one's own clothes was quite a chore; drying facilities were limited, besides which there was always a certain amount of freshwater rationing, supplies being cut off at various times.

It will be clearly seen therefore, that anyone setting up as a dhobeying firm, would have to be in dire need to spend the dog watches rubbing away at someone else's dirties, but there was always a few members of a ship's company who seemed to be in such need, even though they might sometimes have to compensate an owner for something lost in the wash, thus lessening the profit of an evening's work.

I can imagine you saying to yourself, "What losses? "These were losses through pilfering mostly, for it was net uncommon for an article of clothing to be swiped during the drying process, especially if it hadn't been marked with the owner's name.

One last private enterprise deserves a mention, if only for the fact that workwise, it was the easiest of them all.

This was the selling of *Goffers* – or soft drinks – the purveyor mixing his own ingredients in an enamel bucket and finding a ready sale for his wares, especially in the warmer climates.

I was never able to find out from whence the word goffer originated in this instance. Could it be from the word *Quaff* I wonder, which the dictionary defines *as to drink in copious draughts.*

Not every commanding officer would grant permission for the sale of goffers, one I know, putting forward the reason that even at one penny per glass; the profit margin was far too high.

Big business eventually began to move in on the goffer salesmen however, the N.A.A.F.I. following the American pattern and installing soda fountains and ice cream bars in H.M. ships – such is progress.

PART II
SHIPS & SHIPMATES

Prologue to Part II

The idea for a title to the second part of my story, comes to mind from a happening many years ago, long before I ever thought of putting pen to paper; when a messmate of mine, out of sorts with the world, and his own shipmates in particular, came on to the mess deck after someone had upset him and said; "When I get out of this mob, I'm going to write a book and call it, *Ships I have been in and Bastards I have met.*

Whether he ever did so I can't say: I have never seen such a title on the bookshelves. Perhaps he is still turning the idea over in his mind, and should this be the case, I have no wish to use his words, so have condensed them to *Ships and Shipmates;* better in a way I think, for one did not serve *in,* but aboard a ship, and not all shipmates were bastards.

Chapter 14

Ganges, Viscount and *Marlborough*

HMS *Ganges* 9th November 1923 – 19th March 1925

Life as a new entry has been adequately described in the opening chapters of part one, so here I will deal with some of the more personal aspects of this period.

It soon became apparent that friendships between the boys were seldom likely to be of a lasting nature. During my early weeks I became great pals with the son of a Manchester butcher. His name, Bob Crossley, does not add to, or detract from my story, neither does the fact that his father was a butcher; but if ever he should read this, I wonder, after the passing of so many years, whether he still remembers the cockney boy with whom he used to share parcels, in the days when we never seemed to be able to get enough to eat.

My moving on to advanced class did much to bring an end to this friendship, he remained with the original bunch, but this move of mine meant that I also lost an instructor who was a townie.

If one should have a pal who came from the same hometown as oneself, it could prove an asset when it came to proceeding on seasonal leave; but being townies with an instructor had proved to be somewhat of a liability, so losing him was one thing about the move that I did not in the least mind.

Perhaps the reason for it being a liability may have escaped you, but if I say that his showing favouritism had to be avoided at all costs, and that this meant that I was the recipient of a few extra swipes with his stoniky in order to let the remainder of the class know that no such favouritism was taking place, it may make, things a little clearer.

There being three port divisions was another reason for friendships only being of a transient nature, for when it came to leaving Shotley, two boys, if allocated *different divisions,* might never come into contact with one another again. This, I might add, could be equally true of two boys in the same port division, and I personally, after my first ship, served again with only one of my classmates, albeit on two different occasions.

Jack Potter did not aspire to higher rating, and so, on both occasions of our serving together in later years, the friendship of days under training could not readily be re-established, for I had, by then, reached petty officer status, whilst he had been quite content to remain an able seaman, but I do not wish this to appear derogatory; it is only mentioned as an illustration of that side of the service, which of necessity, did not allow of too great a friendship between varying grades.

Another example of this of which I was again concerned was on the occasion of my meeting another erstwhile classmate. Wat Tyler as he was known to us all in class, had, living at Brighton, been allocated Portsmouth division before leaving the training establishment, and I being Chatham, there was always the possibility that we had met for the last time.

It was many years later that our paths did cross again, I as a petty officer, and he, having aspired to a commission, had attained the rank of commander. Recognition was mutual, but he knew that I would not; neither did I presume on our earlier acquaintance.

I did not have an outstanding sporting record to show for my days at Shotley. At rugger I had aspired to the divisional 2nd XV, had also become a useful ¼ miler, represented my division at cross country, and qualified for the Royal Humane Society's bronze medallion. My essay into boxing had not met with much success, having been beaten in an eliminating competition to pick a mess team.

Of this last I have no regrets, having in later years come into contact with several men, who through boxing, had become punch drunk; and who knows, had I been successful in that earlier contest, I might have continued with the noble art to my detriment.

So, my days at Shotley came to an end. Many things which I had learned would no doubt be forgotten, but there would be a great deal more to learn during the years that lay ahead.

HMS *Viscount* – 20th March 1925 – 11th April 1925

Nothing appears on my service records concerning service aboard the destroyer *Viscount*. From the time of leaving Shotley, I was, in effect, on the books of HMS *Marlborough,* time aboard *Viscount* being solely for the purpose of taking passage.

At this particular time, ASDICS were barely out of the embryo stage, and the second destroyer flotilla – to which *Viscount* belonged – had been detached from the Mediterranean Fleet in order to be fitted with this anti-submarine device.

The flotilla was at Portland, carrying out trials under the supervision of the ASDIC School, and so it was to Portland that I and five other boys were sent, in order to join Viscount for passage to Malta.

One thing quickly learned was that we no longer had to call chief and petty officers Sir. The coxswain of *Viscount,* himself a chief petty officer, had put us right on this as soon as we set foot aboard, when, on being asked by him whether we had got all our baggage, a chorus of "Yes Sir!" brought a lecture on who was, and who was not, to be given such a courtesy title.

The non-substantive rating of coxswain was an abbreviation of torpedo boat destroyer coxswain, this emanating from the days when destroyers were called torpedo boat destroyers or T.B. D's.

This title eventually became shortened officially to torpedo coxswain, and unofficially to coxswain, or even 'swain, and this was our first seagoing meeting with such officialdom.

Boy ratings were not then included in the complement of a destroyer, consequently it was not considered necessary to include us in the watch bill, and so, instead of having to work our passage, we were on what one might call a pleasure cruise.

The ship's company looked after us very well, occasionally standing treat for the odd game of tombola, and during the trip my education was also improved, for I was able to learn the rudiments of both cribbage and solo whist.

Someone must have remembered from their big ship days that boys had to be turned in by 2100, and this we had to abide by, but we were also allowed the luxury of a lie-in until "Guard and Steerage" each morning.

By the time the ship had reached the Bay of Biscay, some of our number had changed their minds about it being a pleasure cruise, for we were beginning to realise how uncomfortable life aboard a destroyer could be; and although, since that first time, I have crossed the Bay on several occasions with the sea almost as calm as a mill pond, in this instance, the weather left a lot to be desired.

During this part of the journey, I was to hear for the first time, an injunction from one of the ship's company, to a very seasick young boy, which went as follows. "Bring it all up son: it's better out than in; but if you feel something round and hairy come up into your throat, for God's sake bite on it and hold it back, for that will be your anus, and if you let that g0 you'll be in one hell of a state."

Strangely enough, although not feeling exactly on top of the world, I was not seasick. In a way I suppose that I must consider myself lucky, for I never did suffer from actual seasickness, but the motion of a garden swing, or a swing boat at a fair, always gave me a feeling of nausea.

We got our first sight of Gibraltar on a beautiful sunny day, but it was a great disappointment that we were not to be allowed to go ashore, for although we had no money to spend, I feel sure that a walk would have done us the world of good and been most enjoyable. However, the day of arrival was not one on which leave was granted to boys, and so, on this our first visit, we had to make do with looking at the rock from afar.

Leaving Gibraltar, another three days steaming saw the ship at Malta, and although it was usual for destroyers to tie up in Sliema Creek to make it easier for our transfer to *Marlborough*, *Viscount* was instructed to secure a buoy in Bighi Bay.

Our shipmates of the past few weeks, lost no time in pointing out to us the various battleships in the harbour, with such remarks as – "There's your big ships and you can have 'em."

This, I discovered later, was general throughout the service, some men preferring life aboard the *Battlers,* with all the spit and polish, whilst others – the "Give me the Boats" type – would much rather have the harder destroyer life and a little less bull.

It was not possible for *Marlborough* to be pointed out to us, and we learned that she was in Dockyard Creek alongside the wall at Corrodino, being in the last stages of a minor refit.

In reply to a signal telling of our arrival – relayed by a signal tower overlooking the harbours – one of *Marlborough's* two picquet boats arrived alongside to expedite us on the last part of our journey. As for the send off by the ship's company of *Viscount,* it was almost a voluntary clear lower deck, and a rousing cheer sent us on our way.

HMS *Marlborough* 12th April 1925 – 31st March 1926

I and my companions were met at the head of the ship's gangway by the duty regulating petty officer, and after having been reported to, and inspected by the Officer of the Watch, we were given into the care of a chief petty officer who, we learned, was the senior instructor of the sixty or so boy ratings numbered among the ship's complement.

Having been allocated to various of the messes on the boy's mess deck, we were then required to attend the sick bay for the usual medical inspection, and only after this had been done, was I able to take stock of my new surroundings.

Boys were not allowed to fraternise with the remainder of the ship's company, so they had their own recreation space, this being out of bounds to other ratings, as also were the boy's messes which were situated in the starboard six-inch casemates.

The exception to this ban was of course our instructors, and the mess deck ban being reciprocal, boys were not allowed to visit those of the men, unless of course, their duties warranted them passing through.

This segregation was mainly to ensure that the no smoking rule which applied to the boys was strictly complied with, for as I have mentioned earlier, it was an offence for a boy to just be in the company of someone who was smoking.

On joining the ship, we had been told by our chief, to read the notice board, as there was an item on it which concerned us all. This item as he called it, was to the effect that the ship's sports was to be held during the next two days, and the list of entries showed that we new arrivals had all been included, each having been entered in two events apiece.

Needless to say, after our recent journeyings, none of us excelled, but we did gain points for the boy's division, these being awarded for having finished our heats, which I suppose; was our divisional officer's main reason for having entered us.

My action station was shown on the watch bill as that of a loader number for one of the six-inch guns of which *Marlborough* had twelve, situated in casemates six on the starboard and six to port. I was also a quarterdeckman of the blue watch and second cutter's crew, so my days of training had come to fruition, and now at last, I was an active member of a fighting unit in what was then the largest fleet in the world.

The earliest age at which a boy could join the Royal Navy was fifteen years and three months, but because of age on joining – I was sixteen and a half – and the extra time spent at Shotley through being in the advanced class, I was destined to spend very little time afloat as a boy rating, for I was only six weeks short of my eighteenth birthday.

However, I did have time to sit, and pass the examination for accelerated advancement to ordinary seaman at the age of seventeen and a half, although I was well over this age before the opportunity was offered. But, My Lords Commissioners of the Admiralty had decreed that every boy should have one opportunity to sit; so I was allowed to take the examination, but by the time the results became known, I had already been rated ordinary seaman by virtue of the fact that I had reached my eighteenth birthday.

Fortunately, My Lords also had the answer to this one; my ordinary seaman rating being made retrospective to the date when I was seventeen and a half; although this did, on paper anyway; make me an ordinary seaman four months before I had finished my boy's training at Shotley.

I was a boy rating aboard *Marlborough* for long enough to hear, on more than one occasion, the pipe "Boys to muster through the bath," although such bathing only consisted of a wash down with a bucket of water, with a sluice down afterwards, no other facilities being available. There was no inspection by the duty instructor now that we had left the training establishment, but we were ticked off in his little book as having carried out our ablutions.

My one payday afloat as a boy rating, I well remember, as having money – a whole ten shillings – I was able to set foot ashore the next day, it being a day on which afternoon leave was granted to boys.

I cannot truthfully say that this was my first time putting foot on foreign soil; this had happened some days earlier on the occasion of the ship's sports, but I was now able to visit the capital of the island – Valetta.

It now seems strange, that on this my first visit, although having no prior knowledge of the district, my steps should be drawn to the *Gut*, where at the *Happy Return,* in company with two of my erstwhile classmates, I partook of my first ever alcoholic drink – a port and lemon – served by Jessie the proprietor's daughter, a young girl of similar age to ourselves.

During the ensuing years, I was destined to pay many more visits to this same *Gut,* often calling at the *Happy Return,* on these occasions Jessie always being in attendance, growing older and wiser with the years.

Before being rated an ordinary seaman, I had time to learn of a minor racket between some of the boys and the men. This was to do with the sale of repayment clothing, or *slops* as they were more commonly called. Men needing slops were required to pay cash, but boys were allowed to pick up their requirements and have the cost charged against their credit.

The racket involved a boy picking up something which a man wanted, and then selling it to him below cost; thus saving the man a few shillings and giving the boy a little more spending money. Not very good for his credit, and rather like buying money at a premium.

Being a member of a six-inch gun's crew, I was, on being rated ordinary seaman, moved into a mess situated in one of the port gun casemates; all nice and handy for my action stations, but in the event of the gun having to be fired, or even used for drill purposes, the mess furniture first had to be dismantled.

My new messmates were of varying ages, ranging from some not much older than myself, to old timers nearing time for pension. Some of these old timers I felt really sorry for, they being what one might call victims of education.

By this I mean that they had at one time held a higher rating, but through some misdemeanour they had been disrated. Not an uncommon occurrence, and after a lapse of time, usually from six to twelve months, they could have been reinstated.

Unfortunately for them, before such a reinstatement could take place, authority decreed that an educational test was to be included in the examination for higher rating, and obeying this edict to the letter, commanding officers were not allowed to reinstate any man unless he first passed this educational test.

There were three of these unfortunates victualled in my mess. Two had been leading seamen, and the leading seaman in charge of the mess was a one-time petty officer; excellent seamen all, but hopeless with the three Rs, and now having to carry on indefinitely in the lower rating.

I was made cooking oppos with a two-badge able seaman who I am only able to remember as *Curly,* a title by which he was known to all and sundry, he being as bald as a coot.

My pay as an ordinary seaman was two shillings and nine pence a day, so I had received a rise of one shilling per day – seven shilling per week – and I was now looking forward to my first pay day in man's rating, for I would then be paid all the credit which had accrued to me.

Wisely, before payday arrived, the paymaster commander, through his chief writer, suggested that I put some into savings. The amount involved was £20, not a large sum by present day standards, but for comparison, in the days of which I am writing, it would have been enough to buy a motorbike or six good civvy suits.

An ordinary seaman would, in normal circumstances, providing that he was making no allotments, expect to pick up about £4-10-0 a month, and so I decided to draw half of the £20 and put the balance into savings.

There were three methods of saving available to men serving abroad – a regular monthly allotment to the home dockyard bank, a deposit in the ship's savings bank, or an allotment to a relative or friend.

With the first method, withdrawals took far too long for it to be a practical proposition unless one really wanted to save hard, and the second, except in very exceptional circumstances, would only allow for pre-arranged withdrawals to be paid with the monthly payment, and so, once banked, the money usually remained there until the end of the ship's commission.

Allotments were all very well in their way; married men made allotments to their wives of up to six days pay per week, but once made, it needed a letter from the recipient before it could be stopped, such a letter having to state that the money was no longer required.

My choice was the ship's bank. I did have one unsuccessful attempt at a mid monthly withdrawal on an occasion of being broke, but after that I allowed my £10 to remain there, earning an interest of 2% per annum; but unfortunately, I never seemed to be in a position to add to that initial deposit.

Some of my newly acquired wealth was used for replacing my *pusser's* issue with made to measure uniform, a blue serge suit costing about thirty shillings, and a white drill suit about five shillings less.

It was the usual practise to patronise shore-based naval tailors for the upkeep of main kit items, especially when, at a later date, it became possible to make a monthly allotment to the tailor of one's choice, six months credit being allowed as soon as the first payment was authorised. There was no fear of any bad debts, for the rule concerning allotments applied equally well to those made to tradesmen, and a rating could not stop such an allotment until he first produced a letter stating that he was in credit.

Not everyone used such methods for the upkeep of their kit; there were some, mostly the older men – pusser built – who preferred the cheaper ready-mades which were available on repayment from the paymaster's-stores, and others who patronised the jewing and snobbing firms set up by members of the ship's company.

During my time aboard *Marlborough*, allotments to shore-based tailors had not yet become fashionable for the English firms had not opened up at Malta to any great extent and the Maltese were getting most of the business. Unfortunately, these gentlemen did suffer some bad debts, for they were prepared to make a suit and wait until the end of the month for their money, and there were a few bad payers.

My second monthly payment was also well above average, for I was in receipt of six months back pay for my retrospective rating to ordinary seaman. The full payment amounted to £12-10-0, and on stepping up to the pay table, I was asked by the paymaster, "What are you going to do with all this money?" My reply was that I intended to send some home to my parents; there might possibly have been some such idea at the back of my mind, but I never got around to doing it, and the money gradually dwindled.

Sending money home presented no difficulties; postal orders could be obtained from the ship's office, no poundage having to be paid, and I did make use of this facility on subsequent occasions.

Through no fault of my own, I did not get off to a very good start in man's rating, becoming what was known as a *fowl,* the term applied to someone who was always in trouble.

This was because a certain leading seaman, of uncertain morals, and in my opinion, of uncertain parentage, had made suggestions which, to me, were abhorrent. My refusal to comply with his wishes brought the ultimatum that it could be the occasional easy five minutes or a hard commission, and in his capacity as leading hand of the watch, make it hard he did.

It was because of him that I gained first hand experience of being duty watch, duty hand, cook of the mess and under punishment at one and the same time, and at times I was in the unhappy position of being stood over on one charge because I was already undergoing punishment for another.

In those early days, any rating on a charge was, on being taken before the officer of the watch, placed in the commander's report, or, a rare happening indeed, he had the charge against him dismissed. If it was the former, the commander would deal with the matter if possible, although the offender sometimes had to be passed on to the captain.

Later, with the adoption of the divisional system, where an offender would first be placed in his divisional officer's report, I doubt if any youngster would have found himself in the position that I did, for such an officer would I feel sure, have made it his business to find out why a boy, intelligent enough to pass an examination for accelerated advancement did not know enough to keep himself out of trouble, and could only rate a moderate abilities classification as an ordinary seaman; however, I survived, managing to get a few runs ashore in between punishments.

Before leaving Malta for the first summer cruise, *Marlborough* had to coal ship, taking in some 1500 tons. Most of the work was carried out by Maltese labour, the coal coming alongside in large lighters; and the Maltese workmen, numbering many dozens, and chattering away like monkeys, carrying it up a gangplank in small baskets. Only a few of the ship's company were required to assist, some trimming the bunkers, and others shovelling the spillage from the baskets into these same bunkers.

Prior to the coaling, *Marlborough* had been painted and this I could not understand. Why should a ship be painted overall shortly before taking on coal? An operation during which the paintwork would get smothered in coal dust.

The answer was obvious once I had been told that no matter how well a ship is washed down after coaling, some of the coal dust would still be about for quite an appreciable time, and for this reason, if a ship was due for painting such painting would always be carried out before coaling, thus ensuring that no dust got painted over.

The cruise took us to the Aegean Sea and the Grecian Archipelago, but apart from Piræus, allowing for a visit to Athens; leave was only in the nature of picnics in the more remote places.

One place visited and worth a special mention though, was Navarino Bay, for here the fleet came together and I was able to witness my first naval regatta. *Marlborough's* crews had already been in training when I first joined the ship, so I was not an active participant – the only regatta during the whole of my service, in which I was not a member of a representative crew.

One or two of the more affluent members of the ship's company opened up a book on the events, strictly illegal of course, but this was before the days of the tote.

I am afraid that *Marlborough* did not do too well, but two sister ships – *Benbow* and *Iron Duke* – carried off a few of the honours, so the coal burners were not disgraced.

The cruise nearing its end, preparations were made for another coal ship; a different proposition this time, all the work having to be done by the ship's company; no one, unless they happened to be on the sick list, being excused.

Preparation took place the day before. All ventilation shafts were sealed up so as to prevent coal dust from finding its way below decks; derricks were rigged, and scratch meals were prepared so that too much time would not be wasted with cooking on the day.

In the evening a collier secured alongside so that an early start could be made next morning; and early start it was, the hands being called at 0500.

Notices posted on the various notice boards had informed the men of their duties, and at "Hands fall in," the commander only had to say "Coal Ship" and we were off.

The four parts of ship – Foc'sle, Fore Top, Main Top and Quarter Deck – each took over one of the four holds of the collier, and from then on, the keen competition between the parts of ship became most apparent, each vying with the others in their efforts to get the most tonnage out.

Rope handled two hundredweight sacks were used, one man holding open the sack and three or four others filling it; twelve full sacks would have a wire strop rove through the handles, and then, by a combination of *Marlborough* and the collier's derricks, they would be hoisted in board – one hoist one ton – there to be trucked away to the bunkers by miscellaneous ratings.

I can imagine the more mathematically minded of you saying, "But twelve times two hundredweight is not one ton" to which I must reply that the sacks were not completely filled, this to make it easier for the slinging of them. The sack holding job was mostly given to the boy ratings, although they sometimes spelled the shovellers. One ton hoists simplified keeping a tally of the output from the four holds, and from time to time one would hear injunctions such as "Come on lads: we're all behind," or, "We're leading the field boys: keep it up." We were also in competition with our sister ship *Iron Duke,* coaling from another collier, the tonnage taken on by each ship being made known by flag hoists at the yard arm.

The Royal Marine band, although taking no active part in the actual coaling, did their bit, suitably attired in boiler suits, moving around the ship to various vantage points and treating us all in turn to renderings from their repertoire.

Coaling completed, there began the task of cleaning the ship, high-pressure hoses helping to disperse the coal dust covering the upper deck and adjacent paintwork.

Only after this was done – a hard day's slog of some ten hours – were we able to take stock of ourselves. Covered in coal dust from head to foot, this same dust having permeated our clothing, what we needed was a nice hot bath and a good soak, but no such luck; bathing facilities being what they were, a wash down with a couple of buckets of hot water were the only means available, but even so nothing could be done about the clearing of our nasal passages, and for some days afterwards, the act of blowing one's nose would still bring down a certain amount of coal dust.

The return of the fleet to Malta always brought out a large crowd of onlookers; Barracca Gardens, looking out over the Grand Harbour being an ideal vantage spot. Dhobeying firms and the like lost no time in getting back aboard, hoping to get enough work to make up for the loss of income which they had sustained during the period of the cruise.

Completion of the summer cruises did bring a lucrative time to the island, for apart from occasional exercises and firing practices, the fleet remained at Malta from October until February.

Coincidental to the fleet's return, was the arrival of the marriage ships, passenger liners bringing mothers and their marriageable daughters to the island in the hope of a suitable match being made for them during the ensuing season.

Before the year's end, we learned that the last of the coal burning battleships were to be dispensed with as units of the Mediterranean fleet, returning to the U.K. in order to recommission as sea going training ships for boys. They were to be replaced by the R. class battleships, the changeover to take place during the spring cruise, with *Royal Sovereign* taking over from *Marlborough*.

An amusing incident concerning *Marlborough's* gunnery officer and the Royal Marine crew of 'Q' turret occurred during one of the autumn gunnery practices; amusing that was, for all except the gunnery officer himself.

His cabin was situated in the after superstructure, and at his own expense he had had it tastefully decorated in pale blue and gold.

After a practice shoot, 'Q' turret had one left up the spout after training fore and aft, and through some fault in the procedure managed to fire it. At the range of a few feet, the projectile had no difficulty in-penetrating the after superstructure and entering Gunnery Jack's cabin: fortunately, it was only a projectile from a sub calibre fitted into the parent gun, and only weighed a few pounds.

That Gunnery Jack was not a popular officer can be gathered from the remarks which followed – "A pity he wasn't in there at the time," and, "Too bad it wasn't the real thing," being but two examples – the real thing weighing nearly one ton.

A spell in dockyard hands because of a minor defect resulted in the majority of the ship's company being able to proceed on a one-week camping expedition to Ghain Taffia, which was some fourteen miles from where the ship lay.

Once again, the competitive spirit between members of the ship's company became apparent; each part of ship forming it's own company, and then, fully equipped with rifles and field order, leaving at regular intervals and marching against the clock.

Camp was a change from working ship: working hours were spent playing at being soldiers, whilst most evenings saw the men in the wet canteen, either taking part in a singsong, or playing tombola. Incidentally, it was at this camp that I first became a member of the beer drinking fraternity, although I was not much taken with my first sampling of the ale.

Although I was only reckoned to be an ordinary seaman with moderate ability, I had successfully passed the technical examination required of me in order to be rated able seaman, and in due course, my captain's request to be rated as such was granted, and with a pay rise of one shilling and threepence per day, I was now, as a fully fledged able seaman, in receipt of four shillings per day.

It was whilst serving aboard *Marlborough,* that I was able, without becoming personally, involved, to discover a trait in the character of several of the elder of my shipmates, which trait, I was later to find, was fairly general throughout the service: this was the practice of an older man taking unto himself a *winger.* By this I mean that he would take a younger rating under his wing; being a kind of father confessor to him, and on occasion, somewhat of a sugar daddy.

Although the majority of these associations were quite harmless, sometimes jealousy would become apparent, and it was because of one such occasion, that aboard *Marlborough,* a not so eternal triangle led to a punch up.

Nutty Coupland, a staid able seaman and a veritable bully, had taken under his wing an ordinary seaman by the name of Gibson. Such was Nutty's possessiveness that the youngster could not even bathe without him also being in attendance.

Came a certain Sunday afternoon and Nutty, looking for his winger, could not find him anywhere. The reason for this was obvious to many of the ship's company, for he had gone on afternoon leave with another able seaman.

Whether anyone told Nutty, or whether he sensed it, makes no difference to my story: sufficient to say, that getting cleaned to go ashore and being unable to contain himself until the next liberty boat, he broke out of the ship and went on what proved to be a fruitless search.

Returning aboard some hours later, and finding that his erstwhile quarry had also returned, he proceeded to beat them up in no uncertain manner – and so ended a beautiful romance.

The spring cruise, and combined exercises with the Home fleet brought me my first glimpse of the Balearic Islands. Not as a visitor, for on this occasion, the ship never got near enough for one to get an idea of what going ashore might hold in store.

A target of some kind, in a battle between the Red and Blue fleets, a blur on the rain-swept horizon, Majorca looked anything but the sun-drenched paradise advertised in the present-day travel brochures.

As with all spring cruises, the combined fleets, in their respective ways, berthed at Gibraltar, and sporting activities took place.

During these periods of fleet meeting fleet, several hurried requests to change ship might materialise; men in one fleet, prevailing upon their counterparts in the other to make the change, perhaps a homesick man in the Med fleet changing with another in the Home fleet who had no ties with the U.K.

All decisions having been made as to which fleet was champion at what, both proceeded on their various ways; the Home fleet back to their home ports to give Easter leave, and that of the Mediterranean carrying out a short cruise before returning to Malta.

In this instance, *Marlborough,* having entered Gibraltar as a unit of the Mediterranean fleet, left in company with *Empress of India* and Iron *Duke* en route to the U.K., the fourth ship of the squadron, *Benbow,* having completed her commission and paid off earlier.

The next few days were uneventful, but, having cleared Ushant, we parted company with the *Empress of India,* she to make her way to Devonport, whilst *Marlborough* and *Iron Duke* continued their journey to Sheerness.

We were not however, to complete our journey without an unexpected delay. The estimated time of arrival would have been too early for the harbour facilities to be available, and *Marlborough's* captain, being senior officer, decided that both ships should anchor in the Downs for a few hours.

The time was about 0200, and the cable party was mustered on the foc'sle. When the captain gave the order to let go the starboard anchor, neither he, nor anyone else for that matter, had the least idea, that not only would the anchor go, but also the full hundred fathoms of cable attached to it.

At the time of letting go, *Marlborough* had been making eight knots against an eight-knot tide. Who miscalculated, or what was the outcome? I never became aware; but there we were two ships in company, both having lost our starboard anchor and cable, for letting go at the same time, had suffered a similar mishap.

In an emergency, it had been known for a ship to slip her cable instead of weighing anchor, but in such circumstances, the end of the cable would be buoyed in order to facilitate it's recovery; but as can be imagined, our loss caused quite a delay, for divers had to first go down in order to carry out a search, this search taking all the longer because they could only work when the tide was at it's slackest.

Eventually, anchor and cable recovered, both ships got under way and continued their journey, arriving at our destination some thirty-six hours late.

Sheerness was as near as we were able to get to our home port of Chatham, this being a bone of contention amongst the crews of Chatham manned battleships, ships of such tonnage being unable to navigate the shallower channels of the Medway, so, never allowing them the amenities of docking or refitting in their home port. Having been gone over by the customs officers, there now began the final phase of paying off, that of stowing our baggage in the Royal Naval Barracks at Chatham, this having to be done before we were allowed to proceed on foreign service leave.

A tender of the Royal Fleet Auxiliary took part in this operation, the paddle steamer *Harlequin,* which usually ferried libertymen between Sheerness and Gillingham pier, on this occasion changing her itinerary so as to disembark us at Chatham Dockyard steps.

Here, lorries were waiting to transport the baggage to the barracks, and we, having loaded them, were marched through the dockyard into these same barracks, where, after recovering and storing our own personal baggage, we were free to proceed on leave.

My foreign service had only been of eleven and a half months duration, and by virtue of the fact that leave was granted on the basis of seven days for each period of six months, I was about to proceed on a leave of thirteen days.

A point worth mentioning here perhaps is that any man who had served in the Home fleet for the same period, would have had forty-two days seasonal leave, besides the odd weekend or two.

All other things being equal, it would appear that a man on foreign service fared the worst so far as leave was concerned, and although it was said that home and foreign service were equally apportioned, I, for one, have always had my doubts.

Chapter 15

Pembroke, Tetrarch and *Victory*

HMS *Pembroke* 1st April – 28th April 1926

It was with mixed feelings that I alighted from the train at Chatham station, for having finished my leave; I was about to join Chatham Barracks for the first time.

Sometimes called the stone frigate – as were all shore establishments – but better known as HMS *Pembroke*, many were the tales I had heard whilst serving aboard *Marlborough,* tales of the pitfalls in store for the unwary, many of them I was to learn, having some element of truth.

But first the joining routine. First a visit to the Seamen's Main Regulating Office, where one was allocated a mess number and put into either the Red, Yellow, Green or Blue watch and given a card to denote the same.

This card was almost a licence to breathe. It had to be hung on at all costs, for to lose it would mean having to go through the whole of the joining routine again.

Without this card a man would be unable to go ashore, neither would he be able to draw his pay or take up his soap and tobacco ration.

It also had to be produced if one was caught in the act of committing some misdemeanour. Petty Officers and leading hands would collect them from the members of any working party which they happened to be in charge of; in order to be certain that no man in such a working party absented himself if the job was not to his liking, the cards only being returned when such a job was completed.

Now, the card having been issued by the regulating office it had to be completed by having the spaces on the inner pages stamped by the relevant departments.

This entailed going through the rounds of the establishment, and it took about two days. It was during these rounds that I learned the parade ground could only be crossed during working hours at the double, exceptions to this rule being officers and chief and petty officers.

Visits were paid to the Sub-Regulating and Drafting offices so that6ne's particulars and drafting availability might be checked; the Anti Gas School so that gas masks could be tested in the gas chamber, and the Sick Bay and Dental Department for both medical and dental officers to carry out their inspections.

Each of these departments had their own rubber stamp, and an impression would be made in the appropriate space, but this was not the finish; there was still one more stamp to come, that of the clothing department and this could only be obtained after the undergoing a most stringent kit inspection.

At this particular time, this kit inspection was the most dreaded part of the barrack joining routine, for it would often end with a man being placed in crown debt.

A clothing officer – a lieutenant – was in charge, and it was he who carried out the final inspection to see that the kit was complete and that every item was properly marked with the owner's name, but before this happened, the Clothing Gunner – a warrant officer – who must have forgotten that he was himself once an able seaman, really went to town with his inspection of the individual items of clothing.

He would condemn a cap because it had a wire instead of a cane grommet (the stiffener in a naval cap), a collar because the three rows of tape were fractionally too close together, a pair of trousers, the bottoms being a little too wide, a jumper cut too low in front, lanyards because the knot was sliding instead of fixed, and various other items, which having been brought ashore, did not conform completely to a uniform pattern, although they had passed muster whilst the owners were afloat.

The condemned items would all have to be replaced from the clothing store, the cost being charged against the man's pay; very few men left the clothing department without some such condemnation, and many in crown debt, the cost of replacements being more than their entitlements could defray.

These kit inspections took between two and three days to complete, but once completed, the joining routine was also, and all one then had to do was to conform to the barrack routine, hoping never to hear the command, "Give me your card!" Such a command could come from many of the barracks personnel regulating staff, barrack guard, any chief or petty officer if he were so minded, and of course, the officers.

Any man hearing such a command would have been unfortunate enough to have contravened some barrack regulation, perhaps one that he had never been aware of, the plausibility of his excuse being the deciding factor as to whether he would get his card back or have to appear before the Officer of the Day as a defaulter.

The disposition of all ratings in the establishment depended to a great extent on their non substantive rating; higher gunnery rates being mostly employed in the gunnery school, and a few of the higher torpedo rates likewise at the torpedo school.

Of the remainder, many would be employed on special duties – main gate staff, messengers, barrack guard and chief and petty officers' messmen to mention a few – any not so detailed forming the barrack working party.

These last were easily distinguished from the special men, for they would be wearing their white duck suits – No.5 dress and the rig of the day for working parties – for special dutymen being their blue No. 3 uniform.

As with all ships and establishments, *Divisions* was the main parade of the day, and after inspection and prayers were over, the gunnery school and training classes were marched off, leaving the working party to be detailed for the various jobs in and about the establishment. The commissioned gunner in charge of the Seaman's Main Regulating Office was in charge of this operation, although the actual duty was that detailing was done by the Chief Bosun's Mate, a chief petty officer of some seniority.

The whole group were fallen in; leading seamen and petty officers to the front, and the men would be chopped off from one end by the chief – "One, two, three, four, five, six – one leading hand – one petty Officer – ROADS." "One, two, three, four – one leading hand – WARDROOM." He would carry on with this procedure until the whole of the working party had been disposed of, the majority of them to jobs necessary for the well being of the establishment, but others to jobs which could only be considered as time wasting.

For this, my first essay into barrack life, I was not destined to stay over long; four weeks in all, but I did, in that short time, experience three of the most unwanted jobs ever. The sweeping of the parade ground was probably the most irksome, but sweeping the drill shed, and cleaning the drill shed windows were a close second and third.

Each of these employed six men and one petty officer, but, I cannot say that they were kept busy; for any one task – could have been completed in an hour, the remainder of the time was spent in trying to look fully occupied; and then, in the afternoon, another party would be detailed to do the same thing all over again.

These were the jobs which no one, not even the petty officers wanted; but it was no use holding back, for it would never be known at which stage in the proceedings the Chief Bosun's Mate would say, "One, two, three, four, five, six – PARADE GROUND, DRILL SHED, or whatever.

After two weeks of working parties, I was given the job of petty officer's messman, and this I kept, until two weeks later, I was drafted to HMS *Tetrarch*, a destroyer of World War I vintage.

Not until after I had left the petty officers' mess and joined my new ship, did I learn that messmen were paid three pence per day from the mess funds; a debt to me of three shillings and six pence which was never settled.

HMS *Tetrarch* 29th April 1926 – 6th January 1927

The ship was already in commission and lying in Chatham Dockyard. I was being drafted, in company with another able seaman, as a replacement for a man who was time-expired, my fellow draftee being much older than I was, he being in possession of three good conduct badges.

There being only the two of us, for the transport of our baggage we had to make use of the barrack baggage party. This was a party of eight able seamen and two leading seamen who, when not toting baggage, sat around in the drill shed reading the daily papers, although for the record, with the advent of a new barracks commander, they became responsible for the drill shed window cleaning also.

For a draft of two, a handcart and two men of the baggage party were all that we required, and having collected our draft chits, we departed.

The elapse of about ten minutes saw us alongside *Tetrarch,* and, our baggage unloaded, the two men of the baggage party went in search of duty free cigarettes – a perk of the job when they could be obtained before returning to barracks and their newspapers.

I and my new shipmate learned from the remainder of the crew that *Tetrarch* was normally based at Port Edgar, South Queensferry: not a unit of a flotilla, but a tender of sorts; her main function being to sail in attendance on the aircraft carriers *Furious* and *Argus*.

I believe that I am right in saying that these two ships were the first of the Royal Navy's aircraft carriers; the first that is, that allowed aircraft flying on and off. Prior to these, seaplanes had been carried in upper deck hangers, the ship having to be stopped, and the planes hoisted out for take off. There had also been experiments with planes flying off a platform built over the 'A' turret of battleships, but once airborne, these were unable to return to their ship and had to return to dry land.

Furious had been laid down as a heavy cruiser and altered during construction, but *Argus* was a converted merchant ship. Neither of them had the superstructure of the aircraft carriers in commission at the present time, the smoke being ejected through stern vents: as a matter of fact, *Argus* looked so much like a huge box floating on the water, that she was nicknamed the *Floating Ditty Box,* a ditty box being a wooden box with a hinged lid, which, before the advent of the attaché case, was issued to the men of the lower deck for them to keep their personal belongings in.

It was to be some weeks before we saw Port Edgar, for the General Strike was imminent, and *Tetrarch,* together with other destroyers in Chatham dockyard being sent to key points, our destination was Swansea Docks.

Our reception was not exactly a friendly one – probably because the local inhabitants thought that we were there on strike breaking duties and for this reason, no leave was allowed during the early days of our stay.

After a few days, the mood appeared to be less hostile, afternoon leave was allowed, and from then on, a happy state of affairs existed, we interfered with no one, and no one interfering with us.

The strike over, we at last made our way to Port Edgar; the route taking us round the north coast of Scotland via the Minches and Pentland Firth.

Port Edgar being within easy reach of Edinburgh gave me an opportunity to visit relatives living in that city, relatives I had not seen since I was five years old; but for my sins, although opportunities for further visits were more than adequate, other attractions took priority, and my first visit was also my last; unfortunate as it turned out – or unthoughtful – for one of those relatives was my paternal grandmother, and it so happened that I was never to see her again.

The Home fleet being in Scottish waters, I learned that another of *Tetrarch's* duties was towing dummy Coastal Motor Boats at high speed as targets for the various units. Hits were scored, but the boat did not sink, they were filled with thousands of table tennis balls.

Another job apart from that of attending the aircraft carriers was that of taking off the crew of the *Agamemnon* when she was to be used for target practice.

Agamemnon was an old battleship carrying a skeleton crew which was just sufficient to bring her out to sea. She was also radio controlled, and after the crew had been disembarked, she was used as a target for full calibre shoot, a target which could alter course as directed by radio by the controlling destroyer HMS *Shikari*.

During the exercises with the aircraft carriers, we were unfortunate in having one casualty when a plane returning to *Furious* ditched.

From our vantage point on the port quarter, the plane seemed to make a good landing, but before it could be secured, toppled into the sea.

Tetrarch always had a boat's crew standing by during these exercises in case of such an eventuality, and although they were able to rescue the pilot and navigator, they could not do anything for a leading telegraphist who was trapped in the submerged fuselage; although we later learned – after his body had been recovered – that he had died as a result of the crash, and not by drowning.

Fortunately, although we were to witness some hundreds of planes taking off and landing, we never again had to send a boat's crew away on an errand of mercy.

We now had boats' crews in training for the regatta which was to take place in Weymouth Bay toward the end of the summer cruise; but I was not involved at this time, my turn was to come later.

Fashionable units of the fleet visiting the more fashionable resorts, *Tetrarch,* not being in this category, except for a visit to Ramsgate, visiting only a few of the minor Scottish ports before calling at Harwich *en route* to Weymouth Bay.

The regatta, when it took place, was hardly worthy of the name, not comparing at all favourably with others in which I was later to take part. Not being a unit of a flotilla, *Tetrarch* only took part in a regatta for fleet tenders, these being all shapes and sizes with different types of boats to boot.

Because of this, competition was not over keen, and our seamen's whaler, after all their training, refusing to take part, the captain, without more ado, had the duty whaler's crew called away to substitute for them. That is where I came into the story, being a member of the duty crew; and it proved to be the only race I know of, where a crew, pulling a duty boat stroke, came in last by some dozens of lengths.

Back to Chatham for summer leave, which completed, saw us once again on our way to Port Edgar and our day-to-day endeavours.

I somehow think that it was the easy going routine aboard *Tetrarch;* easy that is in comparison with *Marlborough* that fostered in me the idea that where possible I would be a small ship man. Not being subject to seasickness I was in my element. True, it was uncomfortable at times, with the mess-decks awash, and with no wash room, one's only means of bathing was a bucket of water behind a canvas screen at the break of the foc'sle, having first gone half way along the upper deck to pump up the water and then heating it in a steam heated copper provided for the purpose.

In harbour with the boilers shut down there would be no steam and therefore no hot water, unless one could prevail upon the generosity of the cook and his back copper, so called because it was situated at the back of his galley range. With this shortage of hot water, it was not unusual for three or even four men to make use of the same bucket of water in order to have a wash; but such hardships were compensated for by the absence of the flannel and red tape associated with the big ship routine.

As it was, my idea of being a small ship man was a long time coming to fruition, for after leaving *Tetrarch*, it was to be more than five years before I again served aboard a destroyer.

Autumn manoeuvres an end, *Tetrarch* once again returned to Chatham; on this occasion for the giving of Christmas leave, a leave I might add, which was to prove disastrous for me, although it was a disaster of my own making.

Seasonal leave was always given in two parts, one half of the ship's company taking first leave, the remaining half being split into two watches, thus enabling them to proceed on night leave on alternate nights, the same also applying during the second leave period.

Christmas leave was so arranged to allow the first leave party to have Christmas at home, returning in time to allow the second party to reach their homes in time for the New Year.

As with all leave, changing was allowed, and providing that the two men requesting a change were of equal rating, such a request would never be refused.

On this particular occasion I was due for first leave, but having been invited to spend my leave with a Geordie pal – he being second leave – and having been unsuccessful in finding another rating to change with me, I had proceeded on leave with an idea at the back of my mind that I would become A.W.O.L. and take part of the second leave also. My leave over, I set out for Victoria Station and the return journey; but I did not catch the Chatham train, knowing that in a couple of hours my pal would be arriving at that same station on his way home. Had I missed him, I would in all probability have returned to Chatham and my ship, being only a few hours late, for which the punishment would have been a couple of days pay and leave forfeited.

However, the dice were cast: my pal, arriving as expected, taking me to his home where I experienced the most enjoyable of New Year celebrations, only then returning to my ship, leaving him to enjoy the remainder of his leave.

I arrived aboard at the same time as some of my shipmates were returning from weekend leave: the duty petty officer met me at the gangway. "Fall in aft," he ordered. "You've managed to get the time right, but you're six days late."

First Lieutenant's Report, Captain's Report, Remanded for Warrant Punishment, all these followed in due course, and then I was leaving *Tetrarch* under escort, bound for the cell block in Chatham Barracks, there to await transport to the Royal Naval Detention Quarters, Portsmouth.

HMS *Victory* 7th January – 1st February 1927

I have, in an earlier chapter, dealt fully with my incarceration in the detention quarters, so will not repeat myself by making further mention of it here.

My service certificate states that I was on the books of HMS *Victory* for twenty-six days, the reason being that Portsmouth Barracks and its environs had a ship name as did all shore establishments: e.g. Chatham Barracks – HMS *Pembroke*, Devonport Barracks – HMS *Vivid* (now Drake) Torpedo School – HMS *Vernon,* etc., that of Portsmouth Barracks being HMS *Victory* now *Nelson*).

My twenty-six days detention had therefore to be shown as *Victory* service, although it was twenty-six days service without pay, all time spent in detention being lost time which had to be made up when a man signed on to complete time for pension.

It was most notable during my service that no Portsmouth manned, or Chatham manned ships" serving together on the same station ever seemed to become *Chummy Ships*. I have found Chatham and Devonport matey, Devonport and Portsmouth, and even two ships manned from the same port, but Chatham and Portsmouth – Never!

Portsmouth ratings were always very proud of their *Victory,* and when she eventually found her last resting place in Portsmouth Dockyard, she was more theirs than ever – or was she?

In my opinion, Victory belongs to Chatham. She was built in Chatham Dockyard by Chatham men, and when I was last there, the place of her launching still bore a plaque giving full details. Could *Victory* then, have unwittingly become the cause of there being no chumminess between these two port divisions?

I spent only one day in Portsmouth Barracks, one day awaiting transport back to my homeport of Chatham after having completed my twenty-six days in D.Q.'s.

Chapter 16

Pembroke and *Ramillies*

HMS *Pembroke* 2nd February – 28th February 1927
Having left Chatham four weeks earlier under escort, it was most gratifying to be returning as a free man; free that that is, so far as shackles were concerned, but not free to go ashore, being very much in debt to the crown because of the stoppage of thirty two days pay, my punishment in addition to the detention which I had undergone.

I had also had thirty two days leave stopped, but this hardly made any difference to me, the twenty-six days detention accounting for all but six of them, and as men in debt to the crown had to muster with stoppage of leave men anyway, I was no worse off.

The barrack joining routine had to be carried out again, with medical and dental inspections, although these had also been done at Portsmouth the day before as part of the leaving routine.

As usual, the clothing gunner was in the clothing department waiting to pounce, but as kit inspections had been a feature of my detention, I was able to get away with it rather well, although, being in the position that I was, a few more £'s in debt would not have been all that noticeable.

I was not destined for too long a stay in barracks on this occasion, and after only two weeks of various working parties, I found myself doing the drafting routine and proceeding on ten days draft leave prior to joining an 'R' class battleship, HMS *Ramillies*

Stoppage of leave did not apply to draft and seasonal leave; this could never be forfeited, and although I was still in debt to the crown, on going round the pay table I was presented with ten days victualling money – amounting to a little less than £2 – just that and no more, and from this I had to pay my fare home.

HMS *Ramillies* 1st March 1927 – 9th September 1929

The ship had been undergoing a refit and was lying in Devonport Dockyard, which meant that the whole of the new ship's company had to make the journey between the two ports by train.

A special train for this purpose had been shunted into Chatham Dockyard, and the journey being an overnight one, at 1830 we were marched through the dockyard gates in order to entrain.

There was no chance of having a farewell drink with any pals we might be leaving behind, for orders had been passed, that the wet canteen, instead of opening normally at 1730, was to remain closed until after the draft had departed.

By means of the various rail networks, the journey was completed without any changes having to be made, and we arrived at Plymouth in time for breakfast.

An advance party had joined the ship some weeks before; the Watch and Station Bill had been prepared, and everything in readiness for commissioning.

On being issued with station cards, mine showed that I was a Foc'sleman of the Blue Watch and 1st Whaler's Crew, with my action station being once again a loader number of a six-inch gun crew.

Unlike *Marlborough*, *Ramillies* had no messes situated in the gun casemates, this because, having a very low freeboard, in any sea at all, the 'R' class casemates would always be awash.

Having embarked, complete with baggage, we now waited for the pipe "Clear Lower Deck, Everybody Aft," a pipe which, when obeyed, saw the ship's company on the Quarter Deck waiting for the Captain to make his commissioning speech.

The speech made, and the commissioning pendant hoisted, the ship was now in commission, a commission which was to last for two years and seven months.

Ramillies being on General Messing, the cook rating were in sufficient numbers for them to be able to carry out the preparation of all meals, and because of this, cook of the mess duties only entailed fetching meals from the galley and washing up afterwards, but as the leading hand of the mess had not yet had time to make out a cooks' rota, "he decreed, that the clearing up after our first meal aboard would be *hands in,* a term which meant that everyone was to do their bit. This was also a method adopted when a ship was in homeport giving leave, when any rota was likely to be unworkable.

My new messmates were a mixed bag so far as ages were concerned. They included several of the more staid able seamen, two of whom had three good conduct badges apiece, not in this instance, men who had previously held a higher rating, but still wishing to make a career of the navy in their role of able seaman.

I was by no means the youngest member of my mess: there were several *jixers,* a name given to ratings that had joined after October 1925, at which time a lesser rate of pay had been introduced for all new entries.

Their pay as an able seaman was three shillings per day as opposed to my four shillings, and whereas my official number had the prefix 'J', with them it was JX, hence the name *jixer.* There were also a number of short service men, direct entry ordinary seamen, *Ramillies* being their first ship.

Recruitment to the seaman branch had always been by way of joining as a boy seaman, entry. being open to them from the age of fifteen and a quarter years, the upper age limit being sixteen years and nine months, although, even at that early age, they had to undertake to serve for twelve years from the age of eighteen.

The short service men were of an entirely new category, joining as ordinary seamen for seven years active service and five years on the reserve, being on a pay rate of three pence per day less that he aforementioned jixer, and having a prefix to their Official number of SSX: they were however, free at any time to sign on for another five years active service – thus undertaking to complete twelve years – and if doing so, their pay would be brought into line with that of a equivalent JX rating. As it was, we had the anomaly of three groups of men, all of the same rating, doing the same work, but of three different rates of pay depending on the J, JX or SSX category.

Prior to her recommissioning, *Ramillies* had been a unit of the Home fleet and was painted Home fleet colour, a darker grey than that which was used in the Mediterranean.

Sailing for Invergordon in order to work up to fleet standard, rumours were abroad that we might remain with the Home fleet all having had ten days foreign service draft leave, but a return to Devonport soon scotched any such rumours, pots and brushes being produced so that the ship could be given a coat of a different hue – Mediterranean grey, this task unfortunately resulting in the death of two crew members – Petty Officer Braid and Boy Barker.

The under part of the mainmast crosstrees was reached by means of a net slung underneath and secured by the four corners; the painting party sitting in this net and carrying on with the painting. In this instance, there remained only about two square yards to be done; two of the party had descended, leaving Petty Officer Braid and Boy Barker to finish off. Another five minutes and they would have been through, but as luck would have it, before they could finish the job, one of the net securing ropes parted, tipping them both out onto the deck fifty feet below. Petty Officer Braid, falling headfirst, was killed instantly but Boy Barker, although landing feet first and surviving the fall, died on the way to hospital.

A court of enquiry could blame no one: the rope securing the net had been new, with a breaking strain far in excess of that which it had been subjected to, but yet it parted. Fate, and a tragedy; but it could have been so much worse had it happened a few minutes earlier, when two other men had also been in the net.

The parents of Boy Barker requested that his body be sent to his home for burial, and the coffin carrying his remains was borne on a naval gun carriage and escorted from the mortuary at Stonehouse Naval Hospital to Plymouth Station, where it was entrained for the journey to London.

Petty Officer Braid was buried with full Naval honours, his mother and brother, himself serving in the Royal Navy as a Chief Petty Officer, being the chief mourners, whilst the whole of *Ramillies'* ship's company – with the exception of a few ship keepers – followed the cortege.

Before leaving for the Mediterranean, *Ramillies* had one more duty to fulfil, that of acting as guard ship for Cowes Regatta week.

In those days, regatta week was more of an occasion that it is at the present time. King George V was present aboard the Royal Yacht *Victoria & Albert*, and being the ardent yachtsman, raced *Britannia* against *Shamrock, Westward* and *Lulworth* these being the big boys of yacht racing.

At night, ships anchored in Cowes Roads were illuminated overall, Ramillies being no exception, the whole outline of the ship being picked out in lights: quite a spectacle I have no doubt, but rather oppressive below decks, all the deadlights having to be closed so that the ship was completely darkened except for the special illuminations.

The ship's company was not given leave to Cowes: it was another example of the ship being wanted, but not the men. Libertymen had to make the journey to Portsmouth if they wanted to spend their leisure hours ashore; otherwise the men had to make do with their normal shipboard pastimes, although some of the seamen petty officers were invited aboard *Shamrock* to take part in the racing, greatly enjoyed by those able to accept the invitation.

A sub lieutenant whose name escapes me – hoping perhaps to enhance his prospects – as soon as it became known about Cowes week, asked for volunteers to sing sea shanties, and these men, suitably attired as sailors of sailing ship days – such attire being of their own making – visited the various yachts in turn, lying alongside and rendering sea shanties from their repertoire.

The only concrete appreciation shown for their efforts was by the owner of an American yacht, drinks being passed down to all the party, the owner perhaps, being only too glad to show hospitality which – due to prohibition – would not have been possible were his yacht in American waters.

On the Sunday, *Ramillies* was visited by royalty, their majesties King George V and Queen Mary coming aboard; he to inspect the ship's company at Divisions, this being followed by a march past at which the queen was also present, my first ever close up of any member of the royal family.

The act of leaving Cowes also brought an end to our sojourn in home waters and found ourselves proceeding on an uneventful journey to Gibraltar and the Mediterranean.

Arriving at Malta before the fleet had returned from the summer cruise, the ship's company had a chance to experience how quiet the usual haunts of the men could be with all the ships being away, and also to find out how much the inhabitants missed them.

We were not to join up with the fleet yet however, *Ramillies* being detailed to show the flag for Great Britain at Navarino, a town in Greece which gave its name to Navarino Bay.

It was in Navarino Bay that the combined Turkish and Egyptian fleets were sunk by the allied English, French and Russians on 10th October 1827, and we were to attend a ceremony to celebrate the one hundredth anniversary of the action.

Besides *Ramillies,* representative ships from both France and Greece were present, but it seemed as though the Russians had either not been asked, or else had no wish to take part in the ceremony, they being most conspicuous by their absence. The ceremony consisted of a parade and the unveiling of a commemoration stone, with long speeches from both Greek and French V.I.P. 's, each in their own tongue and infinitely boring as not one word could we understand.

Then came the turn of the British Consul, he made a speech in English, after which a Greek interpreter repeated it in his mother tongue.

A march past then followed, martial music being played by the Royal Marine band of *Ramillies* and a band comprised of seamen from the French ship. There was to be no celebrations for us however, for the march continued to the harbour where, after embarking in the ship's boats, we returned aboard.

Back at Malta, expecting to at last take part in fleet activities, we remained only long enough to be issued with tropical clothing and also take certain anti-gas stores aboard.

Ramillies had been detailed to sail for Sierra Leone, there to carry out certain anti gas tests, volunteer members of the ship's company to act as guinea pigs in order to make the tests under tropical conditions.

Our destination was Freetown, but a call was made at Madeira en route, although we of lesser rating had to content ourselves by bargaining with the occupants of the bum boats, leave only being granted to chief and petty officers.

The ship remained in tropical waters for almost three months, mostly anchored off Freetown, but occasionally putting to sea for two or three days, some of the tests having to be carried out under sea going conditions.

It was during one of these trips that a third death occurred aboard, a death which was to result in a burial at sea.

A certain Stoker Clarke had undergone an emergency operation for appendicitis, the operation being carried out by one of the ship's surgeons. The operation safely over, the patient appeared to be making excellent progress, and everyone thought that he was on the way to making a good recovery.

It came as quite a shock when we heard that Nobby, who we on the foc'sle had spoken to through the sick bay fanlight only that morning, had died at 1130, the reason for his demise apparently being pneumonia.

His funeral took place that evening, and there is something about a burial at sea which words cannot adequately describe: the canvas enshrouded remains covered by the Union Jack, a funeral firing party standing by, the chaplain reading the burial service, engines stopped and everything so quiet, even the seagulls somehow sensing what is going on and keeping their cries to a minimum – or so it seems.

The chaplain reads the words, "We commit his body to the deep," the body slips from beneath the flag and drops with a splash into the sea below, a volley is fired by the firing party and only after the *Last Post* has been sounded do the gulls seem to resume their screeching, as if extolling the virtues of the departed.

Christmas was to be spent at Freetown, and this we were not looking forward to at all, there being very little ashore for our amusement, and it was obvious that any festivities would be only those that were available aboard ship and of our own making.

The captain had made a tentative suggestion that a fun fair of sorts be held on the quarterdeck, and it was asked that suggestions be put forward by possible stall holders. That many of them had not been vetted too well, became apparent on Christmas day when the miniature Wembley funfair was opened to the customers.

Several of them were real catchpennies, with no one but the organiser standing an earthly chance of winning, but the 'Harry Freeman's Soft Drinks Bar' was not at all expensive, this being run by the canteen committee and being exactly what the name implied – free soft drinks for everyone.

The side shows were allowed to run all day and well into the dog watches, but after supper tombola was played, this being the only occasion that it was allowed aboard *Ramillies,* the captain being a nonconformist to the game, but opening up his heart just this once.

During the morning, an amusing incident occurred when an able seaman by the name of Chegwidden, essayed a take over from Charlie Brown.

This Charlie Brown was a character – a native – who had been keeping us amused with his antics from a dug-out canoe, diving for coins and the odd tin of salmon or corned beef. He also had a few stock phrases, such as "Me Charlie Brown" – "Queen of England very good Man" – "Rule Britannia": his only wearing apparel was a 'G' string and stiff white collar, his headgear a black top hat.

So, this was how *Cheg* appeared, blacked from head to foot and complete with 'G' string and collar – the top hat he had to borrow during the take over of the canoe, which was accomplished without much bother.

Really looking the part, it was unfortunate that *Cheg* only remained in the canoe for as long as it took for him to be photographed. A great pity, for we would have liked to try him out with the odd coin or two.

We were not to leave Sierra Leone without another death occurring; a yeoman of signals named Munns waking up one morning with pains so bad that he was literally trying to tear his stomach apart. He was rushed ashore to hospital but died the same morning, being buried in the evening at Freetown cemetery. The ship's company was not informed of the cause of his death, but rumour had it that it was some form of cholera, but if this was so, then it was endemic only to him.

Before leaving West Africa, the ship paid a courtesy to the Gold Coast, visiting Takoradi and Accra, the latter well remembered for the hospitality of the European community; a sports day being organised, with small cash prizes for the successful contestants; prizes which, in a way I suppose, made the winners professional athletes.

Banyan, or feasting parties, were also much in evidence, and although the term banyan has, in this instance, some obscure origin, in naval parlance it was always used to describe a get together at which the food and drink were provided free of charge.

Whilst at Accra, *Stiffy* Gates, an able seaman in the same mess as me, bought an African Grey parrot for thirty shillings and the bird very soon learned to talk. *Stiffy* believed that the value of the bird would be enhanced if it's vocabulary could be confined to word's not likely to give offence; a bit of a problem where swearing was part of a sailor's everyday language, but strangely enough, not one cuss word did it learn, in spite of a few surreptitious exhortations to "Say F*** you old B******."

Our return to the Mediterranean did not immediately see us joining up with the fleet. The World's Fair was due to open at Barcelona, and whether it was to compensate the ship's company for time spent in the not so congenial surroundings of West Africa, or some other reason not apparent, a decision was made that *Ramillies* should show the flag as the representative of Great Britain.

In a way it was fortunate that leave facilities had not been too good at Freetown, for the money that could have been spent was still in our pockets, coming in very useful for a couple of good runs ashore in Barcelona.

About eight per cent of the ship's company were present at a bullfight, one hundred tickets being presented to the ship by the local authorities. These were balloted for, and with a complement of approximately twelve hundred, an eleven to one chance came up for me and I became a spectator to my first bullfight.

Because of the balloting, in which the whole of the ship's company had been included, all members of the duty watch who had won a chance to attend were allowed ashore out of watch, but I am afraid that this was one *corrida* at which the naval contingent rather tended to let the side down. The hundred tickets were in a block, so we were all sitting together, somewhat bored with the proceedings until, in one contest, the bull knocked the matador for six, at which we, the uninitiated, stood as one man to cheer.

Fortunately, the matador was not badly hurt, and it is to be hoped that the *aficionados* put our outburst down to our ignorance of the noble art of bullfighting. A new football stadium had been built as a feature of the exhibition, and I was fortunate in being able to attend it's inauguration where after witnessing a Spanish/Italian rugger match, I was one of the many disappointed spectators of a soccer match in which a Spanish eleven defeated the then F.A. Cup holders Bolton Wanderers by three goals to one.

Ramillies' return to Malta coincided with the commencement of the summer cruise, and a visit to Juan-Les-Pins in the south of France saw *Stiffy* Gates and his parrot part company.

The ship being open to visitors, an English-speaking French woman and her seventeen year old daughter were quite taken with polly, although an enquiry, "Does it swear?" when answered in the negative, only brought the reply, "What a pity!"

The outcome of it was that the next day, a message was sent to the ship asking if *Stiffy* would call at the lady's house, where an offer of £20 for polly resulted in a deal. Not a bad profit margin, but who knows, if the bird had been a blaggard, it might have been a better one.

Visiting day at Juan-les Pins led to another meeting, which resulted in romance, and later, a marriage, between a young French visitor and one Able Seaman Brown, a romance helped on its way by his messmates subbing for his turn of duty whilst the ship was at both Juan-les-Pins and nearby Cannes.

During this time, training was in full swing for the fleet regatta, due to take place toward the end of the cruise. *Ramillies,* although having a full complement of crews in training, was destined to have very little success, due in no small measure to the boats, for these did make an appreciable difference, as was proved on the occasion of a challenge match, boats being exchanged for the return.

The crews were representative of the *Buffaloes* of *Ramillies* and *Royal Sovereign,* the races taking place in Malta's Grand Harbour, *Sovereign's* boat winning with both their own and *Ramillies'* crew at the oars, which rather proves my point.

We did have one good boat however – the 1st whaler – but good only for its sailing qualities. This boat with Leading Seaman Ben Tillet at the tiller, and me as one of the five crew members, made a habit of scooping the pool at the Saturday afternoon sailing races.

The races – for whalers only – took place over a course marked out in the open sea outside of the Grand Harbour, coxswains pay one shilling per boat, and the winner taking the kitty, usually about twenty five shillings, and it became quite a habit for 07 Kl to be first over the finishing line.

Writing in anticipation of a-future event, 07 Kl also proved herself when sailing for the Gibraltar Cup; not winning, having to be content with fifth place, but she did have the honour of being the first home of her class, and that after sailing against the combined fleets.

With the return of the fleet to Malta, preparations were in hand for the autumn season, this being something which we had previously missed due to our commitments in West African waters.

The officers of Ramillies decided to hold a dance on the quarter deck, and this of course meant that the seamen were required to help with the preparations.

A ceremonial awning – which until then had not seen the light of day – was brought up from the canvas room and spread. This awning was of alternate red and white widths of canvas which had to be spread underneath the main quarter deck awning, and as the name implies, was used only on ceremonial occasions – aboard *Ramillies*, only this one time in two and a half years.

All the spare bunting was brought from the signal deck for prettying up the quarter deck and boat deck, the boat deck officer organising, with the aid of bunting and canvas screens, secluded nooks which could comfortably hold two people; nooks, to which any self respecting woman having been brought, it would be obvious to her that it wasn't just to talk about the weather.

These preparations were made during working hours, but after tea came the pipe, "Hands to dance and skylark on the Quarter Deck."

This was to make the surface fit for dancing, men – all volunteers – running and sliding about the deck to their hearts' content, being helped in their endeavours by liberal sprinklings of French chalk.

After this, members of the ship's company took no further part in the proceedings, except that a few of the duty watch, in order that the flow of drinks might be maintained, were detailed for the washing of glasses. Guests were mainly V.I.P.'s and officers wives, and of course, the doting mothers with marriageable daughters who had managed to come by invitations, but reports received via the duty gangway staff, gave the information that several lovelies from the *Gut* had arrived, complete with official invitation cards.

The ensuing months were quite a strain on the exchequer, this being due in no small measure to the amount of night leave given, there usually being some kind of leave or another on three nights out of four.

When a man was broke – usually near the end of the month – a loan might be solicited from one of the more thrifty of his acquaintances, perhaps for sippers of the next day's tot, or even perhaps, out of the lender's goodness of heart.

At times, there would also be the occasional *shark*; a man quite willing to lend, but only at an interest, such interest being five shillings on everyone pound lent: veritable *shylocks,* with the motto 'An eye for an eye, a tooth for a tooth, and a quid for twenty five.'

The following story concerns two messmates; *Lofty* Kendal and *Brigham* Young, both able seamen and both very broke, but badly wanting a run ashore.

Their mess being adjacent to the canteen, they sat at the end of the table from 1630 until 1830, asking everyone who passed on their way to the canteen in order to make a purchase, if they could lend them a halfpenny, giving the impression that they were just that amount short of their needs for making a purchase. There were very few refusals, and in some instances, they received the reply, "I haven't got a halfpenny, here's a penny."

The point of the story is that in two hours sitting there, they raised enough to enable them to catch the last liberty boat at 1930. They tried it again on a later occasion, but it did not work a second time; the story had got around.

This same *Brigham* Young had a hatred for all artificers, not having a good word to say about one of them.

Apparently, he had, prior to an earlier commission, become engaged to a girl in his home town and made an allotment to her; the money to be saved for his homecoming and their ultimate marriage. They did of course keep up a correspondence until, about two months before his homecoming she stopped writing.

A letter asking his mother to make enquiries brought the following telegram in reply: XXX married XXXX (an artificer) six weeks ago "And," said *Brigham,* relating the story, she kept my bloody money as a dowry."

Hence his hatred of all artificers, but he appeared to have no hard feelings against the girl, still having her photograph on display in his ditty-box.

My request to pass professionally for leading seaman had by now reached a successful conclusion, successful inasmuch that I had got through the examination without difficulty, but had little chance of attaining a higher rating in the foreseeable future, there being seven years waiting time on the advancement roster.

It was during my swotting for the examination that I became involved in my one and only punch up – all over a seamanship manual.

One of the older members of my mess had loaned me a manual, a much earlier edition than my own, which we both thought, gave more details on certain subjects than the later edition which I owned. A pal of mine – Jack Hall, a native of Newcastle borrowed this manual from me from time to time, for he too was going to take the examination.

One morning, a couple of loose pages brought an accusation from me and a denial from him, but my accusation repeated, without more ado he threw the manual at me, and in no time at all we were going at it hammer and tongs, until stopped by one of the regulating petty officers, being told by him that if we still felt the same way about it in the dog watches, we were to battle it out under supervision, with the gloves on.

I am glad to be able to relate that it did not come to this, the dog watches seeing us the best of pals once again. This friendship lasted until well after the ship paid off, but, as so often happened in naval life, we eventually lost track of one another.

Christmas day 1928 was much like any other Christmas afloat. An open gangway meant that the watch ashore did not have to wait for the routine liberty boats, but could proceed ashore as the fancy took them, an abundance of dghaisas being available for this purpose.

It was on this Christmas night that I broke out of ship: a stupid thing to do in any event, but in this instance even more so, for I was watch ashore.

The time was about 2045 and life aboard was absolutely dead. Nobby was duty watch, but they had been mustered in order to clear up for rounds and would not be required again unless in an emergency.

My suggestion that we go ashore brought the reply – "How can I, I can't get anyone to sub for me, and in any case, the gangway closes at 2100." A further suggestion that we break out, did not meet with any objection, so we proceeded to put the project into operation.

In practice, it was not really the problem it may seem, for the ship was lying alongside the dockyard wall on the Cospicua side of Dockyard Creek, close by a flight of steps known as The *Hole in the Wall*.

A visit to the dockyard heads with collars hidden away, collars put on in the heads, a walk along the dockside until an accommodating dghaisa could be found, a short journey to the steps, and we were ashore; a few beers and a sing-song later, returning to the ship by the same route, fortunately undetected and without being missed.

Was it worth it? Well under the circumstances I suppose, yes! But if we had been caught out? Well, we weren't, so who knows?

Christmas and New Year celebrations over, a few exercises in readiness for the meeting of the combined fleets, and we were off on the Spring Cruise.

It was during this cruise that I was belatedly awarded my 1st good conduct badge: belatedly, because in a way, I was still being punished for my absenteeism two years earlier, having only now completed the required period of *Very Good* character, a period which would have been completed some nine months earlier had I not transgressed.

The award carried with it another three pence per day, so now, as an able seaman with one good conduct badge, I was in receipt of four shillings and sixpence per day.

During the spring cruise, part of my working day was taken up with an Acting Seaman Gunner's course, which satisfactorily completed, would result in a recommendation to qualify as a Seaman Gunner when next in Chatham Barracks; this non substantive rating carrying another three pence per day.

After the Red and Blue fleets' had again done battle, all units put into Gibraltar for the usual get-togethers, and then, after splitting up in order to go their various ways, *Ramillies* visited several of the Algerian ports, including Algiers itself, with my essay into night club life mentioned in an earlier chapter.

Returning to Malta, many of the ships had boats' crews in training for the regatta, but we of *Ramillies* were taking no part this time, for we were due to leave for the U.K. before it took place.

So, in mid-June we sailed. The commission had been a few weeks short of the usual two and a half years, with the first five months in home waters, and because of this, our leave entitlement was to be only twenty eight days instead of the customary thirty five which was to be expected after the completion of a full two and a half years.

Ramillies did not pay off immediately; we were to remain in Devonport Dockyard for six weeks before this happy event took place.

The reason we gathered was because of the forthcoming Navy week, a battleship in dry dock being one of the attractions *Ramillies* was to be that attraction.

Had she been a Devonport manned ship it would not have been too bad but being Chatham manned, the majority of the ship's company were from south and south east England, many with their homes actually in Chatham and neighbouring Gillingham.

Weekend leave was given, but free railway warrants were unheard of in the 1920's and 30's. The service fare from Plymouth to London was thirty shillings, a whole week's pay by my standards, and after one visit to London, I reached a decision that thirty shillings could be spent on a much better advantage by enjoying myself locally: but then, I was unattached.

Before relating an amusing incident that occurred during my one week end in London, it would be as well to make it clear, that apart from half a pound of duty free tobacco or its equivalent in cigarettes, no customs concessions were allowed to men returning from abroad, customs officers having no hesitation in charging the full amount of duty on any gifts which had been brought in.

So to my weekend in London, and another pal, Arthur Case, had decided to take some silk underwear with him although he had not paid duty on it; defeating any customs enquiries by wearing it under his uniform: perfectly straightforward if he had remained sober, but having a night on the town, Arthur became incapable, so much so, that I, and my other pal *Nobby* Hall, had to get him to the Union Jack Club and turned in, divesting him of the silken underwear in the process.

What would have happened had he not had friends with him I shudder to think, for I feel sure that anyone else – police or patrol – would have got the wrong ideas about the underwear.

During my sojourn at Devonport, I met an interesting old boy of eighty-four who had left the navy on pension some forty years earlier. According to his story – and I had no reason to doubt it – he had asked to commute his pension for a lump sum of £200 in order to start up a business, only to be told that he would not live long enough to draw that amount. "But;" he said, taking a drink from a pint of his favourite porter, "Here I am and well and still drawing it."

The day of paying off eventually dawned and we were pleasantly surprised to learn, that because of the delay, a further seven days leave had been awarded, although this was due, in no small measure, to the efforts of Mrs Page-Chapman, wife of an able seaman; she having got some of the other wives together in order to lobby their M.P.'s.

Another special train; this time from Plymouth: another all-night journey, bags and hammocks stowed in Chatham Barracks, and leave had begun.

Chapter 17

Pembroke, Curlew and *Cyclops*

HMS *Pembroke* 10th September 1929-30th March 1931
During the two and a half years that I had been away from Chatham Barracks, several changes had taken place.

There were of course, new faces in the clothing department, and although, as before, a clothing gunner was in attendance, there was more tolerance, and not nearly so many condemnations.

Men employed as messengers now had to wear an armband embroidered with a capital M, and also carry documentation to the effect that they were so employed.

Prior to this it had been possible for a man, if he were so minded and also had the effrontery, to don a blue serge suit and, carrying a sheaf of any old papers, walk about the barracks the whole day long supposedly as a messenger, but actually having one hell of a loaf. So, it would appear, with the advent of the armbands and documents, someone higher up had got wise to it at last.

After a couple of months employed on various working parties, I became a member of the baggage party, only to learn that there had been a change here also, and that they were now the drill shed window cleaners. This meant that instead of reading the various *Dailys* between jobs, I, like the others, had to busy myself cleaning these windows; windows which must have been the cleanest in the establishment.

As far as I was concerned, this state of affairs did not last long, for I was drafted to the Gunnery School in order to qualify as a Seaman Gunner.

By the long arm of coincidence, in spite of the number of instructors that were available at the Gunnery School, and the comings and goings due to drafting requirements, my instructor was the one I had been townies with at Shotley, and so we renewed our acquaintance – but not for long.

I had been on course only a few weeks when, volunteers being required to form a field gun's crew for the Royal Tournament, I and a few of my ex *Ramillies* pals put our names forward.

The outcome was that one cold February morning, together with ninety-nine other volunteers, I was marched off to East Camp, this being the site of the field gun course.

In the initial stages, the competition allowed fifty men, these to form two crews and reserves. Later, when their capabilities became known, the fifty would have to be reduced by ten. These were the rules which governed the competition, and all participating units had to abide by them.

On this particular morning the idea was to whittle the one hundred volunteers down to the allowable fifty. The men were split into pairs, and then a trial of speed and strength between each pair began – the winner in and loser out. For this survival of the fittest the course was the same as for a field gun run, the two contestants starting at one end, climbing the first five-foot wall, clambering over the chasm and running up to the second wall, also at five feet. Here, two-gun wheels weighing one hundred and twenty pounds each were on the ground, and these had to be picked up and thrown over the wall, the contestants following. They then had to retrace their steps to the first wall, where a second wheel had to be disposed of in a like manner, after which the contestants themselves had to surmount this same obstacle.

As I said earlier, only the winners were in, but why the whole business could not have been runoff against the clock with the fastest fifty being accepted escapes me, for on this day I am certain, that many of the winners had their betters in losers of other heats.

I will never know how this might have affected me: suffice to say, that as a winner, I was taken off course at the Gunnery School and mess changed into the newly formed field gun mess.

The field gunners were messed on their own so that their victuals could be increased by twenty-five per cent, this being thought necessary because of the strenuous nature of their endeavours. We were also excused from all duties, but it could hardly be said that because of this we were to live in the lap of luxury, for the training programme was to be most exacting.

There was road work before breakfast; no one excused, even libertymen having to return that much earlier in order to take part. After breakfast, either P.T. or swimming, with the remainder of the working day being spent on the field gun course; first doing the run-in stages, swapping the men about so as to get the best combination; eventually doing the complete run.

Now came the moment of truth, for in order to comply with the rules, some had to go. Not the ten originally expected; a few had already fallen on the way: two of their own accord, not being able to stick the pace; a third, sacked for dodging road work, whilst a fourth was in hospital, having lost the top of his index finger in an accident when taking the limber over one of the walls.

Minor accidents were quite common; especially in the earlier stages of training, and I for one, had my share; a split finger necessitating three stitches: crossing the chasm on the limber without being properly aboard, in consequence of which, when it was slipped on the opposite side, my leg being underneath, I hobbled away with a badly bruised shin; fortunate in fact, that things had not been worse. Accidents supposedly happening in threes, on another occasion; again crossing the chasm, this time on a gun carriage with three other men, the No.1 man slipped it too soon, but whilst the other three managed to hang on to the traveller, I finished up in the chasm with the trail of the gun carriage in the small of my back: rather painful, but then again, it could have been much more serious.

All these little snags having been ironed out, and training now being with a view to getting the run time down to something like competition standard, I found myself in the probable No. 1 crew.

Unfortunately, without being involved in any further accident, my hopes of appearing in the arena to compete with crews from other establishments were to receive a bitter blow, for I was knocked out by a sore throat.

Many of the bumps and bruises sustained during training would, in other circumstances, have put a man on the sick or light duty list, but to prevent this, a leading sick berth attendant had been prevailed upon to tend such injuries without the injured party first having to see the M.O.

So, with my sore throat, I went to see him; thinking that some sort of gargle was all that I required. It was not so simple however: he informed me that I was suffering from tonsillitis, and there was nothing for it but to see the medical officer.

The outcome was that I finished up in the Zymotic ward of the Royal Naval Hospital at Gillingham, under observation for diphtheria.

A patient for ten days, swabs were taken during the early stages, being incarcerated in a glass cubicle until tests proved negative; after which, I was moved into an open ward.

Time and treatment saw me fit once again, and I was discharged to duty, returning to the field gun mess.

That I was medically fit one must agree, but my physical condition was another matter, and being given a run with the No. 2 crew the following day, my shortcomings in this respect were most noticeable.

So, for me, the ensuing training periods were spent on the sidelines watching the two crews going through their paces, but the physical training and road work were helping me to regain peak fitness, and after a time, a broken leg sustained by one of the crew members resulted in my joining the No. 2 crew, and there I remained until we all left for Olympia and the Royal Tournament.

A new rule, instituted midway through the training programme, had caused a bit of a furore; the rule stating that the representative crew must include at least one petty officer.

There had been no volunteer petty officers in the original intake, so of course, there were none in training. A call for petty officer volunteers brought only one response, so it was a case of 'Hobson's Choice,' and also fortuitous in a way that an accident to one of the pole numbers left an opening for him.

Both crews went to Olympia: The No. 1 crew taking part in the competition, whilst the reserve crew acted as gatekeepers and ushers, all being paid four shillings per day from the proceeds of the tournament admission charges.

The guns used in the tournament were authentic twelve pounders, but for competition purposes the elevating mechanism had been removed, the barrel then being secured to the carriage by means of a hand spike, which jammed into the breach and made fast to the trail with a wire strop.

To do away with such an unwieldy process, the ordnance artificer attached to the Chatham crew had developed a small gadget working on a spring and plunger basis, which, when – fixed to the gun carriage served exactly the same purpose. Unfortunately, this little gadget had not been declared as required by the rules, and this was later to lead to a disqualification.

Two trophies were awarded for the field gun run, one for the best aggregate and the other for the fastest time. The competition had a keen following, with results being signalled daily to units serving abroad. The event nearing the halfway mark, Chatham had a nice lead on the aggregate, so much so that they would have had to do some very bad runs if they were not eventually to win it.

This state of affairs prompted the Portsmouth crew to lodge a complaint to the effect that the gadget was giving an unfair advantage, and the outcome was disqualification from the aggregate competition: – not for using the gadget, but for failure to declare it.

So incensed at the decision, and Portsmouth not having run that evening, the Chatham crew borrowed their gun and proceeded to break the then existing record, putting up a time of three minutes fifty-two seconds, a time which won for them the fastest time cup, it not being beaten during the remainder of the competition

Having won this cup, a triumphal return to Chatham met with rather an anti climax when the crew, following the usual procedure, marched on to the parade ground expecting to be congratulated by the commodore, only to be given a dressing down before the whole assembly and accused of gamesmanship which had deprived Chatham of a much coveted double.

The two crews did not immediately disband. Organisers of the Derbyshire Bakewell Show had asked for a naval display, we being given the job; and only after this show was over did we return to our normal endeavours, which in my case meant remaining at the Gunnery School to complete the course for seaman gunner.

The course satisfactorily completed, I was drafted to the reserve fleet destroyers which lay in Short Reach, a reach of the river Medway just off Gillingham Pier.

These destroyers, six in all, were manned by a care and maintenance party, the party living aboard one of them and carrying out various jobs on the others – keeping the moth balls renewed as it were.

This sinecure of a job lasted for nine months and might have lasted for longer had I not put an end to myself by volunteering for sea service.

Time served with the reserve fleet was classed as home shore service, and having been so based for eighteen months, and knowing that it could not be long before I was given a foreign draft, I tried for one – of my own choosing – HMS *Dragon*.

Dragon, a light cruiser of the West Indies station, was paying off at Chatham and was due for recommission, again with a Chatham crew; I put a volunteer chit through, but the West Indies being a plum station, many others had the same idea. I was drafted to a light cruiser though – the *Curlew*, commissioning at the same time for service in the Mediterranean.

HMS *Curlew* 31st March 1931 – 4th January 1932

No special train was required to transport the men for this commissioning, the ship being in our home dockyard.

My commissioning card told me that I was to be a Maintopman, with my action station on a three inch H.A. gun, but it was not long before I discovered that I was in fact, a supernumerary and in excess of complement as a seaman gunner, the job being one normally carried out by a trained man holding no gunnery rating, although, at the time this did not worry me unduly, for I was still in receipt of my seaman gunner's pay of three pence per day.

The ship had not been long in commission when we became involved in an uprising on the island of Madeira. Historians would in all probability be able to produce the full facts, but it had something to do with the foreseeable dictatorship of Salazar, a certain element of the Portuguese on the island wanting independence

Our role was simply to look after the inhabitants of British nationality and to this end, an armed party was landed, the British population were moved into two hotels, and we of the landing party became their guardian angels.

The uprising was short-lived, a little sniping between the rival factions and a Portuguese gunboat firing the odd shell or two being all the action we saw.

Eventually the rebels asked for asylum aboard *Curlew,* which was given insofar as a passage to the Portuguese mainland was vouchsafed to them. Of what happened to them after they were landed, I have no word. Doubtless they were arrested and tried, but whatever the outcome, no word of it ever reached *Curlew*. Rejoining the fleet, our sporting achievements were variable. Regatta-wise, the gig appeared to be almost unbeatable, winning practically every race in which it was entered; but this, together with the fact that we had a couple of good whalers' crews was not sufficient to win the cock, having to be content with third place behind *London* and *Sussex,* two county class cruisers of more modern design.

Curlew did however, bring off one quite notable achievement, winning two of three fleet sailing cups; a success which needed some celebrating, and the pipe "Sailing boats crews lay aft," saw us being served with drinks, on the officers and by the officers, the captain also becoming a waiter for the occasion.

Shortly after this there occurred something which gave no cause for celebration. I am referring of course, to the reduction in pay, the reduction which resulted in the Home fleet going on strike.

At this time the Mediterranean fleet was split up, so it was not possible for meetings to be held, as was the case with men of the Home fleet at Invergordon.

We of the lower deck felt sure that the reduction was an attempt to level down the 1919 rates of pay to the 1925 rates, the one shilling a day reduction doing just that.

If it had not been for the men of the *Hood* and the *Valiant* refusing to weigh anchor and sitting on the cable in order to make certain that the officers couldn't either, this levelling down of the two rates might have become an established fact.

As it was, the trouble brought about a review, the outcome of which was a further statement to the effect that the reduction was only to be considered as a loan, repayable at a later date, which in fact it was. But who boobed? Was the text of the first signal wrong, or did the strike in the Home fleet bring about a change of mind?

Readers may think that far too much fuss had been made about a shilling a day, but it was a twenty-five per cent decrease in an able seaman's flat rate, and would those shillings have made much difference to the country's exchequer, which was in a sorry state under a minority Labour government.

Aboard most ships, shore going usually developed in groups of men, a small party going ashore together. Seldom were there loaners, unless such a one was a womaniser going ashore solely for the purpose of soliciting female company.

As I have mentioned before, shipboard friendships did develop, and *Curlew* being no exception, I became quite chummy with one Dick Dovey. Dick hailed from Norwich, and we were of an age; but friendly though we were, neither of us did a lot of shore-going, we both having matrimony in mind, and needing to save.

During my eighteen months shore-based service, I had met and become engaged to Elsie, who was eventually to become my wife. It had been my intention to be married when *Curlew* paid off; but Dick had other ideas, for he had arranged for his fiancée to come out to Malta after the spring cruise, with a wedding taking place at the Anglican cathedral in Valetta.

All the arrangements had been made, and Dick had asked me to be his best man; but as things turned out, this duty had to be carried out by somebody else, for I was drafted to HMS *Cyclops,* a submarine parent ship, arrived back in England before the bride to be had even left for Malta. I did have an opportunity to see her; however, meeting her in London when she arrived from Norwich and escorting her to the boat train at Waterloo.

HMS *Cyclops* 5th January – 29th April 1932

My draft to *Cyclops* came about because I was supernumerary aboard *Curlew;* such drafts from ship to ship being not uncommon, for depending on the need and availability, these movements on the station obviated the sending out of an occasional relief from the U.K.

With the job of Wardroom Flat sweeper, and my action station being in the navigation party, I failed to see why it had been a drafting for a seaman gunner, when both jobs could have been done by a trained man.

I was annoyed to say the least, for the whole idea of my wishing to complete the commission was to accumulate capital as it was, after only nine months aboard *Curlew,* and three and half aboard *Cyclops,* I was homeward bound again, and would have to make a fresh start.

It would have been possible to recommission *Cyclops,* but I was not enamoured of a further stint aboard a coal fired submarine parent ship, having in three and a half months, savoured of the work involved aboard a ship, which being a parent,' had eight submarines in her brood. I therefore elected to payoff and once again join *Pembroke*, to await whatever draft might be coming my way.

Chapter 18

Pembroke and *Daring*

HMS *Pembroke* 30th April – 30th November 1932.
Very few changes had taken place during the year or so that I had been away from Chatham.

Working parties were as usual, and, some of the barrack stanchions – men so called, in a sarcastic manner because they gave the impression that the establishment would fall down if they received a draft chit – were still in evidence.

One notable exception was the driver of the horse and cart, the horse having been retired and a pickup truck doing the duties which had been performed by dobbin.

I suppose I should have mentioned before, that the driver of the horse and cart was a staid able seaman, the cart an open two wheeled one, the whole combination being used for various transport jobs in and around the establishment; but now, with progress, mechanisation had moved in.

I spent three months in the working party, and during this period I was twice detailed as a member of a field gun carriage party for the burial of naval pensioners who lived locally.

In the days of which I am writing, it was the prerogative of a deceased pensioner's next of kin to be allowed the use of a field gun carriage to bear the mortal remains to the last resting place.

As the need arose, eighteen men from the working party were detailed for this service, a commissioned gunner being in charge of the proceedings.

On the two occasions of my being a member of the gun carriage crew, the commissioned gunner was one *Guts* Everett – so called because of his corpulence – and he made sure that the route back was by way of the *Monarch* public house, the crew being accommodated for the serving of drinks although it was after hours, *Guts* apparently, having an 'Open Sesame' no matter what the hour.

Three months in the working party and I was given a quiet number, that of Main Gate Messenger.

Any man having a quiet number would know that any duties out of working hours would be in that same capacity, whereas members of the working party would, when duty watch be detailed off for any one of the various jobs which had been carried out; fire Party, Duty Baggage Party, Town Patrol, Room Sentry and Canteen Sentry being but a few.

It was an absolute certainty that the Fire Party would be required to carry out an exercise; twelve stalwarts manhandling a hand operated fire engine to the scene of the imaginary fire, closely followed by another party complete with fire escape.

How efficient they might have been in real emergency was never put to the test, but it may be of interest to the reader, that on the occasion of a quite large fire in the adjacent dockyard, the Chatham and Gillingham fire brigades were quite able to cope, without any assistance being required from the duty barrack fire party.

The duty baggage party had to be available to assist any late drafts arriving or leaving, and on occasion they would be called upon to carry out other jobs where a certain amount of humping was required.

Men detailed as Town Patrol spent their evening patrolling the main streets of Chatham and Gillingham, wearing belt, gaiters and armbands as badges of office, and being in the charge of a petty officer; he also being duty watch.

Their jobs consisted mainly of telling the liberty men to take their hands out of their pockets or to put their caps on straight; but if a group of three or more happened to be standing and talking they had to be moved on, for it would never do to have liberty men cluttering up the pavement. Occasionally the arrest of a drunk and disorderly rating would be made, the offender then being taken to the patrol house and turned over to the standing patrol for a night in cells.

Room patrols took over in the various mess rooms at 2100, working in two-hour shifts and being armed with an order board telling what they had to do in certain eventualities.

The hours between 2400 and 0400 could be most eerie; the sentry in all probability being the only one awake, with about one hundred men asleep in their hammocks, some snoring, others talking in their sleep; an atmosphere which a written description cannot give a true idea of.

At times the sentry would not be the only one awake, for it was during these nocturnal hours that a sneak thief might be most likely to operate; going through his roommates' clothing in the hope of finding some spare cash, or even perhaps, taking cigarettes and personal belongings.

The prevention of such nefarious practices was one reason why the room sentries were posted, but another was because of fire hazards; especially in the winter months, when the only means of heating the rooms was by open fires.

The Officer of the Day went the rounds in one of the accommodation blocks during the middle watch, usually as soon as possible after midnight so that his night's rest would not be too much disturbed.

It so happened that at this particular time, a certain Lieutenant Commander Bocket-Pugh was Senior Officer of the Day. Not the most popular of officers – it was said that he sent moore libertymen back for haircuts than all the other O.O.D's together – he, when doing his rounds, went to great length hoping to catch the room sentry out, even entering the barrack room with his shoes off in the hope of catching the sentry dozing.

This officer more commonly referred to as *Bucket of Spew,* which speaks for itself with regard to his popularity – one night met his match in a quiet junior able seaman.

I am almost punning when saying met his match, for it was a match that came into it in the following manner.

Finding the sentry wide awake, and having received the report "Post correct Sir," hoping to test the sentry further, he struck a match and threw it to the floor, at the same time shouting "FIRE" thinking no doubt, that the sentry would carry out the instructions on his order board and rouse the men in the vicinity before going to the nearest phone and informing the Main Gate.

Not so however, for the sentry, being equal to the occasion, stamped on the match, sprang sharply to attention and reported "Fire out Sir!"

So much for the chores of the duty watch. My own job of Main Gate Messenger had no such onerous involvements, being that of a runner for the Officer of the Day and the Chief Petty Officer i/c Main Gate.

Being employed in this capacity, I was enabled to learn much of the perks which came the way of the higher hierarchy by virtue of the position which they held; perks however which, being a junior rating, I was not allowed to share.

I held this job for four months, after which a posting for foreign service had me once again proceeding on ten days draft leave; the draft being for service with the Mediterranean fleet, the ship HMS *Daring,* one of a new class of destroyer being manned for the first time.

HMS *Daring* 1st December 1932 – 24th October 1934

Daring was not commissioned with a complete new crew from barracks, and when I joined, the majority of the crew were already aboard, having transferred from HMS *Wryneck,* a V&W boat of

World War I Vintage, she having returned from the Mediterranean solely for this purpose.

Each of the 'D' class destroyers were commissioned in this way; as they became available from the builders, a V&W boat of the first Destroyer Flotilla returned from the Mediterranean in order to transfer her crew to the new ship.

The 'D' class having a greater tonnage and more armaments, they also needed a larger complement, which was why I, and twenty-four others, came to be joining a ship in Chatham Dockyard when she was one third of the way through a Mediterranean commission.

Being a new ship, the problem of getting rid of the dockyard workmen and their paraphernalia did not arise, and we were soon on our way down the Medway to Sheerness, en route for Portland and working up practices.

Daring was due to sail for the Mediterranean on 23rd December, and this would have meant spending Christmas day at sea; rather unusual in the peacetime navy, organisation usually allowing for all units of the various fleets to hold their Christmas celebrations in port.

However, as things turned out, we did not sail until after the holiday, being delayed by condenser trouble.

The job delegated to me was that of quartermaster, so, being a watchkeeper, and therefore entitled to lie in until "Guard and steerage" when not actually on watch, I was victualled in the watchkeepers' mess, away from the hustle and bustle of the early risers.

Daring was only the second of the 'D' class to have arrived on station, so the First Flotilla at the time was an odd and incomplete one; some of the V&W's being in company, with others in the U.K. for the change over; but eventually we did become a complete nine boat flotilla, eight 'D' class and the leader *Mackay*.

Arriving in the Mediterranean early in the year allowed ample time for the organising of boats' crews for the flotilla regatta, although training did not immediately start; for too early a beginning would mean a crew reaching their peak of fitness too soon, and staleness before the regatta took place.

The combined fleet exercises during the Spring Cruise took place in the most atrocious weather, and we were glad when they had reached a successful conclusion and we were able to put into Gibraltar.

Before returning to Malta, the ship visited several of the Tunisian ports, but they were not then the holiday resorts that present-day tourists seem to enjoy visiting.

In Malta, the ship's company were regulars of the *Great War Bar,* at Sliema, this being mainly due to the fact that a shipmate – Able Seaman Alf Wilmshurst – was a son-in-law of the proprietor, and any man wearing a *Daring* cap ribbon was able to buy *Farson's Blue Label* for three pence a bottle instead of having to pay the usual four pence.

Farson's was a beer brewed in Malta, and a brewery run was one of the island's highlights, everything being free. Arrangements had to be made beforehand: first with the brewers, and then aboard ship for leave to start early.

The run started at the Farson office in Valetta; a special bus, amply provided with their own brand liquid refreshment being laid on for the journey. On arrival at the brewery, a grand tour, with more sampling and further refreshment for the return journey. Perhaps I should add that snacks were also provided; this to prevent too much drinking on an empty stomach; but even so, the party returned with beer literally oozing from their ears.

These brewery runs must have been purely promotional, the market in earlier years being mainly for Simmonds and McEwans beers.

The summer cruise saw *Daring* winning the flotilla regatta, albeit without winning a single race, our boats finishing second or third in all but two of the races, these exceptions being communications fifth and officers sixth. The regatta over, and the summer cruise nearing its end, in my capacity as quartermaster I was to be the first man aboard *Daring* to take part in a chain of events which lead to an unexpected dash to the Persian Gulf.

In harbour at the time, and during the middle watch, the ship of the senior officer in company started to make *Daring's* pendants – H 49 – in Morse code.

Apart from the auxiliary watchkeeper in the engine room I was the only one awake, and realising that it was our pendants that were being made, I proceeded to rouse the duty signalman, shaking his hammock and saying "Bunts, she's bobbing;" a phrase commonly used to tell any signalman (bunting tosser) that some other ship was making his pendants with a signal lamp (bobbing).

Bunts aroused; and I taking down the message as he read, it became apparent that we would soon be on the move, and the captain being given the signal, the engineer officer called, and steam raised, we were very soon on our way to the Suez Canal en route for the Persian Gulf, where at Basidou, a Persian gun-boat had had the effrontery to haul down the British flag.

Basidou – or *British Bloody Basidou;* as it came to be known after we had been kept in the Gulf for two and a half months – was only a small trading post, and by the time we arrived the gun boat had been long gone.

We did however, visit other, more important places in the Gulf; taking various sheiks, together with their entourage, for a day put; loosing off guns and torpedoes in order to impress them with our fire power.

A visit to Bahrain coincided with the sheik's birthday so a guard of honour was landed, and after a march past they were regaled with sherbet and chapatis – a celebration feast.

No proper leave was given during our stay in the Persian Gulf: beer was carried on the ship, but this could only be sold and consumed on the beaches during a two hour dog watch period, both beer and men being transported ashore for this purpose.

Before finally leaving the Gulf, a trip of some sixty miles was made up the Euphrates River to Basra where a large Royal Air Force contingent was stationed.

Their welcome to us came in the form of a signal, which read – Ships company invited to a dance at 1930; beer and dancing partners provided. Lack of leave during the preceding weeks brought a ready response to the invitation, but also some disappointment, for although the beer was the real thing, dancing partners were in fact R.A.F. personnel masquerading as members of the opposite sex.

A visit to Aberdan allowed of a visit ,to the oil installations by the chief and petty officers, whilst the wardroom officers were entertained by the European colony; the remainder of the ship's company gaining solace by – on this one occasion only – being allowed to buy, and drink, beer aboard ship.

One other visit, outside of the Persian Gulf, was made before returning to the Mediterranean.

Muscat, an independent state in the Gulf of Oman, being very pro British, it was considered advisable after our earlier activities, that the proper thing would be for our captain to make a courtesy call on the Sultan.

Whilst he was performing this duty, the skip's company were able to disport themselves by partaking of their first swim in over two months, the waters hereabouts apparently being free of water snakes, sharks and other denizens of the deep likely to make bathing a hazard, and for this reason, being the only safe waters for miles around.

One last task was to comply with a long standing custom; the painting of the ship's name in large white letters on the surrounding cliffs, a party being sent ashore, armed with paint and brushes, in order to add *Daring* to the many names of ships which, had gone before.

It had been my contention, that as a quartermaster, with my hours of duty being mainly spent under the eyes of the officers, provided such duties were always performed in an efficient manner, the job could be nothing but an asset to me; but what a disillusionment when, being put in the captain's report for being absent from place of duty; I was awarded fourteen days No. 11 punishment and relieved from my job.

I maintained then, as did many others, that in at least ninety-nine cases in a hundred, with the circumstances being identical, no such charge would have been made; but I give the full facts here so that readers may form their own opinion.

It all happened over a jug of cocoa; and if it had not been me on watch at that particular time, then it would have been one of the three other men carrying out the duties of quartermaster, whichever of them happened to have the first watch.

To my knowledge, it had always been the practice for a first watch quartermaster, before calling his middle watch relief, to make a jug of ship's cocoa so that a nice hot cup would be available to that relief when he came to take over; but aboard *Daring* it had progressed still further, for the wardroom officers, before turning in, would also partake, taking their turn at providing the ingredients.

This then, was my absence from place of duty, making cocoa for the officers and my relief in the officers' galley, this galley having direct access to the upper deck and the starboard gangway.

So the captain found me: a call of "Quartermaster" would have had me at his side in seconds; if the Guard Boat had come alongside, I would have heard it, and yet I was absent from place of duty.

The captain himself put me in his report, or at least, he told the first lieutenant to, ironically having at that moment arrived for his cocoa.

Why the captain couldn't sleep, and so happened to be wandering around at that hour is anyone's guess, but if he had been a quarter of an hour later he wouldn't have found me, for I would have been on the mess deck calling my relief.

Here I will pose a question. How can a man; in, silent hours more often than not the only one awake; whose rounds every hour take him to all parts of the ship, having to go below decks in order to call reliefs and early risers, how can such a man, when only two yards from the upper deck, be absent from place of duty? I was but what hurt me most was the fact that the first lieutenant, all too willing to drink my cocoa, said not one word in my defence. Perhaps he feared adverse comments in his commanding officer's confidential report on him.

Earlier, I mentioned the Guard Boat; so perhaps a further explanation of this is called for.

With a group of ships in company, one was always detailed as Guard Ship. An Officer of the Guard would be detailed, and a boat put at his disposal to enable him to make the rounds of the ships, hence the term Guard Boat.

In silent hours especially, the Officer of the Guard would be out on the catch; but an alert quartermaster, seeing a boat heading his way, would, as with all boats approaching, make the hail "Boat Ahoy!" in this instance receiving the reply "Guard Boat!"

If no such hail was forthcoming, the boat would come alongside, and if still unchallenged, the Officer of the Guard came aboard and removed some small object to take away with him; and this meant, that next morning, after he had made his report, the ship concerned received a signal, and the luckless quartermaster had a lot of explaining to do.

The foregoing will give some idea of what I meant when writing of being able to hear such a Guard Boat if it came alongside; but I was not to remain a quartermaster much longer, it being thought that as a watchkeeper I would not be able to carry out the extra work that fourteen days No.11 entailed; and so I was relieved and mess changed to the seamen's mess deck.

Shortly after this the Admiralty decreed that commanding officers could, at their own discretion and within reason, rate as Acting Leading Seaman unpaid, any able seaman who was passed for the higher rating and nearing advancement.

This unpaid promotion became known as *Getting the Hook Repayment*, and the captain made use of his new powers on two occasions, both of the men being junior to me in the time passed for higher rating. I was not unduly worried about this, for I was only just getting over the contretemps concerning the cocoa, and could hardly be called a blue-eyed boy, and in any case, I was not losing financially over it; or so I thought.

There was some cause for alarm however, when both these men had their advancement sent out from the U.K. after only four years passed in the rating.

We of *Daring* had known that the waiting time for advancement had lessened considerably over the years, but never thought that it had almost halved since I had passed the examination in 1928. It did not need a mathematician to work out that I had been passed over, so I immediately put in a request to challenge the advancement roster, only to be told by the captain that this would not be necessary, as the reason for my not being advanced in rating was that he had not recommended me. This meant that my name was stationary on the roster, whilst those of other men, with less seniority but so recommended, were passing me to reach the top, and promotion, as my two shipmates had done.

At this time I had been passed in the higher rating for over five years, and if I had received the half yearly recommendations, my advancement would have come through some nine to twelve months earlier, long before the cocoa episode, so it was not that which had been my undoing: I could only conclude therefore, that for some reason unknown to me my face did not fit, at least, not so far as the captain was concerned.

I could hardly believe that I was still being punished for the *Fair* character which I had received when I was eighteen years of age, although this would have come to the captains notice when he granted me my second good conduct badge some twelve months earlier. The question was what could I do about it?

A request to state a grievance could get to the Commander in Chief and beyond if put through the proper channel, but I knew of no one who had, ever done this, and all reports gave one the impression. Then anyone doing so would be a marked man: a mistaken impression I have no doubt, but learning that the captain was shortly to be relieved of his command, I decided to make the best of it, and hope for better things in the future.

Our new commanding officer was to be Lord Louis Mountbatten, then holding the rank of commander, *Daring* being his first command.

A great many sailors held the opinion that Louis, as he was popularly called, was a bit of a show off, but these are only those that had never served with him.

His many shipmates became endeared to him because of his drive and understanding, together with the fact that he would never expect anyone to do that which he was not capable of doing himself.

On the first Sunday morning under our new commanding officer, The hands were *Mustered by Open List*: this meant that the men – and no one was, excused – lined up as for pay parade, but when their names were called, instead of replying with their ship's book number, each man in turn stated his official number, rating, non substantive rating, and the number of good conduct badges held.

During the preceding days, Louis must have made a detailed study of the ship's company's service certificates; for from time to time, as the need arose, he was able to recapitulate on a man's past history.

When my turn came, the coxswain called "L.A. Harris," I stepped forward. "J108868 – Able Seaman – Seaman Gunner – Two Good Conduct Badges."

"'You have been passed for Leading Seaman for some time?"

"Yes Sir." I replied.

"Your last captain wouldn't recommend you?" "No Sir."

"Well – the first lieutenant thinks that you should be, so we will put that right; Carry on."

"Thank you, Sir." And off I marched, more than pleased with the turn of events under my new skipper.

Readers of – *Mountbatten – His Life and Times,* and viewers who saw the programme on television, may recall, that apart from giving a mention of *Daring* as Lord Louis' first command, little is said of the happenings during the last few months of that commission, the biographer going on to mention the new commission and the changing over to *Wishart*.

He then writes about *Wishart's* prowess in the regatta, but it was a pity that no space could be found to give a word or two about the difference that one man made to the crew of the Officers' Whaler for the second regatta in which *Daring* took part.

You will remember that we won the previous year's flotilla regatta without winning a single race, a victory not to be repeated on this second occasion; for although winning two races, our overall points total placed us second to *Diamond,* a reversal of positions, she having been runner up the year previously.

Of the two wins, that of the Seamen's 'B' Whaler, which I had the honour of stroking to victory, was nothing out of the ordinary, as having been second the year before, only one place had been gained.

This is of course, leading up to the other win; that of the Officers' Whaler, which a year earlier our previous captain had coxed into sixth place.

They now had to make changes. The bow oar became coxswain, the remainder of the crew each moving forward one place, and Louis taking over as stroke oar, he urged them on to a resounding victory; not only in our own flotilla regatta, but in the fleet races which followed.

Also at this time, *Daring* could boast two members of the Royal Navy polo team – Lord Louis, and Lieutenant Commander 'Dickie' Onslow, our first Lieutenant.

Members of the ship's company were invited to be spectators at the annual Navy v Army match; an invitation which was probably regretted by the organisers, the decorum usually associated with such an event being sadly marred by jolly jack, in no uncertain manner, inciting the Royal Navy team to "Bowl those bloody Squaddies over," and. to "Get stuck into them."

I now had a job as sternsheetman of the motorboat, and in this capacity, I came into closer contact with Lord Louis and his many guests than did the remainder of the ship's company.

Lady Louis and her two small daughters were quite often passengers in my stern sheets; Noel Coward was also a frequent visitor, on one occasion sailing with us on a four-day exercise off Malta. But although the exercise was to last four days, Noel Coward's stay aboard didn't.

He may have been a good sailor aboard a larger ship, but bad weather during the exercise proved to be too much for him destroyer-wise, *Daring* slipping into St. Paul's Bay to put him ashore, although passage in a small motor boat was not exactly a pleasure trip for him either.

I have since wondered, had the weather been a little more kind, whether we of *Daring* might not have been characters in a new play.

The summer cruise saw us carrying a supernumerary in the shape of Lord Louis' private chauffeur, and also an extra boat; this being a speed boat which he was to operate whenever his employer wished to go water skiing, this being another accomplishment of his at a time, when speedboat wise, being towed on a surfboard was about as much as high society holidaying on the Riviera could manage.

It was during this cruise that I almost blotted my copybook through what was originally intended to be a leg pull.

On passage with the rest of the flotilla in company; Captain 'D' had, after evening quarters, carried out general drill for two days in succession, taking up about three quarters of an hour of the first dog watch with some form of exercise; much to the annoyance of the ship's company.

Evening quarters over on the third day, and no signal concerning general drill having been made by Captain 'D', I, having the first dog watch as bosun's mate had been told to pipe – "Hands to tea and shift into night clothing."

Following the men on to the mess deck, and thinking to have a little joke, I instead piped "Hands fall in for General Drill," meaning to stop them before they had gone too far by following up with "Belay the last pipe. Hands to tea and shift into night clothing."

What I did not know was that the Chief Bosun's Mate had gone on to the mess deck to speak to one of the ratings, and as he heard my general drill pipe, he followed up with "Come on then, at the rush, fall in for general drill," and I was left high and dry.

The First Lieutenant and the Navigating Officer had not yet left the upper deck, and seeing the men making their way aft with all speed, they must have thought that they were about to become involved in a mutiny; until my pipe was explained to them.

I quite expected to be put on a charge, but No. 1 accepted it in the spirit in which it had been meant, although the joke was on me eventually.

"Joke," the First Lieutenant said; "So you want to joke? Well you've had yours, now I'll have mine," and with a grin he continued, "Go all round the ship and pipe – Do you hear there; Able Seaman Harris is a bloody fool!"

That then, was what I had to do; he followed me in order to see that his instructions were properly carried out.

Daring did not complete the second part of the summer cruise, sailing for the U.K., and as far as I was concerned, twenty-five days foreign service leave. – During the cruise my banns had been called, for I was to be married once I arrived back in England.

The ship arrived at Chatham on August 25th, relatives and friends of the crew being allowed into the dockyard to welcome them; a more or less routine happening now, but not so in those days, *Daring* being one of the first ships to have this privilege extended to the ship's company.

The ship did not pay off completely, there being so many volunteers to recommission; this itself I suppose, being ample justification for the remarks made earlier about Lord Louis and the men who served under him.

Foreign service leave was given in two watches and being in the first group I proceeded on leave on September 4th, my wedding taking place four days later.

After three weeks as a married man, I returned to *Daring* and learned that whilst I had been on leave my *hook* had come through, but even advancement had to be different where I was concerned.

It was the usual practice for a man whose promotion had come through to appear as a Captain's Requestman, requesting to be advanced to the new rating. The request being granted, he would then be told by the Captain, the date from which the advancement was to take effect; but not so in my case.

After dinner, at "Hands fall in," I fell in with the rank and file, only to be told by the first Lieutenant to "Come out front." "You are now an Acting Leading Seaman" he said, "See the coxswain sometime and he will give you the date and all the griff."

The postman going into barracks solved my immediate problem, that of getting a set of badges denoting my new rating; which, the coxswain informed me, was dated from September 1st; one week before my wedding, and so, in effect, a wedding present from the Admiralty.

My pay was now six shillings and sixpence per day: an allotment to my wife of thirty-two shillings each week, plus ten shillings monthly to a naval tailor, would leave me going round the pay table each fortnight for approximately twelve shillings.

Those of us due to leave joined barracks on 25th October, a little sad at leaving perhaps, for *Daring* had been a happy ship, reason still unknown, she had cost me some months seniority as a leading seaman.

I thought that I had always pulled my weight; being a member of a racing boat's crew, the cross country and athletic teams, besides which I had played rugger for the flotilla: all things which would supposedly have stood one in good stead; but not so far as I was concerned, this being a mystery which was never solved.

Chapter 19

Pembroke and *Skipjack*

HMS *Pembroke* 25th October – 29th October 1934

For after only four days had elapsed I was back in the dockyard, this time to join HMS *Skipjack,* a modern minesweeper, Chatham manned but based at Portland, returning to her home port only for the giving of seasonal leave, and – as in this instance – also in October in order to give seven days minesweeping leave.

HMS *Skipjack* 30th October 1934 – 13th January 1937

I was on my own when joining the ship, being a relief for a leading seaman time-expired who had already left for Pembroke and Civvy Street.

Taking stock of my new ship and shipmates, I realised that I would be serving with two *old ships,* both leading seamen.

One, Jack Hobbs, had served with me aboard Curlew when we were both able seamen, and I learned from him that the marital bliss in Malta of my erstwhile friend Dick Dovey had not lasted very long; his spouse having to return home after a few months, the climate not agreeing with her. They had however, been together long enough for her to return to England as an expectant mum, but I never met up with Dick again, so was never to know whether the happy event produced a boy or a girl.

The other old ship – Jack Hodge – had only served with me in barracks, a one-time messmate in the field gun mess. There was one other leading seaman in the complement, a Leading Seaman R.N.V.R., originally an Edinburgh tram conductor, but having now volunteered for one years' active service.

Before sailing for Portland I was able to spend one weekend with my wife, who, like me, was not very happy at the coming separation, especially as we had been hoping that some period of time in barracks would enable me to take advantage of the three week end leaves out of four which was a feature of life at Pembroke.

Normally, drafting allowed for such a spell after a man had returned from a foreign commission; but it wasn't to be so for me.

The minesweeping flotilla did not carry out any fleet operations but proceeded to sea on three days each week in order to carry out minesweeping exercises in West Bay; returning to harbour in time for tea and night leave.

I was coxswain of the ship's motorboat, but as the ship usually tied up alongside the wall each evening, the boat was put to very little use whilst the ship was at Portland.

Two different routines were worked aboard the ships of the flotilla; one, when they were not bound for West Bay and exercises would be normal daily routine, but on exercise days a special minesweeping routine was worked; the men not going to breakfast until the ship had got under way and the necessary preparations been made.

This breakfast usually coincided with the ship's arrival in the Races, a turbulent stretch of water off Portland Bill, this rather tending to make the meal somewhat of a hazard.

Then it was "Hands to Sweeping Stations," all available men busying themselves with such things as Sweep Wires, Orepesas, Kites, Otter Boards and Dan Buoys.

Suffice it to say that this was the gear necessary for bringing mines to the surface – this being what mine sweeping was all about – the mooring wire being severed by means of the serrations on the sweep wire or the cutters which were attached to the Orepesa; the mine then floating to the surface to be disposed of by gunfire.

In theory a floating mine is not dangerous because the activating mechanism, held open by the strain on the mooring wire, closes when the strain has been taken off with the severing of this wire.

It would not do to take chances on this; however, for long immersion, and the marine incrustations resulting there from, might very well cause the mechanism to seize up and remain open, thus making it just as lethal as one moored below the surface.

All the time that the sweeps were out they had to be tended, the men not having a proper dinner hour, but taking their mid-day meal a few at a time. We were compensated for this by not having to work any early morning routine, being allowed to lie in until well after the usual "Guard and Steerage.

A few weeks of exercises and it was back to Chatham and Christmas leave, when I saw my wife of three and a half months more than pleased to see me but feeling so lonely and deserted. We had taken an unfurnished flat in Enfield for which the rent was thirteen shillings per week. This had been furnished without the aid of hire purchase, the furniture having been paid for with money saved during my foreign service commitments.

As things turned out, this had really been a wrong decision, for after my Christmas leave the furniture spent more time in the store than it did in a home.

Several of my shipmates had their wives staying in digs at Portland, and having put the proposition to my wife, she being in agreement, we decided to emulate them.

I was able to obtain a bed sitting room with the use of a kitchen, the rent for which was twelve shillings and sixpence per week. It was impossible to pay both this and the rent of our flat, so the furniture had to be put into store and the flat given up, a further outlay of four shillings each week for the storage, and that much less for the family exchequer; but it did mean that we were together for most evenings and weekends.

Our arrangements still had to meet with a snag, for on the day that my wife was to arrive, *Skipjack* was ordered to Portsmouth, there to be attached to the Torpedo School for four days exercises. My wife was met at Weymouth station by my new landlady, keeping her company until the four days had elapsed and our plans at last materialised.

To help my finances a little I decided to stop my tot and draw the three pence per day instead: a sad wrench, but the blow softened a little by the fact the navigating officer – a sub lieutenant – was presenting me with a bottle of beer a day in appreciation of my doing his chart corrections; a job which he himself should have done, but which I apparently, could do better. Hurrah for Advanced Class!

This happy state of affairs lasted until we had been married for a year. I was now a fully fledged leading seaman, having been confirmed in the rating, and to lift us a little further above the breadline, my wife had taken a job as a daily help, for which she was given her mid-day meal and paid ten shillings per week, thus enabling us to afford an occasional visit to the cinema at Weymouth.

Then Mussolini threw a spanner in the works, for not knowing what the outcome of the Italian invasion of Abyssinia might be, units of the fleet had been ordered to Alexandria, the Portland Minesweeping Flotilla also, there being no minesweepers active with the Mediterranean fleet

Having learned just a few weeks earlier that I could expect to become a father in March I was by no means pleased at the move, but it was the navy's job to be mobile, and I, like many others, thought that we would be home again long before my happy event took place.

But what a disillusionment. Eight months away, and practically the whole of the time spent anchored in sight of the Ras-el Tin lighthouse, which had been taken over as a signal station.

There were but two bits of excitement during this period: one when an Italian liner caught fire in the harbour and was gutted, the other when a destroyer moving about the harbour was in collision with a Sunderland flying boat which was building up speed for a take off. Fortunately there was no loss of life, although, as can be imagined, the flying boat was a write off.

The formation of a Fleet Club did much to relieve the monotony, and one must be grateful to the members of the European community who gave up their time to run it.

The club did not go down too well with the local bar owners however, for the majority of the libertymen preferred its atmosphere to that of the local establishments, a quiet drink and a game of tombola being available without having to be pestered by purveyors of dirty postcards and pornographic books; or touts offering a guided tour of Sister Street and the brothels.

Chief and petty officers were offered a chance to visit Cairo and the Pyramids, at their own expense of course, and had the invitation been extended to junior ratings, it would have been beyond my pocket.

Fishing over the ship's side became an additional pastime, there being one type of fish, similar to a mackerel in appearance, which seemed intent on committing suicide.

All that one required was a length of cane, a short line fitted with a hook and a supply of cigarette papers: one of these papers was attached to the nook which was then trailed along the surface of the water. Soon there was a bite, a snatch, and one more fish had given up without a struggle, this doing much to augment the supper ration.

Invitations to attend their cinema performances were extended to us by the larger ships in company, and what with this, an occasional visit to the Fleet Club, and the inevitable soccer matches, time moved on without boredom becoming too apparent.

As soon as my wife realised that there was to be no early return, she had gone to stay with her mother, and arrangements had been put in hand for her to remain there until the birth of our baby, giving up the accommodation in Portland.

In the February I was given a scare when I received a cablegram via Ras-el-Tin lighthouse. This was from my sister and it read – *Elsie seriously ill. Temperature 103°. Come at if humanly possible. Florrie.*

An urgent request to be sent home on compassionate grounds did not meet with much success, as the following dialogue will show.

First the coxswain. "Leading Seaman Harris, sir. Request to return to U.K. on compassionate grounds – Documentary proof."

"What proof," asked the Captain.

"Cablegram Sir." I replied, handing it to him.

"This is not from a doctor – Who is Florrie'?

"My sister Sir."

"Well," said the Captain, "Cable your sister and tell her that we must hear from the doctor before any action can be taken – Can you afford to fly?"

"No Sir."

"If we hear from the doctor, the Canteen Fund might lend you the fare – Stand Over."

A cable to my sister brought the following reply. *Elsie greatly improved. No further cause for alarm. Florrie.*

The reason for the first cable as I later found out, was that inflammation of the bladder, together with the nearness of our baby's arrival had given rise to complications, and there had been a crisis. It was the doctor who had told my sister to send for me, but by the time the cables had been sent and received, the crisis had passed.

So, things sorted themselves out. I did not get into debt with the canteen fund, neither did I miss the examination board for higher rating, which would have been the case if my request had been granted and, happy ending, I passed professionally for petty officer.

A few weeks later, working in the motorboat with my crew, the duty signalman called to me and said – "Cablegram for you at Ras-el-Tin." Without more ado I cast off and got the boat underway to collect it.

The First Lieutenant, choosing that moment to come up onto the upper deck saw the boat on its way inshore, and turning to the quartermaster asked, "Where is the motor boat going?"

"I don't know," he replied, "I never called it away."

"Tell the coxswain to report to me as soon as he gets back," he ordered. This I did, only to be asked why I had taken the boat away without permission.

A look at my cablegram was the only answer necessary. It read, *Daughter born to Elsie 7 – 30 a.m. Weight 7 1bs. Both doing well. Florrie.*

"Congratulations," he said. The date? Friday 13th March.

Another two months were to elapse before I saw the new arrival for the first time. In the interim, leaving mother," my wife had taken our bits and pieces out of store and installed herself once again in unfurnished rooms; actually the top half of a house which was more or less self-contained. The rent was twelve shillings and six pence per week and the accommodation was within easy reach of her family home.

The increase in our family also brought an increase in our income, the Admiralty paying an allowance of five shillings per week for young Patricia.

Skipjack's return to the U.K. saw us first at Chatham for leave, and then back to Portland to continue where we had left off when Mussolini had interrupted the proceedings.

The one difference was that my wife would not this time be with me, mother and daughter staying put; although they did, on several occasions during the following six months, spend a couple of weeks at Portland; once, all three of us living, eating and sleeping in a fisherman's cottage at Chiswell, with a paraffin stove for cooking and candles for illumination; the washing being put out to dry on Chiswell Beach.

A return to Chatham for Christmas leave saw me leaving *Skipjack,* the advancement roster having improved to such an extent, that after only nine months passed in the rating, I was promoted to Acting Petty Officer, this putting me in excess of complement.

So, once again I left a ship to be domiciled in Chatham Barracks; but this time with a few extra privileges such as not having to double across the parade ground, being allowed to proceed ashore until 21:00, entitled to an extra half hour's leave in the morning, and having my kit-bag and hammock humped for me.

Chapter 20

Pembroke and *Emerald*

HMS *Pembroke* 14th January – 19th April 1937
I was not destined to become a member of the barrack working party on this occasion; for having completed the joining routine, I was posted to the barrack guard.

Never really being disposed to becoming a member of the *gate and gaiters* fraternity – this probably emanating from my earlier days when being on the receiving end of a gunnery instructor's stoniky – I was not greatly enamoured of the job; but it had it's advantages, for being a watchkeeping job meant that I was able to get home other than at weekends.

The time had now come for me to make a big decision, for my twelve-year engagement was nearing its end. Now I had to decide whether to become *time expired* and a civilian or re-engage for a further ten years in order to complete time for pension.

What qualifications had I to hold down a good job in Civvy Street, always supposing that such a job was available?

I was a fairly able motor boat coxswain, also capable of handling a boat under sail, and quite expert at tying bends and hitches with both eyes shut and my hands behind my back; but civilian qualifications? None whatever.

Quite truthfully though, Civvy Street was what I really wanted, for I had decided some time earlier that, so far as I was concerned, the navy was no place for a married man. One job that did appeal to me was that of a conductor on the London buses. At this time, being a member of a London bus crew was quite a job. They had their own flying club – that in itself being somewhat of a status symbol – and a conductor's wage of three pounds ten shillings a week was way above average at a time when skilled men on the dole would have thought themselves indeed lucky to be offered something within the region of two pounds ten.

So, full of hope I wrote, stating that I would soon be leaving the navy after twelve years service, I had attained the status of petty officer, and would they please consider me for employment as a London bus conductor. The reply which I received was stereotyped. It stated that there were no vacancies; neither would there be any in the foreseeable future.

Disillusioned that, although experienced in most matters nautical; able to steer all types of ships under any conditions, but was not to be allowed to conduct a bus, and viewing the three million or so unemployed with some misgiving; not wishing to become one of them I signed on the dotted line and proceeded on fourteen days re-engaging leave.

That I had made the right decision did, I think, become apparent some two years later; for had I not re-engaged, I would almost certainly have signed on the reserve and so been called up with all the other reservists when war with Germany became imminent.

It almost seemed as though the drafting office had been waiting for me to take the steps I had, for returning from my re-engaging leave, I was immediately sent on ten days foreign service draft leave. This was not altogether unexpected, as I had been on home service for two and a half years; mostly afloat though, and eight months of it *at home in Alexandria,* no allowance having been made for that extra bit of service in the Mediterranean.

Knowing that a foreign draft could not be far off, my wife and I had earlier discussed the matter; and although I had had my fill of

Malta and the Mediterranean, we both thought that a further period might be ideal from a matrimonial point of view, passage to Malta for a dependant costing only nine pounds, with accommodation being available on the island at quite reasonable rent.

But it was not to be. Whether the drafting office earthed my volunteer chit of earlier days; on which I volunteered for service in the West Indies I don't know; was so, then they had certainly misread it, for I was to commission HMS *Emerald*, for service in the East Indies.

HMS *Emerald* 20th April 1937 – 15th August 1938

The ship lay in Chatham dockyard, so commissioning her from the barracks presented little difficulty.

An advance party had already joined, and the remainder of the new ship's company loaded their baggage onto lorries before they themselves were marched out to the ship.

To say that I had no qualms would be an understatement, for although we were all new boys together, I was joining my first ship as a petty officer, and only with an acting rank at that, this being most noticeable, due to the fact that an acting petty officer continued to wear his blue jacket, or square rig, until he had been confirmed in the rating.

This gave rise to a few more butterflies than had been the case when joining *Skipjack* as an acting leading seaman, for in that instance, as far as the junior ratings were concerned, I might have been a leading seaman of some years seniority, there being nothing in my outward appearance to denote other wise.

I was, I think, fortunate in being given the job of chief quartermaster; what one might almost term a quiet number, being in charge of the watchkeeping quartermasters and bosun's mates, with my working day duties being concerned with things navigational. The duties of quartermaster were carried out by four leading seamen, one of whom, senior to me in years, but not in rating, had to be put in his place quite early in the commission, this being the only time I had to show rank – even if it was only acting – , but it did get things into the right perspective, and there was never any more trouble in my department.

The ship now in commission; preparations were put in hand to make her ready for the trip to far eastern waters, but the dockyard workmen seemed reluctant to let us depart; and it was not until the middle of June that we made our way down the Medway to Sheerness, there to take on ammunition and swing ship to adjust compasses.

These tasks completed, and all our goodbyes behind us, we at last set sail on what, at the time, were thought to be a two-and-a-half-year commission in waters east of Suez.

The passage was quite a leisurely one; calls being made at both Gibraltar and Malta before proceeding to Port Said at the northern end of the Suez Canal.

Here a pilot was embarked for the journey through the canal and Bitter lakes to Port Suez, and I, by virtue of being chief quartermaster, spent very little time away from the wheelhouse until this journey was completed and the pilot dropped.

The ship commenced the working of tropical routine as soon the Red Sea was entered. This meant that the hands were called at 0515 instead of 0545, and dinner, instead of being at 1200 was at 1300; the remainder of the afternoon being free so as to avoid having to work during the hottest part of the day.

More often than not it would be an afternoon's head down on deck; but although awnings were spread, one would always wake up in a pool of sweat, yet in spite of this heat, when the opportunity offered for a game of football at Aden, there was no lack of volunteers.

It was at Aden that the ship's complement was completed by the taking aboard of twenty-four Somali seamen.

They were paid one rupee (one shilling and sixpence) per day, and it was to be their job to work about the boat deck and ship's side and on any other job where it was considered that the heat was likely to prove too oppressive for the European members of the ship's company.

The living quarters for these Somalis was a hut which had been built on the boat deck, and the men themselves appeared to be very devout, for they were always to be seen, morning and evening, washing themselves and praying to Allah.

Eventually the ship arrived at Colombo; actually, it was in early August, so the journey had taken almost two months.

Although we were later to spend quite a lot of time at Colombo, on this our first visit we did not stay long, the ship being expected at Trincomalee on the north east coast of the island.

This was to be our main base whilst on station, and it boasted very little else but a large natural harbour at the time, although there were several projects in the course of construction.

During the ensuing weeks there was only one little bit of excitement, this being when a Royal Fleet Auxiliary vessel ran aground in a spot where, according to the charts, it shouldn't have.

She was re-floated without much difficulty, and it then fell to my lot to go out to the area with our navigating officer in order to take new soundings, which I have no doubt found their way to the hydrographic department, eventually to appear in the weekly Notices to Mariners.

Apart from this there was very little but routine activity: the men working ship during the morning and forenoon, landing for bathing and other sporting activities in the afternoon, and, if finances permitted, going ashore again in the evening to drink a few bottles of lukewarm beer in the naval canteen.

It was during this period of inactivity, that the idea of forming a ship's concert party was born. I suppose that being an active participant I should not say this, but in my opinion, it became one of the best concert parties that any ship had produced.

Our two female impersonators had to be seen to be believed: one impersonated the more seductive type of female and had all the wiggles and come-hithers off to perfection. With a stage name of *Daphne,* it was hard to believe that his real name was in fact, Leading Cook Tough.

Mary acted the more blasé ember of the opposite sex, and this, he too did with perfection. Although billed as *Mary,* he was actually a Stoker Grogan.

An ordinary seaman and a royal marine did a song and dance act, the ordinary seaman taking the part of the girl, but it is unfortunate that their names now escape me.

A Leading Seaman Hart was billed as second Bing, one of his songs I remember, being *Pennies from Heaven,* in which the chorus – yes, we had chorus girls – suitably manoeuvring with colourful umbrellas, danced to his vocal accompaniment.

Another double act a la the *Western Brothers* as performed by Able Seaman Sims and Stoker Cheadle; a Stoker Burgess sang the songs of the late Harry Champion and one or two of his own; the P.T.I. did a club swinging act using cutlasses instead of clubs, and everyone doubled up for various sketches in which I also took part; usually as a dame, but I was also the hero in a miming melodrama entitled *Joe Buckskin's Girl,* in which the cast mimed to a story related by another member who was standing in the wings; the miming having to be overdone in order to make it appear more humorous.

The whole show was stage managed by Able Seaman Hopkins, assisted by Leading Seaman David; they also were quite adept at scene painting.

Apart from the Grand Opening at Trincomalee, shows were staged at Madras, Port Blair – the capital of the Andaman and Nicobar Islands – up country at Diyatalawa in Ceylon, and vocal turns went on the air from Colombo Radio.

Normal working of the ship, together with rehearsals and our Grand Opening, had now brought us well into October and the winter cruise.

The course was by way of Madras and the Bay of Bengal to Calcutta; this last necessitating a seven-mile journey up the Hooghly River, a journey on which I was once again very much in demand on the wheel.

We arrived at Calcutta in time for the Christmas Celebration, such celebrations being carried out in a grand manner; but not so far as we of the lower deck were concerned.

Emerald had taken over the flag of Vice Admiral Sir A.M. Ramsay, the flagship, HMS *Norfolk* having returned to the U.K. on the completion of her commission; and the admiral, together with many of the ship's officers, had a full list of engagements, but we, as usual, were left to our own devices. Members of the petty officers' messes were fortunate in being offered the hospitality of the garrison sergeants' messes, many of the members having been in Calcutta for a number of years and glad to see new faces.

It was in the company of two of these sergeants, that I and a Petty Officer Joe Moat partook of a marvellous curry in a low dive which I doubt if I would have been able to find by myself; or if I had found it, would have probably thought twice about entering. No implements were provided with which to eat the meal; one's fingers had to be used, warm water and a towel afterwards being provided. Our sergeant friends told us that it was their opinion that no better curry could be obtained anywhere in Calcutta, and I am inclined to agree, for it was far better than any I have eaten before or since.

The festivities ended with a New Year's Day parade on the Maidan and here the Viceroy took the salute at a march past of many units of the Indian Army and members of the British armed forces in India at that time.

Emerald provided a naval contingent for the event, but other members of the ship's company, not needed for this, were allowed ashore as spectators; I being one of them; and I must say that it was one of the most colourful parades it has ever been my good fortune to witness.

The Viceroy arrived for the review at 1000, but preparations had been set in motion long before; *Emerald's* contingent landing at 0700.

Festivities over, and our presence being required elsewhere, the ship returned to Colombo in time for us to act as hosts to the German cruiser *Emden,* recently arrived on a courtesy visit.

Beating them at football and then laying on a beano for both team and supporters, the only way in which they were able to return our hospitality was by inviting us aboard *Emden* to partake of their beer.

This was indeed a novelty to us; beer on tap aboard a man of war; but it was all they were able to offer, being allowed no money to spend in foreign countries, their pay being in the form of tokens redeemable only aboard their ship and back in Germany.

At Colombo we had an open invitation to make use of the garrison sergeants' messes, and, also that of the European members of the Ceylon Police.

I suppose that we were a little envious of the fact that they had their wives with them, but it was also nice to know that we were accepted as equals by some members of the European community.

At certain times for the payment of an entry fee, the ships company were allowed the use of a swimming pool in the basement of the Galle Face Hotel. There was a well stocked bar alongside the pool, and this gave Joe Moat and Nobby Clarke – a Petty Officer Telegraphist – an idea for a new sporting event; that of a beer relay.

The idea was for the teams to line up at one end of the bath, and at the start, one member of each team would swim to the other end, drink a pint of beer and then swim back to let the next man go: it sounds easy enough, but believe me, it was most exhausting and the race was never repeated, at least, not by members of *Emerald's* ships company.

By this time HMS *Norfolk* had returned from the U.K., and we sailed in company with her for Singapore, calling at Penang en route.

Singapore was actually off station so far as the East Indies squadron was concerned, but we were to take part in the official opening ceremony of the King George VI dock, reputed to be the largest dry dock in the world, which alas, was to be destroyed only a few years later, when Japanese occupation became imminent.

Also in attendance were two cruisers of the China Station and a squadron of American cruisers, *Emerald* being paired off with the U.S.S. *Milwaukee,* for a reciprocal entertainment programme.

Our entertainment for the Americans consisted of a slap-up supper and excerpts from our concert party repertoire, whilst they in turn, also gave us supper, and a cinema show with far more up to date films than were available to us.

One thing learnt from our visit to *Milwaukee* was that our victualling, at least in this instance, was far superior to that of our American counterparts. This may have been because *Emerald* was on canteen messing and the individual messes could put on what they liked within reason and availability, whilst the Americans were on some kind of general messing, they all being on cold meat and sauerkraut.

I must tell of one incident aboard *Milwaukee,* which I doubt would ever have been allowed to happen aboard one of our own ships.

It concerned the American petty officer I was in company with and a junior rating who had not apparently completed a job to his satisfaction; the rating being told that as punishment he was on no account to collect his ice cream ration that evening. The guests however, were allowed to partake of this ration, but this had to be one thing that was not reciprocal, no facilities for ice cream making on a large scale being available aboard H.M. ships.

The ceremonies over, our American friends departed, but the R.N. units remained to carry out exercises against the Singapore defences.

Several undetected landings were made, one by way of the Johore Strait, but apparently no great lesson was learned by this; for the Japanese did the same thing four years later.

That they would have done so in any case I have no doubt, but better defences in that area might have caused a delay that could only have been in our favour.

As it was, the defences were mostly against landings from seawards, landings which, as far as I am aware, never materialised.

On our return to Colombo, arrangements were made for the ship's company to spend two weeks at Diyatalawa, up country and some six thousand feet above sea level.

The journey was by train and necessitated all night travel, this developing into an all night drinking party, the men having been allowed to order drinks for the journey, such drinks being more than adequate, in consequence of which there were a great many hangovers when the train reached its destination.

Very little work was done during our stay, the camp being for relaxation. There was a two day hunting party organised for the petty officers, which unfortunately ended in a native guide losing his licence, one of our party having shot an out of season deer: rather a harsh punishment we thought; but there was no appeal.

A party of men volunteered to *weed the fox*; this fox cut into the mountain side being a landmark for miles around. It had been put there many years before, when the crew of HMS *Fox*, relaxing as we were doing, became cut off for some months because of a landslide.

Many of us played golf on a nearby golf course. Perhaps I should have tried to play golf: it certainly made me realise how far a golfer has to walk during his round, especially when, as in my case, the flight of the ball always seemed most erratic.

The return to our ship brought us near to another cruise; a cruise which was to last for nearly three months and end at our home port Chatham.

The reason for this was that the admiralty had decided to relieve us and our sister ship *Enterprise* with two modern cruisers, the *Liverpool* and *Manchester*: *Enterprise* was already in the U.K., having completed her commission, and so in May we set off.

Our cruise was to take in the Seychelles first, and then several East African ports before once again entering the Red Sea, this time for Port Suez and home.

It was whilst on passage to the Seychelles that our Crossing the Line Ceremony took place, but as I have given full details of this in an earlier chapter, I will make no further mention of it here, but pass on to our arrival at the Seychelles.

These Seychelles are in actual fact, a group of islands in the Indian Ocean, about ninety in number, the largest being called Mahé, the capital, Victoria.

The highlight of our visit was a cricket match with the local club, whose players consisted of both Europeans and Creoles, the latter being of mixed blood, and extremely good cricketers.

Our course continued via Lindi, Zanzibar and Mombasa, then to Berbers, the then capital of British Somaliland, before calling at Aden to refuel and disembark our Somalis.

At Mombassa the local Europeans laid on a swimming gala and high tea for the ship's company, the only hospitality which had been, shown to the men of the lower deck by any of the many European communities we had come into contact with in the various ports adjacent to East Indian waters, with the exception of the previously mentioned garrisons and Ceylon police of course.

From Aden into the Red Sea, but a visit to Hodeida on the Arabian coast was more in the capacity of a peace keeping force, there having been some border incidents.

Whatever these might have been, the outcome was that *Emerald* was required to give a demonstration of firepower; after which, our one and only seaplane was catapulted off on a demonstration flight. What deterrent this might have been must be anybody's guess, the plane in question – a Sea Fox – being capable of a top speed of only 85 knots.

Next on the itinerary was the island of Kamaran, rather isolated, but of great importance; it being a quarantine station for would-be pilgrims to Mecca.

No leave was given, as our stay was only to be of short duration; but the ship was visited by several local bigwigs before we moved on to Massawa, which at this time was an Italian naval port giving access to Eritrea.

As Emerald was the first British warship to visit the port since the Abyssinian trouble, there was some speculation as to the reception we could expect, but our welcome was most warm.

The ship's football team played three matches: winning two and drawing the third. The ship's company were invited to visit the Italian ships and shore establishments, a party of officers and petty officers being taken to Asmara on a three-day visit.

The capital of Eritrea, Asmara was undergoing a great deal of modernisation, many Italian workmen having been drafted from their mother country in order to carry out the work.

Whether it was something of which they were proud I cannot really say; but our Italian petty officer guides made it their business to let us see just how the sexual needs of these workmen were catered for.

It must, I think, have been a state-run brothel: whether it had certain opening hours I can't say, but at the time of our visit it was well patronised.

The whole of the proceedings were as if a time and motion study had been instituted: a man and girl would go upstairs together, and after ten minutes a bell would ring in their room thus telling them that time was up: down the man would come, the girl shortly after, and then the proceedings would be repeated; same girl, different man.

There were, I think, eight girls in all, and our guide informed us that they're expected to do a six months stint, for which they were extremely well paid then returning to Italy.

So much for Massawa and Eritrea. There were no further calls to be made in the Red Sea, and so we continued our way to Port Suez and the canal.

Nearing Port Said for the trip through the Mediterranean to home waters, we were counting the days to our arrival at Chatham, where our friends and relatives would be waiting on the dock side to welcome us.

There was however, to be an unexpected delay: a bomb-throwing incident at Haifa necessitated urgent reinforcements for our troops and so *Emerald* was ordered to alter course and proceed with all speed.

On arrival, two-thirds of the ship's company were landed as an armed party, their presence I feel certain doing much to keep the peace.

We learned HMS *Repulse* had also been diverted but having further to come would not arrive until twenty-four hours after *Emerald*.

A decision that it was not necessary for both ships to remain allowed *Emerald* to continue her interrupted journey and, stopping at Malta and Gibraltar only long enough for refuelling, we secured a buoy at Sheerness on schedule.

After "Finished with Main Engines," it was my job as chief quartermaster, to clear all the charts, sailing directions and other navigational aids from the bridge, and securing at Sheerness being no exception, this I proceeded to do.

It came as quite a surprise to me, when the navigating officer, my immediate boss, who had not yet left the bridge, turned to me and said – "A successful conclusion, I think. Will you join me in a drink?" – this being the first time he had ever invited me to partake.

It was not such a successful conclusion for me however, when a request to be recommended to qualify for torpedo coxswain was Not Granted, the inference being that I was too junior a petty officer to hold such a position.

Two days later, *Emerald's* arrival at Chatham was witnessed by a large crowd, passing into the dockyard for relatives and friends having been organised beforehand, this now being the rule for ships returning from abroad.

We did not pay off immediately, our arrival coinciding with preparations for Navy Week, during which *Emerald* was to be open to visitors.

I had many relatives and friends visiting during that week, and I believe to this day, the thing that sticks out most in their minds about

Emerald is the number of cockroaches we had managed to accumulate in the petty officer's pantry.

When the time for paying off did arrive, it was not without some regrets, for we had been a happy ship, and although our commission had lasted for only one year and four months, many of the company would, I think, have willingly completed the two and a half years originally expected.

Chapter 21

Pembroke, Eskimo, Pembroke and *Vernon*

HMS *Pembroke* 16th August 1938 – 1st January 1939
Although I had left barracks sixteen months earlier as an Acting Petty Officer and in a blue jacket rig, I was now established in the rating, having been so confirmed aboard *Emerald,* at the same time being allowed a grant of ten pounds with 'which to change my rig.

For this money I had to get a cloth suit, two serge suits, two white drill suits, three white shirts, two black ties, six collars and two peaked caps.

This was possible if everything was purchased off the peg from the paymasters stores; something not often done, especially with the No. l cloth suit, so consequently, further outlay had been necessary from my own pocket; but I had joined barracks fully kitted up with my new rig.

It seemed rather ironic, that having been unsuccessful in my efforts to obtain a recommendation to qualify for a torpedo coxswain, my next job was indeed to be that of a coxswain; coxswain of the steamboat which operated from Gillingham Pier.

Although I was born on the books of *Pembroke* for pay purposes, the job was on Lodging and Provision Allowance: which meant that the crew were paid an allowance instead of being provided with accommodation and victualling.

No difficulties arose in these matters; however, for the hut which was at our disposal when not away with the boat, gave us ample room for slinging our hammocks, and the midday meal we had delivered by a nearby cafe at quite reasonable cost. Other items we scrounged, or else they were given to us in return for favours which we were able to do for our various passengers.

Besides me, the crew consisted of a stoker petty officer, a leading stoker and two able seamen. The boat plied between Gillingham Pier, Chatham Dockyard steps and Sheerness; not the routine trips servicing the ships moored in the reaches: these duties were carried out by the Medway Ferry Service, boats manned by naval pensioners and operating under Commander 'M' of the dockyard.

We operated as required by the Officer in Charge, Gillingham Pier; our only regular commitments being that on two afternoons each week, training classes for Leading Seamen would be taken out in order to practice power boat steering.

That the job for me, did not last longer, I have I suppose, only myself to blame; for still being desirous of qualifying as Torpedo Coxswain, a request to the commander of the barracks only brought the reply that a sea going recommendation was necessary, and I have not the least doubt, that my request was the reason, after a few months, that I was drafted to HMS *Eskimo,* a Tribal Class destroyer about to commission in Chatham dockyard for service with the Home Fleet.

HMS *Eskimo* 2nd January – 27th April 1939

It was not usual for boy ratings to be numbered among the complement of a destroyer, but the Tribal class were to carry twenty, and aboard *Eskimo,* I was to be their instructor, with a leading seaman to assist me.

Apart from discipline, my main job was to get them to a state of efficiency as seamen, in order that they would be able to pass their test for able seaman: the leading seaman, being messed with them, was responsible for their mess deck endeavours, learning how to cope with food preparation, mess cleanliness etc.

It had long been apparent to me that life for a boy rating was not nearly as hard as it had been in earlier years. For one thing, they were now allowed to smoke, and were therefore allowed to mix with other ratings in the recreation spaces.

Corporal punishment had been discontinued, so there was no fear of a boy being sentenced to being on the receiving end of the cane.

Also, if a boy was to be taken up on a charge, on occasion, the officer whom he was appearing before, would almost put the complainant in the wrong for bringing the charge, this doing much to bring about a laxity of discipline, junior ratings getting away with what would normally be a chargeable offence.

A competition to find a motto for the ship won me a voucher to be exchanged for goods at the N.A.A.F.I., although, in my opinion, the winning effort – *Cool but Courageous* – was so obvious as "to warrant a certain amount of duplication, but apparently this was not so.

Whether my brain child was adopted, or my endeavours as an instructor came to a successful conclusion I was never to find out, for an early request to the captain for a recommendation to qualify as Torpedo Coxswain was approved, and when the ship returned to Chatham for Easter leave, my relief joined and I was once again on my way to barracks.

HMS *Pembroke* 28th April – 29th September 1939

I did not go immediately to the Torpedo School to qualify, before this happened, I was to spend five months as a New Entries Instructor and also to become involved in a removal.

Neville Chamberlain and his *Peace in our time* had decided my wife and I on the move, and taking a house in Gillingham, we completely furnished it with the idea of letting rooms to other naval personnel and their wives, this type of accommodation being very much in demand; no married quarters being available in those days.

The move was from Hertfordshire, where my wife had been installed quite comfortably in a self – contained flat. Perhaps we may

I came across several members of this class in the ensuing years, and most gratifying it was to meet up with two of them who had attained the status of Petty Officer Gunner's Mate.

My next class comprised direct entry Sub Lieutenants (A), and these I had to teach the rudiments of seamanship, although they were destined to become pilots in the Fleet Air Arm.

Before I could be allocated another class, I was drafted to the Torpedo School at Portsmouth, for it was here, at HMS *Vernon*, that I was to carry out my long-awaited Coxswains course.

HMS *Vernon*. 30th September – 6th December 1939

I was not a little surprised to find that four of the would-be coxswains in my class were acting petty officers, for it still rankled somewhat that the commander of *Emerald* had considered that I was too short in seniority to be considered for a recommendation.

However, as time passed, acting petty officer coxswains were to be much in evidence: the commissioning of reserve fleet destroyers, fifty clapped out American destroyers, and the corvettes and escort vessels building each requiring a coxswain in their complement.

I knew of one instance – and there may have been others – where a commanding officer refused to accept an acting petty officer as his coxswain; understandable in away, for a destroyer coxswain, if not a chief petty officer in his own right, had to be given an acting rate as such, and I suppose that in this particular C.O.'s estimation, acting petty officer to acting chief was a bit much, especially as it also meant a change of uniform.

The course itself consisted of school, signals and destroyer work, examinations having to be taken in each of these subjects.

School work involved navigation and the keeping of victualling accounts, for until the advent of the larger destroyers; coxswains had always been responsible for the ordering, issuing and account of Paymaster's provisions: in later destroyers, a Supply Petty Officer was included in the complement, the Paymaster's stores then becoming his prerogative.

Signals are self-explanatory: there also had to be a first aid qualification, but it was the destroyer work which was the most important to a candidate.

Each would-be coxswain was posted to a destroyer for four weeks. Here, under the watchful eye of the ship's own coxswain, he would put what he had learned ashore into practice afloat, ultimately being accepted by the commanding officer as proficient. If such an acceptance was not forthcoming, the embryo coxswain would develop no further, packing his bag prior to being sent back as failed.

My proficiency at navigation I owed, firstly to my having been in the Advanced Class as a boy, and secondly, because much of my service had been concerned with matters navigational.

Successful in the examination, I give the results, not because I wish to appear pretentious, but to show that if I was proficient, the same can hardly be said for the person responsible for entering the details on my history sheet.

My marks were 98/100 for schoolwork, 44½/50 for signals and 179/200 for destroyer work, qualifying so my history sheet says, with an average of 89%.

By my arithmetic however and accepting all the rules pertaining to fractions and percentages, I made the right figure to be over 91%. I raised no query however, pleased to have qualified and so be entitled to a wage increase of one shilling per day.

My pay now, as a Petty Officer Torpedo Coxswain with three good conduct badges, was seven shillings and nine pence per day, and with my extra wealth I returned to Chatham Barracks, there to await whatever draft might be in store for me.

Chapter 22

Pembroke and *Harvester*

HMS *Pembroke* 7th December 1939 – 23rd April 1940
During the course at Portsmouth my wife had lost her lodgers, the husband being drafted and the wife returning to her hometown.

The uncertainty about the early stages of the war, and the fact of being left on her own once again, caused my wife also to leave Gillingham and return to Hertfordshire, our home once more going into storage. After a few days in barracks I was elected Vice President of the Petty Officers Mess, a job which would have been far more beneficial to me had I still been domiciled in Gillingham, for in my capacity as mess official I was excused from all normal barrack duties.

The Mess President was appointed by the Commodore of the barracks, usually for a period of two years, but all other officials, Vice President, Secretary, Caterer etc., were elected by the members of the mess.

When first taking over office, the President had introduced me to the Petty Officer cook in charge of the Petty Officers galley, saying as he did so – "You must look after him, for he looks after us"

As one of my duties was to draw and issue the daily rum ration, the inference of his words was quite apparent, and, I was soon to find out, a few extra tots to the Petty Officer cook brought me among other things, the week-end joint, as I have no doubt, it did to other mess officials also.

Should you be wondering how these extra rations were available to be so disposed of, perhaps I should now clarify the situation.

With all the comings and goings at this particular time, the victualling office was hard pressed trying to keep pace with the paperwork from the drafting and joining offices.

As far as the Petty Officers Mess was concerned, the joining and leaving book kept in the mess office was a much better guide to the number victualled, and adding a few to allow for a margin of error, the victualling office was always prepared to accept this figure for the issue, which somehow or another, always seemed to be in excess, thus giving a surplus for certain exigencies.

The other items? Well, all messes appeared to be over victualled, much of the food being cooked and finishing up as pig food; much better in my opinion, that such items should become the perks of office

Dishonest? In a way I suppose it was, and when a gallon jar of rum was stolen from the mess office, it was a theft that was never reported to higher authority, the reason I think, being fairly obvious.

We were now experiencing the period which was to become known as the *phoney war*, with the expected air raids not materialising and the civilian population becoming a little complacent, allowing many of the evacuee children to return to their homes.

This feeling did not exactly reach epidemic proportions, but it was catching, and my wife having returned to Gillingham, moving from one digs to another without finding anything really satisfactory, we decided to set up house once again.

Unfurnished property to rent was quite easy to come by in those days, so we took a house in Gillingham, de-stored our furniture, took in another naval couple, and we were together again, but only for a couple of months.

A few tots of rum had got a messman out of a draft, but the same could not happen for me, coxswains being in short supply; but I was given a choice: I could either go to Motor Torpedo Boats immediately, or the destroyer HMS *Harvester* in a month's time. I chose *Harvester*.

HMS *Harvester* 24th April 1940 – 19th March 1941

I joined my ship at Barrow in Furness, where she was still in the hands of the builders.

Harvester was one of six destroyers, which, at the outbreak of war, was in the process of being built by the Brazilian navy.

Needless to say, our need was now greater than theirs, so they were to be commissioned under the British flag.

I joined the ship in advance of the main party in order to prepare for this commissioning: the Gunners Mate, Torpedo Gunner's Mate, Chief Stoker and myself, together with a few other key ratings, were the only crew members who had so far joined, working aboard ship during the day and living ashore after working hours, the ship not yet having been taken over.

Several of the key ratings had been at Barrow for some time, as they were concerned with various installations, but I, being needed only to prepare for commissioning, was there for only two weeks before the main party arrived.

Having travelled overnight, the ship's company arrived at Barrow in time for breakfast, this being laid on at the station buffet – but only, they were told, when all their baggage had been off loaded from the train and reloaded onto lorries.

The job almost completed; on going into the buffet to warn the staff of the impending arrival of some one hundred and eighty hungry men, I was surprised to see two of their number already tucking in skulkers both; but they posed me a problem.

Should they be my first two defaulters, charged with being absent from place of duty, or should I just give them a dressing down and let it go at that.

The latter prevailed: but only after breakfast was over and the men were fallen in ready for being marched to the ship.

Calling the two offenders to the front, I then showed them up as behaving in a manner which would not in future be tolerated, and I flattered myself that the message was received and understood.

A sister ship, HMS *Hurricane was* also building at Barrow, not so far advanced as Harvester, but during the pre-commissioning period I had got along quite well with her First Lieutenant. When her coxswain eventually joined, this first lieutenant sent him along to see me in order to pick up a few tips, which to me seemed rather amusing, for here was I carrying out a coxswain's duties for the first time, being asked to give a few tips to a coxswain of some years standing who had also been a one time president of the Petty Officers mess at Chatham. I must certainly have created quite an impression with that first lieutenant.

Acceptance trials completed to everyone's satisfaction, *Harvester* now left Barrow for Plymouth and Portland. This was to carry out working up practices so that the ship would become efficient. In this instance however, because of coming events, the programme was destined never to be completed.

It was late May. We were exercising off Portland with a submarine, carrying out simulated attacks in preparation for the time when it might become the real thing.

The receipt of a signal resulted in the submarine being brought to the surface and sent back to harbour, *Harvester* then proceeding with all speed to Dover.

En route the Captain cleared the lower deck and gave us the news: members of the British Expeditionary Force were cut off and we were on our way to evacuate them. It was the Dunkirk evacuation, but the enormity of the task was not yet apparent.

Remaining at Dover only long enough to refuel, we sailed for Dunkirk, arriving before dawn so that the panorama opened up as the daylight improved.

Many stories have been written about Dunkirk; by far more able writers than I, so I will confine myself only to events as they applied to *Harvester*.

Our captain decided to pick up from the beaches rather than the pier, and to this end boat the motorboat and whaler were lowered.

The ferrying had not been long in operation when the capsizing of the whaler caused a delay in the proceedings. If the coxswain of the whaler's story is to be believed, this in itself was a tragedy, for he was adamant that fewer men surfaced than had been in the boat when it capsized, understandable perhaps, for many of them were still wearing packs.

Various other small boats had been carrying on with the ferrying, and we had at last embarked enough men to warrant our return to Dover. When first arriving at Dunkirk we had landed a beach party of one officer, one able seaman, and the captain's steward; but we now sailed without them.

We must have been fortunate, for the trip back was almost without incident, but back at Dover one of our young able seamen was involved in an accident that resulted in his death.

Many of the troops had embarked, bringing their rifles with them, and these they had taken on to the mess decks. When leaving the ship at Dover however, they had left these rifles behind and one of them unfortunately, still had one up the spout. A party detailed to collect these rifles numbered among them one Ordinary Seaman Greenfield, and picking up the loaded rifle and pulling the trigger, he sent the bullet on an errand of death, hitting the able seaman in the groin and proceeding in an upward direction.

Death was not instantaneous, but he died a short time later in hospital at Dover. Ordinary Seaman Greenfield was awarded fourteen days No. 11 punishment for negligence, and although he was not the only one who was negligent, the real culprit, the soldier, probably never even realised that he had left his rifle loaded.

On returning to Dunkirk things had warmed up considerably: ships carrying out the evacuation put up barrages against the enemy aircraft, but even so, a paddle steamer lying at the pier ahead of *Harvester* was hit but we escaped unscathed.

Embarking troops from the pier we had been able to fill up much more quickly than previously and were soon underway again.

On this occasion however, the trip was not to be without incident in both its early and later stages.

A flotilla leader, HMS *Codrington,* was leaving just ahead of us and I received the order from the bridge to "follow *Codrington* not an unusual order when two ships were steaming line ahead.

I followed as ordered; being able to see her quite plainly, the early morning sun being dead astern. Suddenly *Codrington* disappeared in a cloud of smoke and spray: "Poor Bastards," said someone on the bridge, for it certainly looked as if she was a goner; but when the upheaval had subsided, there she was steaming merrily on, for it had been the nearest of near misses.

Then it was our turn, an aircraft being spotted approaching from the stern; but before it could get within bombing range, 'X' gun had proved its undoing. It was afterwards rumoured that it was one of our own aircraft, but I have extreme doubts about this, for no pilot in his right mind would have approached a friendly ship down sun.

The extra top weight of some hundreds of men was doing much to upset the manoeuvrability of the ship, the feel of this being most noticeable on the wheel, and we now had to run the gauntlet of the shore batteries at Nieuwpoort, which had by now fallen into enemy hands. Avoiding action was out of the question, and we were thankful that perhaps a combination of bad marksmanship, together with the enemy's unfamiliarity with the guns, enabled us to pass without mishap.

The white cliffs of Dover once again: the harbour, the jetty and *Crash!* We were alongside, but with a damaged bow.

Most readers will know that a heavily laden vessel continues to have way for longer than one not so loaded; and so-it was with *Harvester.* A normal approach and then – "Half Speed Astern Both" but no appreciable slowing of the ship's way – "Full Speed Astern Both" – but too late, for it wasn't the engines that stopped the ship, but the jetty.

After the troops had landed there was to be no collecting of rifles from the mess deck, for being wise after the mishap to our crewmember, these, after being unloaded, had been piled on the upper deck.

Damage to the ship's bow was sufficient to keep her in dockyard for a few days and this enabled to have a run ashore at Dover, a run ashore gave me a bit of a shock, albeit a pleasant one.

I was in a pub when I heard someone say – It, What are you drinking Gus?" – and turning round, who should I see but one Jim Bellinger, a petty officer who had been a classmate of mine on the coxswains course. He had been coxswain of the *Hotspur* at Narvik, and by all accounts had been killed in the action. He was no ghost however, although it had apparently been a close thing, but he was able to confirm that a Petty Officer Harrison, an old shipmate of mine, had been killed in the encounter.

We had both served as able seamen aboard *Daring,* and it was his promotion to acting leading seaman which had prompted my request to challenge the roster.

Dunkirk was over so far as *Harvester* was concerned. The evacuation had continued during our time in dockyard hands, and although we did not realise it at the time, it was over by the time we were once more operational.

As a matter of fact, when ordered to Sheerness to await further orders, we quite thought that these orders would be to proceed once again to Dunkirk, instead of which we were to proceed to Chatham and the three days leave which had been granted to all personnel who had taken part in the evacuation.

True, our effort had not been as great as that of others, but I suppose, putting it statistically, we had, for every member of the ship's company, repatriated some ten soldiers.

Of our beach party, only two had returned to the ship; the officer and the able seaman: the captain's steward we never saw again, and he was posted missing.

All the ship's company were sent on leave together, one mess deck being left open for ship keepers detailed from barracks.

I was the last to leave, being responsible for the locking up of all other compartments and this done, with the keys handed over to the officer in charge of the ship keepers; I proceeded to my home in nearby Gillingham.

Instead of the expected welcome from my wife and small daughter, I was greeted by our lodgers with the news that they had both gone away, supposedly, it was thought, to the wife's mother.

Off to Hertfordshire, but still no wife! It then dawned upon me that in mid June she was to look after a sister-in-law, in child, at Gomshall, a village midway between Dorking and Guildford.

I could only assume, rightly as it turned out, that some complication had made it necessary for her to go earlier, and so I continued my journeying.

The time almost midnight; on arriving at Guildford, I was lucky enough to find a taxi, the driver being willing to take me the five miles or so to my destination, where, on arrival, he would take no more than the bare fare, refusing the customary tip.

Needless to say, the family had to be knocked up; everyone was pleased to see me, but one of my precious three days was almost gone.

The leave over, it was now June 9th and *Harvester* was once more at sea. It had been rumoured for some time that we would eventually operate from Plymouth; not without reason I suppose, for the ships' accounts were carried at *Drake,* and it became apparent that such buzzes may have had an element of truth in them when, on sailing into Plymouth, we saw that two of our sister ships were already there.

Harvester's stay was of quite short duration however. A couple of hours and we were off again, bound for Le Havre, which we were to enter next morning, tie up alongside and await the arrival of a V.I.P., name unknown to us.

It seemed to be business as usual at Le Havre; although the sound of distant gunfire could be heard: but we sailed at 1200 without the

V.I.P., our orders being to this effect, but there were quite a few French nationals on the dockside who would very much have liked to be sailing with us, even being willing to pay for a. passage.

It was not to be a wasted journey however: several thousands of British troops had been cut off at St Valery-en-Caux, a coastal town mid way between Le Havre and Dieppe, and these we had to try to evacuate.

To assist in the operation we had picked up two merchant ships, and the modus operandi was as follows. Leaving the two merchantmen out of range, *Harvester* was to go close inshore, pick up as many as possible by using small boats and then ferry them to the merchant ships.

As coxswain I was at the wheel for the whole of the operation so being able to hear everything that was happening on the bridge above.

"There are tanks on the cliffs shelling our men on the beach," said the yeoman of signals.

"We can't have that can we?" said the Captain, and then – "All guns with S.A.P. load" – " Target tanks on cliff" – "Salvoes."

When the order came to "Cease Fire," it seemed "that *Harvester's* gunnery had had the desired effect, for we were able to pick up some six hundred men and ferry them back to the waiting merchantmen. Returning for more, with the cruiser *Ceres* following in order to give us the support of her heavier armament, it was a different story.

As we neared the shore, beaches seemed deserted and things were quiet; too quiet as it turned out, for suddenly, at almost point-blank range, guns which had been camouflaged until that moment, opened fire without warning.

"Hard a Starboard," ordered the captain; "Full ahead both" – "Let's get to hell out of here" – "Yeoman. Make a signal to *Ceres*" – "Further evacuation impossible."

We escaped unscathed; but it was not until our return to England that it became apparent how badly the mission had failed, when on going ashore at Portsmouth we saw the newspaper placards which read – 6,000 British Troops Cut Off and Taken Prisoner.

Harvester paid one more visit to the other side; this time a little further south, waiting in the Gironde Estuary for what were probably the last ships to sail out of Bordeaux for the U.K., all the time expecting an air attack – an attack that never materialised, the ships and cargoes being safely escorted to their destination.

From then on it was incessant night patrols; what one might almost term anti invasion patrols; the invasion which was so long expected but missed the boat.

For these patrols *Harvester* was based at Southampton, patrolling the Channel at night and spending the daylight hours alongside the wall in Southampton Docks; two hours leave being given, from 1200 until 1400.

This invasion scare also saw my goods and chattels once more in store, with my wife back in Hertfordshire: not at all a good move as it turned out, for she later joined me at Liverpool, and although the Medway towns suffered, little from enemy air activity, Liverpool, as everyone knows, took a real pasting.

Liverpool was the main base for the North Western Approaches; a command consisting mainly of destroyers and flower class corvettes which were employed as anti submarine screens for westbound convoys.

It was really a kind of shuttle service, for the convoys would be escorted to a latitude of 14° West where a change over saw the return journey being carried out in the company of a homeward bound group.

When not actually required for convoy work, anti submarine patrols might be carried out, and except for boiler cleaning periods there would be very little respite, perhaps twenty-four hours in harbour, sometimes even less.

This then was the job allocated to *Harvester and* sailing from Plymouth we arrived at Liverpool early in July 1940.

The speed of the convoy was decided by the speed of the slowest ship, and although, at the pre sailing briefings the ships' masters would admit to being able to maintain such a speed, there was always the straggler which had to be chased up by one or other of the escort vessels.

Bad weather would keep the U-boats down, but it also had its disadvantages, for it would cause the convoy to split up, and after such a blow had subsided, the escort vessels, like sheep dogs rounding up their flock, would be here there and everywhere, endeavouring to get the ships back into formation once again.

Harvester made many depth charge attacks on suspicious echoes, without being able to produce sufficient evidence to claim a kill.

Then, on October 30th an attack was made; an attack which produced more than enough evidence, this being in the shape of 29 survivors.

Bad weather had split up the convoy; when I say bad I am guilty of an understatement, with mountainous seas that really gave one the impression that the ship was sliding down the side of them.

When we did run out of the heavy weather the convoy was well and truly scattered, and now began the task of rounding them up.

Closing a merchant ship, which turned out to be the *S.S. Balzac,* an echo on the asdics was reported by the operator as being fish, but almost immediately, Midshipman Rushbrooke, happening to glance in the direction of the starboard lookout Ordinary Seaman Greenfield, saw him, open mouthed, gesticulating in the direction of the starboard bow.

Himself looking out, and not being tongue tied as was Greenfield, the midshipman immediately reported a periscope on that bearing, for a U-boat was taking his sights on the *Balzac*.

All this happened in far less time than it has taken me to describe, and by now, probably realising the danger, all trace of the U-boat had disappeared; but the hunt was on.

The operator still had a firm echo on his so-called fish, which was of course our U-boat; so the cat and mouse game began. For two hours the hunt went on, numerous depth charges were fired in patterns, the echo lost, picked up again, another pattern, so it went on; but still no wreckage – Then – the U-boat surfaced.

"Full speed ahead" came from the Bridge, "Stand by to ram", but she had not surfaced to fight it out, the crew were abandoning ship, sinking her had not become necessary and before long she was gone of her own accord, the crew swimming towards *Harvester* for succour – Twenty nine survivors from a crew of thirty two.

Although they had been hunting them but a short time before and would have had no qualms about sending them to a watery grave, the men of *Harvester* showed great concern for the welfare of our prisoners, and made sure that they were amply provided with cigarettes.

The crew of the U-boat were to be disembarked at Greenock, and it so happened that in the approaches we passed quite close to *Ark Royal,* which, on three occasions, Lord Haw-Haw had given out as having been sunk. It was most gratifying to see the look of disbelief on the faces of the U-boat men when they saw with their own eyes, that the *Ark* was well and truly afloat and operative.

These prisoners were only one class of supernumerary with which *Harvester* returned to port from various of her patrols and convoying.

The U-boat war was hotting up; survivors from torpedoed merchant ships were being picked up, the boats then being sunk so that no other ships would stop to investigate them. Blazing and derelict hulks were being disposed of by gunfire to prevent them being a menace to navigation.

Returning to Merseyside in late October, we soon realised that something was wrong, for it was obvious that the pall of smoke was not only from industrial sources and it soon became apparent that Liverpool, the night before, had suffered its first air raid.

Harvester was not to remain in harbour long enough to give leave, for she was under sailing orders to proceed with an outward bound convoy, but the captain allowed those of the ship's company with a wife ashore, to land far two hours in order to ascertain their well being.

This raid was the first of many, and it became a debatable point as to whether we were safer at sea or in harbour, and those of us who had our wives ashore, hearing, on our return their stories of the raids, we did, when back at sea, fear as much for their safety as they did for ours.

Because of one raid, I was paid £11 salvage money for a salvage in which I never took part. *Harvester* had gone over to the Birkenhead side of the Mersey and was lying astern of a merchant ship.

During the raid, a bomb, due to some unaccountable delayed action, did not explode until it had first penetrated the stern of this ship. Although the water cushioned the force of the explosion, there was enough damage caused for help to be solicited, and in consequence, a party from *Harvester* boarded her and assisted with the necessary shoring up.

I was ashore at the time, as were many others of the ship's company, but on my return the captain asked for a list of the names of the men who had rendered assistance.

The outcome of this should have been an award of salvage money to the men whose names were .on the list, and it was quite a surprise, when same months later, Admiralty Fleet Orders stated that salvage money was payable to *Harvester,* for this meant that the whole crew would benefit, from the captain right down to the most junior rating, and my share was the £11 already mentioned.

Nearing Christmas and escorting a homeward bound convoy, we had encountered heavy weather: not sufficient to split up the convoy, but we did suffer damage to our degaussing gear; damage which made it inoperable. Not wishing to take a chance on magnetic mines in the Mersey approaches, the captain therefore took the ship into Londonderry for repairs; the common sense thing to do under the circumstances, but it ruled out Christmas at Liverpool, where, had things gone according to plan, we would have made a Christmas Eve arrival.

Christmas Day dawned; the routine was normal, and Bob Butler, a Chief E.A., Petty Officer Fedarb, together with the Canteen Manager and his assistant, requested permission to go ashore in order to attend church service.

As I have said, routine was normal, so permission was granted; but shortly after they had landed, *Harvester* was put on three hours notice for steam, and then given sailing orders for 1300.

Time enough for our churchgoers to return, so there was no cause for alarm; at least not until it neared the time for us to proceed in execution of previous orders – and they were still ashore.

We sailed without them, and fourteen days were to elapse before we were to see them again, but in the meantime, someone had to be responsible for the running of the canteen, which, as well as dealing with the day to day needs of the men, *Harvester* being a canteen messing ship, the various messes were in need of provisions.

The captain appointed me acting canteen manager; a job which I had to perform in addition to my own, and later, a grateful N.A.A.F.I. awarded me the sum of ten whole shillings.

Nothing drastic had happened to them: after the service, a couple in the congregation had offered them Christmas hospitality which had been accepted.

Their punishment? Thirty days leave stopped apiece. They had not been absent over leave, for church parties could not be classed as leave, and in any case, when going ashore, nothing had been said about the time of their return. Neither could they be charged with committing an offence with the ship being under sailing orders, for *Harvester* had not been under sailing orders at the time of the landing.

The ultimate charge was – Being absent without leave, thereby missing their ship on sailing – the period of absence being from the time of the church service ending until the time of their reporting to the naval authorities ashore.

The bad weather still continued, and because of this we were to lose one of our number overboard. Stoker Thomas was employed as Engineer Officer's servant, and making his way aft to the officers' quarters, although making use of the lifelines which were rigged; a heavy sea took him over the side. Although he was seen to go, very little could be done to help him: no boat would have survived the seas which were running, even had it been possible to launch one, and because of these same seas it was not able to manoeuvre the ship close enough to effect a rescue.

Unlike civilian life, no collection was taken for the dead man's next of kin. Money was raised however, by the sale of his effects.

Officially called *A Sale of Dead Mens' Effects*, it is an auction of a dead man's uniform clothing which is carried out aboard the ship in which the man served, the proceeds of such a sale then going to the next of kin of the deceased.

Different again from an ordinary auction, the highest bidder for an article rarely took it, and it would be put back into the sale, perhaps being put up three or four times before-the person officiating, usually the Master at Arms or the Coxswain, called a halt by that –"This article is not to go up again."

Alternatively the sale might be run in the dog watches on three consecutive days, the highest bidder on the last day being compelled to take the article he had bid for.

It had to be done like this or else the sale could go on indefinitely. No money changed hands; the amount bid being charged to the bidder's credit.

I now had to conduct such a sale but need say very little more about it except that in this instance, a uniform kit which could be purchased new for well under £25, although second hand and some of it well worn, raised over £200.

Carrying out a lone patrol and being in the vicinity of Iceland, my eyes were opened to the abundance of fish that were in these waters; an abundance which besides putting the men, on a welcome fish diet, gave the P.O. Cook a bit of a headache trying to cope with the fry up.

Off Reykjavik, the captain decided to drop a depth charge, and I am certain that the result exceeded even his expectations. An area which I can only estimate as being a quarter of a mile square was literally carpeted with dead fish of many varieties. A boat was lowered, and within twenty minutes more than enough had been collected for our needs, hence the P.O. Cook's headache.

Even so, more was left behind than we had gathered in: what would British housewives have given for some of it.

Some were to be fortunate however, for full use was made of *Harvester's* limited refrigeration, and a few days later, many parcels of fish were taken ashore, which could, I suppose, be considered as perks that went with the job.

My service aboard *Harvester* was now coming to an end. The writing had been on the wall for some time; difficulty on occasion, in hearing helm orders making it obvious to the captain that something was amiss.

A resultant medical disclosed that I was suffering from a 20% hearing loss in my left ear, this being diagnosed as gunfire deafness.

Perhaps such a defect will be a little more understandable if I say that the voice pipe from the bridge to the wheelhouse was always positioned just above the helmsman's left ear. This meant that all orders from the bridge would be received via this same ear, but more than that, so would other sounds from up above; other sounds including those of gunfire from the forward guns, which was funnelled down the voice pipe directly into one's ear. Earplugs could not be used, for if they were helm orders would not be heard, and so it was something that an action helmsman had to put up with.

Whether all war time coxswains suffered from deafness could only be ascertained by survey. It may have been some weakness inherent in me; but suffice to say, my relief was applied for on medical grounds.

Petty Officer Fitzgerald joined shortly before *Harvester* was due to sail with a convoy.

As it had been with me, this was to be his first ship as a coxswain, and there being no time to turn things over to him, the ship sailed with two coxswains aboard.

For most of the trip I became a supernumerary killing time by taking a class of ordinary seamen to seamanship instruction, thus leaving my relief to feel his way around, making it my business to be available to him only when he solicited help.

I was more than a little upset at leaving *Harvester;* much had happened in the eleven months I had been aboard, and she had been a very happy ship.

Others left as time went on, but when, some two years later, she was sunk by the German submarine U432, many of her original ship's company perished; as did my relief, Petty Officer Fitzgerald.

Although until now my writings have been all first-hand information, I think perhaps that the sinking, as it was related to me by Petty Officer Pash Baker, one of the original crew members, and a survivor, is worthy of repeating.

* * *

The story has its beginnings on the 9th March 1943, when an eastbound convoy HX228, five days out from Newfoundland and some 200 miles S.W. of Iceland, was attacked by U-boats.

A large convoy, the escort vessels were eight in number, comprising an assortment of British and Polish destroyers, three Free French corvettes and an American aircraft carrier.

At 0800 that morning, a plane from the carrier had sighted and attacked a U-boat on the surface ten miles ahead of the convoy, although the attack was unsuccessful.

Air protection was not to be available for much longer however, the carrier running short of fuel and having to turn back.

This attack came at 1930, an ammunition ship blowing up lighting up the surrounding area: another ship was also hit, with the crew abandoning, a corvette was detailed to pick up survivors.

Harvester searched diligently, trying to establish contact with the attackers, but without success.

Thinking perhaps that one U-boat at least might surface in order to shadow the convoy preparatory to making another attack, the commanding officer of *Harvester* decided to drop back in order to be in a position to shadow the shadower.

Rightful thinking as it turned out, for shortly after midnight, dead ahead, a U-boat had surfaced.

Action alarm was sounded, but there was very little doubt that the U-boat had also seen *Harvester,* for she lost no time in diving.

"Stand by depth charges" – "Shallow setting" – came the order from the bridge – "FIRE".

The depth charge pattern dropped into the swirl of the U-boat's dive; but even so it was not a kill: she surfaced and tried to escape into the darkness, but *Harvester* still pursued the attack, guns blazing, and eventually there she was, five hundred yards ahead, wallowing in the swell, her crew scrambling out of the conning tower and jumping into the sea.

"Stand by to ram" – came the warning. A terrific jolt and a crunching of steel – the U-boat was doomed, but it was to prove a ramming which was also the *Harvester's* undoing.

The U-boat was tangled up with *Harvester's* stern, after compartments were flooding and she was stopped – A sitting target for any other U-boats that might be in the vicinity.

Freed at last from the U-boat, her position was grim. Port propeller shaft broken, starboard shaft damaged, with various compartments flooded both forward and aft – a sorry state, but now, free of the U-boat, she was able to creep along on one engine.

The French corvette *Aconit,* dropping back to render assistance, was ordered to rejoin the convoy, which she reluctantly did, leaving *Harvester* to limp along in rear; a straggler if ever there was one.

At 0400 *Harvester* stopped to pick up survivors from a torpedoed merchant ship – S.S. *Gorgas*; fifty American seamen, glad to be rescued, but joking half-heartedly about the rescue ship being a lame duck.

Dawn. broke – a grey dawn, with flurries of snow doing much to lessen the visibility; and that the inevitable happened – the starboard engine had gone the way of its mate, and *Harvester* was once again stopped, this time with no help at hand.

By this time *Aconit* was some twenty miles ahead. *Harvester* captain caused a signal to be sent as follows – "Am stopped – Stand by me." Then there was nothing to do but wait.

Time dragged slowly by. It was now 1100 and "Up Spirits."

Then it happened: A terrific roar, the ship shuddered, black smoke mingled with hissing steam from the boiler room. The torpedo had struck port side amidships.

The damage sustained by the ramming and now this – It was too much – *Harvester* began to heel over – she was sinking.

"Abandon Ship" – ordered the captain. Men at their abandoned ship stations launching the floats and rafts, the survivors from *S.S. Gorgas,* torpedoed for the second time in twenty four hours the captain and the first lieutenant, together with the men allocated to the whaler, struggling to launch it against the list of the ship – speed was essential, for *Harvester* was going fast.

There then occurred that which survivors could only describe as cold-blooded murder. Another torpedo struck close to where the whaler party were working, penetrating the ship's side and exploding in the fore magazine, men in the vicinity being blown to bits.

Aconit arrived on the scene in reply to *Harvester's* last signal, but men were to die from exposure before any rescue attempt could be made, for, getting an echo on the U-boat, she went into the attack, an attack which proved successful, Twelve of the U-boats' crew surviving.

Only then did *Aconit* carry on with the operation of rescuing the survivors from *Harvester* but from a total crew of two hundred officers and men, plus the fifty American seamen from *Gorgas,* only forty-seven survived.

Although extreme cold was responsible for many of the deaths, but for the second torpedo more would have survived.

With the crew already abandoning, was the second torpedo necessary? Obviously not; but a neutral observer might also say, neither was the ramming by *Harvester* when the U-boat" crew were also abandoning.

And Pash Baker; what brought about his survival? When the first torpedo struck, he had just arrived in his mess with the rum ration. The order to abandon ship came and thinking to himself that no one would be likely to come for their ration in the circumstances, he took one almighty swig.

Medical opinion may differ on this, but he was certain that it was only because of this surfeit of rum keeping out the cold, that he was able to survive.

* * *

Leaving *Harvester,* I collected my wife and daughter, and we departed from Liverpool in the middle which the city had experienced one of the biggest raids which the city had experienced.

We were bound once again for the peace and quiet of Gillingham, our accommodation being assured, for Bill Fedarb, his wife being with him at Liverpool, had offered me the loan of his house; an offer which was gratefully accepted.

Chapter 23

Pembroke and *Aster*

HMS *Pembroke* 20th March 1941 – 31st July 1941

Having been relieved from *Harvester* on medical grounds, I was obviously unfit for sea service.

I had to surrender my Acting Chief Petty Officer's rate, reverting to Petty Officer and joining up with the barrack working party.

So for 11 months I carried out the normal barrack routine; taking charge of various working parties by day, getting home most evenings, and in addition, attending Gillingham Royal Naval Hospital on three days a week in order to undergo specialist treatment for my hearing.

Some good must have come of this, for I was once again classed as fit for sea service and it was not long before I was on ten days draft leave prior to joining a flower class corvette – HMS *Aster*.

HMS *Aster* 1st August 1941 – 11th August 1944

The ship was already in commission and based at Freetown, Sierra Leone. For the necessary passage I was to join HMS *Dunnottar Castle* a Union Castle liner which had been fitted out as an armed merchant cruiser.

A long dreary overnight journey to Stranraer now had to be undertaken, for the ship was at Belfast and I had been routed via Larne.

Leaving Stranraer, I little dreamed that many thousands of miles would be travelled, and two years and eight months were to elapse before I set foot in England again.

The voyage to Freetown was uneventful, *Dunnottar Castle* sailing on her own, no calls being made en route, and relying on her speed to keep her out of U-boat trouble.

On arrival, *Aster* being at sea, I had to transfer to *Edinburgh Castle*, another ship of the Union Castle line, which in this instance was doing duty as a depot ship.

It was two days before *Aster* returned; looking less like a man of war than any other ship I had served aboard.

Two-thirds of the ship's side had been painted with a red lead; a first coat after having been chipped down to the bare metal; this usually being done to prevent rust corrosion.

I soon found that I had a lot to learn about the *Wavy Navy*; earlier, when based at Liverpool, I had seen a signal from the Naval Officer in Charge and addressed to Commanding Officers Corvettes, advising them to be guided by their coxswains on matters concerning naval procedure, a signal which, so far as *Aster* was concerned, could well have been repeated at Freetown and re-worded so as to include first lieutenants in the address.

The ship had been in commission three months – three months from new, which made it all the more surprising that it was considered necessary to chip and repaint the ship's side.

She had been without a coxswain for almost the whole of this period, he having gone sick shortly before *Aster* sailed from Belfast to Freetown – so short a time in fact, that it had not been possible for a relief to join before sailing.

Aster's complement of officers was five: The Commanding Officer – a Lieutenant Commander R.N.R., a First Lieutenant with the rank of Sub Lieutenant R.A.N.V.R. a Sub Lieutenant R.N.R. carried out the duties of Navigating Officer, and there were two other R.N. V.R. Sub Lieutenants, both C.W. candidates.

Before the war the Captain and Navigating Officer had been sea-going officers in the Mercantile Marine, but the First Lieutenant, apart from being a weekend peacetime sailor, had very little experience.

The other two officers had been ordinary seamen only a few months before, being selected then as possible officer material – C.W. Candidates – doing twelve weeks at sea and then after a six weeks course at *King Alfred*, being appointed to *Aster* as fully fledged officers.

The ship's company numbered eighty-two. Too few to warrant my being rated Acting C.P.O., but it so happened that only the Chief Engine Room Artificer was senior to me, he was being carried to do duty as Engineering Officer.

It was not long before the First Lieutenant and I fell foul of one another; the very first evening in fact, when sitting in the mess after tea, and talking to my new messmates, a terrific clatter made such talking impossible, for the men under punishment had been put to work chipping the ship's side adjacent to the Petty Officers Mess.

First Lieutenant's reply to my protest – "I will decide where men under punishment are employed" – did little to help matters, but when it became apparent to him that I, as coxswain, had direct access to the Captain, it must have rather dented his ego, especially when he received instructions to employ the men under punishment elsewhere.

Aster's role at Freetown was similar to that of *Harvester* at Liverpool; she and the other corvettes based there acting as anti submarine escorts for passing convoys.

There was no similarity ashore however, for apart from the naval canteen *King Tom* there was very little else, and night leave was out of the question.

The ship's company were fortunate in becoming chummy with a waterborne unit of the R.A.S.C., and their boats were put at our disposal for bathing parties; most welcome, for bathing alongside the ship was not allowed.

Several invitations were also received for the Petty Officers to spend an evening in the sergeants' mess, they also provided the transport, a state of affairs, which we thought, might last indefinitely; – but other plans were afoot.

It was whilst preparing to put to sea on what was to become a mystery cruise, that the inadequacy of the junior officers became apparent to me. When hoisting boats, it was the practice for an officer to take charge of the proceedings; he gave the orders, which would then be repeated by the Chief Bosun's Mate or duty Petty Officer.

"Haul taut singly" – both falls would have the slack taken up by the men manning them. "Marry" – the falls would be married together. "Hoist away" – the men would run away with the falls until the boat was almost at the davit head; so far so good, but no one was prepared for what came next. "Avast lowering".

The Chief Bosun's Mate quickly bellowed – "High Enough" – which was of course the correct order, but the men had heard the officer's *Faux Pas*, not without some comment, as you may imagine.

Having sailed, the captain sent for me and told me that the ship was sailing under sealed orders, and when reaching a certain position he would be in receipt of a signal telling him to open me of three sealed envelopes.

He suggested that it might be a good idea to run a sweepstake on the ship's next port of call, and as it turned out, this proved very popular, although many of the ports listed were in home waters; a matter of wishful thinking I suppose, for originally the ship's stay at Freetown was to be for a period of twelve months, and only five of these had been completed.

Actually the position we were making for should have ruled out all thoughts of home, for the ship was heading for a point well south of the equator, and also there was a tanker in company so that we could refuel whilst still on the move.

I am not aware as to whether any other of H.M. ships carried out a crossing the line ceremony during the war; but *Aster* did.

When the idea was suggested I was against it, contending that such a ceremony would cause a delay in the men closing up at action stations should such a need arise.

The captain did of course have the last word; and being of the opinion that it might be the only chance of Hostilities Only ratings ever being able to take part in such a ceremony, I was asked to convene a court for the following day.

We had the ideal man to take the part of King Neptune – Leading Seaman Cimit, with his large red beard, a beard so beautiful, that when, later in the commission, he requested permission to shave it off, the Captain said that he only wished it was in his power to refuse, the beard being an asset to the ship.

So few of the ship's company had crossed the line before, that the ceremony commenced the next day without either policemen or bears, the first men initiated having to be immediately co-opted to undertake these roles.

Such a ceremony has been fully dealt with elsewhere, so I need say nothing more except the proceedings went off without a hitch or any alarms.

We now knew what our destination was to be, for the envelope had been opened. Many of us would have liked to take a peek inside the other two, but not even the Captain could do this, for they had to be returned with seals intact.

In my opinion" one of them would have said Singapore, for we were at sea en route to our secret destination when news of its possible fall was made known to us.

As it was, we had drawn Simonstown, a South African naval base some twenty miles from Capetown.

When leave was piped there was no dearth of libertymen, all wishing to sample the delights of a run ashore in the well-lit land of plenty.

Firstly though, warnings were given about the penalties which would be incurred for fraternising with the black population, even talking to them in the street leaving one liable for a heavy fine.

It soon became apparent to us that the colour bar was the number one priority of life in South Africa; seats on railway stations being marked *Whites Only,* the same also applying to Cinemas, Bar, Buses, Trains, and anywhere else that segregation was possible.

There was however, nothing against blacks waiting on whites at table, or performing other tasks which would make life for the white South African that much easier.

Many of the whites had black servants who were allowed to cook for them, and do the housework, but when it came to eating their own meal, they had to take it to a shack in the garden, this shack also being their sleeping quarters.

During *Aster's* stay in South African waters, I made the acquaintance of a family in which two sisters were unable to go to the cinema together, one of them being so dark skinned. She was obviously a throw back to an earlier generation when mixed marriages were legal, and I suppose that in away, this is what apartheid is all about.

Our arrival at Simonstown coincided with the need for boiler cleaning and this allowed for time enough for each watch to be given four days leave.

Many stories have been told about the hospitality dispensed to our troops when the troopships called in at Capetown on their way to the eastern theatre of war, and such was the hospitality offered to us. As soon as it became known that *Aster* was giving leave, invitations began arriving from many outlying districts, and needless to say these were gratefully accepted.

The Chief E.R.A. and I settled for Paarl, a fruit growing district thirty-eight miles from Cape Town, where, as the guests of Mr and Mrs Swart, we became the seventy-sixth and seventy-seventh servicemen to be entertained in their home at their expense.

I have no intention of writing a travel brochure, but I suppose that one has read many stories in which the mountains of various countries are mentioned, and I wonder how such a writer would describe those under which Paarl nestled.

Alternating between blue and deep purple according to the time of day – they were a fitting backcloth to the white houses and colourful fruit farms of the area; fruit farms, which, as well as Canning their produce, also supplied a nearby distillery.

Chiefy and I were taken on a conducted tour of this distillery and given V.I.P. treatment, sampling the various brandies; peach, apricot etc, and then being waited on by the chairman of the company himself, he served us with snacks and a full bottle of South African brandy with instructions not to leave any.

Before we left he made me an offer of post war employment, which I said that I would consider, but I realised during the ensuing days, that in order to hold down a good job in South Africa, one must need to be bilingual.

Our host, Basil Swart, was a supervisor at Paarl telephone exchange, and when being shown over the place I noticed that many of the plug sockets had a blue ring painted round them. My inquiry as to why this should be brought the reply that they were Afrikaans speaking subscribers and were only to be answered in that language.

Although we were receiving such hospitality, there was a minority group which was definitely anti-British, if not pro-German, for not all the South African parliament had been in favour of declaring war on Germany in 1939, and these dissentants did of course have their followers.

Aster had very limited facilities for keeping fresh provisions, so after a few days at sea it was usually a case of out with the tin opener, because of this we were always glad to get back to harbour and some fresh meat.

Christmas Eve 1941 was no exception. We had returned to Simonstown from convoy duty at 1500; oil hoses were inboard for refuelling, orders had been placed for fresh provisions, and the next day being Christmas Day, a contractor from ashore had promised to deliver that evening, turkeys and all the trimmings.

Fuelling completed, and the watch ashore waiting for leave to be piped, a shock was forthcoming.

There was to be no "Libertymen fall in" that day: instead it was to be "Special sea dutymen to your stations" – "Hands to stations for leaving harbour" – *Aster* was off to sea again, for a passing convoy was without escort, a role which we had now to take on, the convoy being en route to Durban.

As you can well imagine, Christmas Day was far from merry – dinner consisted of corned beef and biscuits, for not one item of stores had been received before the ship sailed.

In other circumstances it might have been possible to scrounge something from one of the ships in company, this often being done, but we were experiencing such a blow, that making a close approach was out of the question.

Arriving at Durban on a Sunday gave no call for rejoicing either; no amusements available, not even a pub open, the Dutch Reform Church being against such things on the Lord's Day, and they apparently, held sway.

The populace of Durban seemed to have quite a thing about fifth columnists and careless talk, for notices were displayed in all the bars, these stating that standing treat was not allowed.

Some of the bars we thought carried this a bit too far, for a group of shipmates, having a run ashore together, were expected to pay for their own individual drinks.

Three months were spent in plying between Durban and Cape Town, escorting convoys as diverse as troop carriers and slow moving merchant ships: on one occasion we were detailed to escort the *Queen Mary,* but we need hardly have bothered, for once clear of the swept channel she left us standing.

I may have given the impression that *Aster* was alone in carrying out this work, and if so the impression is an erroneous one. Working with ships of the South African Naval Forces, we would sometimes be in company with their ships, although quite often, in the event of the convoy being a small one, we would be the sole escort vessel.

The South African Air Force was also in the act; carrying out anti submarine patrols, and on one occasion we had two sergeant pilots along for the ride, but they were more than glad to get ashore again, preferring to fly rather than roll about all over the place aboard a corvette.

With another convoy, the escorting plane ditched, *Aster* picking up the sole survivor.

The hands were at dinner when it happened; the sound of exploding depth charges taking them hurriedly to their action stations.

Perhaps I should point out that exploding depth charges usually meant that another of the escort vessels was making an attack, and when this happened it was not unusual for the men to anticipate action alarm aboard their own ship and proceed to their stations.

It was not so in this instance however as I have already said, a plane had ditched, and the depth charges under its wings, having a shallow setting, had detonated, blowing it to bits.

The pilot was the only survivor: another member of the crew had been seen in the water, but before a boat could reach him, he had vanished.

The pilot landed at Durban: he had sustained a broken leg but was indeed lucky' to be alive.

At Durban the South African hospitality continued, but not on the same scale as it did at Cape Town, and in any event, the latter was the more popular, for many of the men had formed attachments there; not all of them platonic I'm afraid, the cult of free love being most apparent and more than one of the ship's company had been heard to remark that he would be *"glad to get to sea for a rest"*

Only one succumbed to the charms of the South African girls on a permanent basis however, with resultant wedding bells at a later date.

All good things coming to an end, *Aster* left South Africa for pastures new, and but for fate taking a hand, these might also have been her last resting place.

From South Africa we had arrived at Colombo. A sister ship, HMS *Hollyhock,* unable to sail in execution of previous orders because of engine trouble, *Aster* was ordered to her place. Returning some days later we heard that *Hollyhock,* which in other circumstances would have been *Aster,* had been sunk by a Japanese bomber, there being only three survivors from a crew of some ninety souls.

Colombo and Trincomalee had been given their first taste of enemy air activity, the aircraft carrier *Hermes* had been sunk, but our southbound convoy had missed it.

Aster now had to act as an anti submarine escort for a minelayer which was to mine the passage between the Andaman and Nicobar Islands, this being the obvious route for any units of the Japanese Fleet should they have a mind to follow up the air attacks.

It was a job which we were all glad to see completed, and I doubt whether any of the ship's company could honestly say that they were not a little bit scared.

The Andamans were already in Japanese hands, the operation was carried out on a bright moonlit night, with the sea as smooth as sheet of glass: the visibility was so good that we could see splashes being made by the dropping of the mines, and for all we knew, the Japanese fleet, or at least some units of it, might be heading our way, and *Aster* had an armament of one four-inch bow gun and one two-pounder pom-pom.

Our fears were groundless, and the operation safely complete, *Aster* returned to Trincomalee, not to remain for long though, for our next job was to be an errand of mercy; evacuating Indian troops from Rangoon and taking them to Madras.

The ship was now overdue for boiler cleaning, and this was to take place at Colombo. Invitations had been received for members of the crew to spend a few days at up country estates, and in a way, this was to lead to another of the differences of opinions, which from time to time had arisen between the First Lieutenant and me.

He was forever making changes in the Watch and Quarter Bill, moving a man from one station to another, for no apparent reason except that it pleased him to do so.

During my four days up country he had excelled himself, reorganising practically the whole of the ship's company, so that in the event of any action we would have men doing jobs to which they were not accustomed. I was all in favour of a man being proficient at another man's job; but this was ridiculous.

I had no recourse but to see the Captain, and he issuing an as you were decree, things between No 1 and myself were a little strained, his remarks that – "If I were Commanding Officer I would not want you as my Coxswain" – receiving the reply, "And what makes you think that you could hold the job down anyway?"

He had by now been promoted to Lieutenant R.A.N.V.R., and our Captain going sick, a chance to prove one wrong was denied him when a Lieutenant R.N. was appointed temporarily in command.

Readers may think that I am biased against the wavy navy, but this is not so. Many such attained their own commands, but only after undergoing an extensive Senior Officers course at Greenwich College.

No my grouse about this particular First Lieutenant was that in spite of his lack of experience in matters nautical, he always thought that he knew best.

That my opinion of him was shared by at least one other member of the ship's company, when the following rhyme appeared on the mess deck notice board, became most apparent.

> Jimmy had some soldiers
> He took them with him to bed
> Tired of playing with his sergeants and corporals
> He played with his privates instead

Of course, I had to take it down and try to find out who was responsible, but without success.

Aster had now been in commission for twelve months, the thoughts of being relieved were uppermost in the mind of the majority of the ship's company, but enquiries ashore elicited the information that the twelve months stint had only applied to Sierra Leone, and it would be more like two years before any reliefs were forthcoming.

There had been a few changes because of sickness, and we now had some survivors from the *Prince of Wales,* these men having joined as replacements.

In all, fourteen months were spent in these waters, mainly on convoy duties between Colombo and Bombay, with occasional visits to many of the islands which abounded in the Indian Ocean

The reason for these visits were never made known to us, but it seemed obvious that such calls were made to ascertain whether any enemy units were lurking there, a kind of seek and destroy possibly, although it would have been seek and be destroyed so far as *Aster* was concerned; but then if this was the real purpose of the visits, to rout out any enemy, a corvette might have been considered as expendable. Fortunately it was never put to the test, for all such visits proved fruitless.

Leave at Colombo and Bombay was more often than not, restricted to a visit to the cinema. Beer was at a premium. It could be obtained at the naval canteen, but only by ticket, such tickets being rationed. The cost of beer thus obtained was one rupee (1s 6d) per bottle, but more could be obtained in the local bars for five rupees, far beyond our pockets, this being the equivalent of one day's basic pay for a petty officer.

The sergeants' messes at Colombo did not seem to offer the hospitality as had been the case during peacetime, one gaining the impression that they preferred our room to our company. It was after a cinema run at Bombay that I had occasion to put Chiefy and myself in the report for being absent over leave with the ship under sailing orders.

Leave expired at midnight, which meant that one had to catch a liberty boat which would leave the dockyard jetty at that time.

Cinema runs followed a set pattern; starting at 2100, they usually finished at about 2330, leaving ample time to get to the boat before midnight. The film on this particular occasion was entitled – *They died with their boots on* – featuring Errol Flynn as Custer in his last stand; one of the few occasions where he was not depicted as winning something almost single handed.

Leaving after the performance as usual, Chiefy looked at his watch and remarked that it was only 2315, which gave us plenty of time to wander down to the jetty.

The jetty was deserted, but being early as was understandable, until looking at his watch had a shock when it showed 0115.

It then became obvious what had happened; the film had been an exceptionally long one and it had been a quarter of an hour after midnight when we came out of the cinema, already a quarter of an hour adrift without realising it.

It was then a quick dash to the Gateway of India, and after waking up a native boatman; we arrived aboard two hours absent over leave.

Our lapse was a Godsend to a junior rating, also absent over leave, but who did not return until next morning, until just one half hour before the ship sailed. Coming up before the Captain, charged with – being absent over leave six hours thirty minutes. Ship under sailing orders – his punishment should have been three days pay and leave stopped, together with seven days No 11 punishment.

Very, surprised at only receiving a caution, he was not exactly left speechless, remarking to his messmates as he went forward – "Blimey!" – "You could get away with murder aboard this ship."

What he did not realise of course, was that he had only got away with it because the Captain had got it in mind to caution both Chiefy and myself.

Aster had now been attached to the South Atlantic Fleet, which was based at Addu Atoll in the Maldives group of islands.

Whilst here, on two separate occasions, each of our two R.N.V.R. officers, now promoted to Lieutenant, were ordered to sit on an examination board for men wishing to pass for higher rating.

That six weeks officer training at *King Alfred* was not sufficient to make any trainee into an efficient deck officer once more became apparent, when the first of our pair sent for me in order to ask if I would make him out a list of questions and answers suitable for his task; which was to examine Leading Seamen passing for Petty Officer: the subject being Anchors and Cables.

Questions? Yes I could understand that they might need some guidance over those, but set answers were hardly the thing for an oral examination, for in my experience of examining boards, an officer who knew what it was all about, if not getting the required answer, would, by rephrasing the question, get round to it eventually.

At a later date, a similar request came from the other officer concerned, the questions and answers being on Boat Work, the candidates on this occasion being Able Seamen under examination for Leading Seaman.

I helped them out of course, for no blame could be attached to them; the fault was with the convenors of the board for not making use of the many experienced officers who were available.

Two years had now elapsed since *Aster* had left England; a few reliefs had arrived, but many more were required, two thirds of the ship's company having served the requisite time.

We were now to be detached from the South Atlantic Fleet, with the pleasing news that the ship was once more to be based in South Africa, this time at Durban.

So we departed, and calling at Mombasa en route, arrived once more in the land of plenty.

After a few visits to Cape Town, where no time was lost in renewing old acquaintances, and an able seaman named Les Reeve was able to carry out his wedding plans, it was learned that the ship was to undergo a two months refit, and speculation became rife as to where the venue for this might be. Cape Town was of course the wish of everyone, but no such luck: the refit was to be at East London, and for East London we sailed.

The ship arrived on a Sunday, members of a nearby South African Naval Forces Base standing by to make fast our mooring wires.

An invitation from the Petty Officer in charge was gratefully accepted; an invitation to make full use of their mess during our stay, and one that was to prove my undoing later in the day.

Being a Sunday, no dockyard workmen were available to work the crane in order to hoist the brow inboard. Because of this the gap between the ship's side and the dockyard wall was bridged with two planks; a makeshift brow that ever was, but one that would have to suffice until the next day.

Libertymen had gone ashore at a time when the planks were level, but returning later, after a convivial evening with the South African Naval Forces, the tide had risen by an appreciable extent.

The planks had now developed an upward slope of some degrees, thus needing to be negotiated with care.

Dusty Miller, a Stoker Petty Officer who had been in company with me, made the ascent on all fours; but I, the beer being in and the wit out I suppose; decided that a speedy ascent would be better.

My dash got me about halfway before one of the planks tipped, and then I was on my way to the drink, catching my ribs on one of the mooring wires en route.

Such is the efficiency of the grapevine aboard ship, that in no time at all, word got round that the Coxswain was in the drink and very soon, I was fished out, none the worse for my soaking, but with bruised ribs through having come in contact with the mooring wire.

Confined to my bunk, four days were to elapse before I was once again able to make my daily report to the Captain, and he, asking if I had been drunk, was almost apologetic when I replied – "Drunk Sir!" – "How could I have been drunk?" – "It was a Sunday, and pubs don't open in South Africa on Sundays."

During my incapacity I had not been idle: one watch was to be sent on seven days leave, and as use could be made of a free travel warrant, many of the first leave party plumped for the Cape Town area.

For the refitting period, the ship's company were accommodated aboard a Polish liner, the *S.S. Pilsudski,* the Petty Officers receiving V.I.P. treatment, eating in the first-class saloon and being waited on by Polish stewards.

South African hospitality once more became apparent, but the people of East London appearing to be less affluent than those of Cape Town or Durban, there was not so much *Grippos* or *Harry Freemans* to use naval colloquialisms.

Here also the girls bestowed their favours not unwillingly, and two young stokers, returning aboard late one evening, said that they had been picked up by two girls in a car and raped: hardly using the word in its right sense, but true in a way, for the girls apparently had made all the advances.

Having a liking for an occasional flutter at the races, I was able to indulge myself when a meeting at the East London racecourse coincided with *Aster's* spell in the dockyard. I was not prepared for the make up of the fields however, for I found that horses were running twice on the same afternoon.

Not all of course, but I backed my fancy in the second race and it finished second. Seeing that it was also entered in the fifth race I dismissed it as not having a chance, only to see it led from start to finish for a convincing win.

Chiefy and I had decided to take the second seven days leave and spend it with our friends the Swartz at Paarl, but before this could be put into operation, Chiefy's relief arrived, and not caring to go on my own I wrote and put them off, a great pity really, for I was never to see them again. I had been corresponding with them and they told me that their total house guests had now numbered one hundred and twenty five, not including those who had made a second, or even third visit; quite a war effort on its own if you look at it that way.

Many reliefs were now overdue on the two year basis, and although the younger element of the ship's company were prepared to enjoy the South African hospitallty for as long as it was available, there were others, the family men, who were not enamoured of such surfeits, and now only wanted two things; a speedy relief and a quick passage home.

Returning to Durban after the refit, it did not help matters much to learn that we were once more to move on, and having already been based at Freetown, Cape Town, Colombo, Trincomalee, Bombay, Addu A toll and Durban, *Aster* was now to operate from Aden.

Les Reeve, not wishing to be separated so soon from his South African wife, and being overdue for a relief, had a last minute request to stay in South Africa granted, and so with his relief aboard, the ship sailed, having by now, been in commission for two years and five months, with some two dozen of the crew still awaiting relief.

One disgruntled crewmember, putting pen to paper, summarised the *Aster* saga in rhyme, worthy I think, of repetition.

NEC MOIRA NEC REQUIES
(No peace No rest – Ship's Motto)

We think of home and beauty, the country of our birth
Us men who left it many months ago
The few that are remaining, have been halfway round the earth
And where we're going next we do not know

We started off for Freetown, one sunny day in May
The skipper said it wouldn't be for long
Twelve months, perhaps a little more was all we'd be away
But the sailing orders really proved him wrong

Six months was all at Freetown, and then a mystery cruise
Some of the lads they didn't seem to mind
For we finished up at Cape Town, where there was lots of booze
And pretty girls who were so very kind

But one or two had guessed, that it wasn't for the best
Much longer they would be away from home
We only stayed a short time, just for a little rest
Then once again we started out to roam

Colombo was our next base, soon everyone was peeved
For nothing there was like the land of plenty
And instead of doing twelve months, before we got relieved
It had been raised by then to four and twenty

Of course some of the crew, who knew a thing or two
Had worked it so they got a job ashore
But that lucky few, there wasn't much to do
And so they're back in England just once more

We called at many ports, including Trinco and Bombay
With one or two more changes in the crew
For a little over twelve months and then there came a day
When the Captain told us what we had to do

To Mombasa first, then Durban, and we won't be coming back
The lads they thought of home and got romantic
Sam Duddle and Albert Butler were the only ones to pack
And the ship became attached to South Atlantic

Then there came a day, after just two years away
The ship she lay in Durban as you know
And an officer from shore, just stepped aboard to say
Three months more you'll have to do before you go

Then East London for a refit, where another small corvette
Had got reliefs although they were not due
It raised our hopes you bet, and the lads they all got set
To welcome some new members to the crew

After two weeks in East London, reliefs arrived for four
With a rumour that there were some more to come
The number we required, was just about a score
The next batch only numbered one.

Two more arrived before we left, a Bunting and a Cook
But of any more we never saw a sign
So Dusty and the Buffer had their names put in a book
And the Captain wrote the C in C a line

Then we sailed for Aden; we did go back you see
And everyone was feeling very sore
Dusty said to 'Swain, it's not good enough for me
Take my request to see the Commodore

The Commodore was awfully nice I'll do my best said he
You really should be homeward bound by now
So he sent a signal addressed to C in C
Relieve this man he's kicking up a row

At last a letter was received, reliefs had been detailed
And frowns they were removed from many a brow
But they have to come from Durban the place from which we sailed
So they may take months before they reach us now

From Aden the ship operated in the Red Sea Persian Gulf calling at Muscat to add the name of *Aster* to the many hundreds already painted on the surrounding cliffs.

No longer in the land of plenty, fresh provisions were scarce, and we were quite often without potatoes. There was no fresh fruit issue as there had been when serving in the Persian Gulf prior to the war; but there was some consolation I suppose, in being allowed a double issue of lime juice.

Eventually, all the original crew members had been relieved, the last of them having had to wait for two years and four months; but I was to wait even longer; almost two years and eight months in fact, after which, my relief having taken over, I was put ashore at Aden to await passage.

Chapter 24

Danae, Pembroke and *Cowdray*

HMS *Danae* 12th April – 27th April 1944

The time spent awaiting passage at Aden was to be of very short duration, only thirty-six hours; after which, HMS *Danae,* homeward bound and calling in for refuelling, was asked to accommodate me.

I had to work my passage, and being a coxswain, a trick on the wheel was an obvious choice. Unlike *Aster,* where the duties of quartermaster were carried out by able seamen, *Danae,* being a light cruiser, had two petty officers and two leading seamen as her regular helmsmen, and for the passage home I became the fifth, thus making things a little easier for all.

We took the short route via the Suez Canal and Mediterranean, a route which could have proved not uneventful, there still being a certain amount of Stuka activity in Mediterranean waters.

Luckily the voyage was without incident, but calling in at Malta, my first visit for over seven years, from Bighi Bay I was able to count seven wrecks, all resulting from the extensive air raids which the island had suffered.

I was not able to go ashore and find out how my haunts of earlier days had fared, for *Danae* stayed only long enough to embark a few more supernumeraries for passage.

On arrival at Gibraltar however, leave was given, and shopping consisted mainly of oranges, lemons and bananas for the folks at home, unripe bananas costing twice as much as the riper ones, the Gibraltarian shopkeepers being fully aware that only those purchased in an unripe condition would be of much use at the journey's end.

In my opinion, nothing is so striking as the greenness of the English countryside when one first sees it after returning from abroad, and this occasion was no exception, apart from the fact that on this April day our arrival it wasn't England, but that outpost of the British Isles known as Scapa Flow. I was not at all happy about this, for it meant my having to catch a ferry to the mainland, this being followed by a long dreary train journey with several changes en route; for my destination was Chatham, and I was not travelling light, for all my belongings – kit bag, hammock, suitcase and attaché case, together with a large pillowcase full of fresh fruit all had to be transported.

Fortunately, before I could be disembarked, *Danae* received orders to sail for Rosyth, and I was thus able to make my first ever trip across the Forth Bridge to Edinburgh and a fast train to London.

In anticipation of my homecoming, my wife had once again set up home; this time in North London, quite close to the place from which I had, some twenty years earlier, set out for the start of my naval career.

Before leaving Edinburgh I had been able to contact her by phone, asking her to meet me at King's Cross Station with a taxi early next morning; this to enable me to unload some of my personal belongings on to her, and so avoid transporting them to Chatham and back home again.

She went one better than this however, for having become friendly with the wife of a hire car proprietor, it was in his car that she arrived, thus giving me the opportunity to make a detour en route to Victoria and the Chatham train, in order to say a quick hello to my daughter, just over five years old when I last saw her, but now one month past her eighth birthday.

Going through the routine at Chatham barracks did not take long and I was back home again the same evening; not for just a quick visit this time, but with thirty-nine days Foreign Service Leave ahead of me.

HMS *Pembroke* 28th April – 1st September 1944

Returning from leave, the barrack joining routine was soon completed, and I was once again a member of the working party, but I lost no time requesting to challenge the Chief Petty Officers' advancement roster, having learned that Petty Officers of less seniority were being advanced to that rating.

Surprise! Surprise! My certificate of advancement was somewhere between Chatham and Bombay, for it had been sent to *Aster*. My date of advancement should have been 15th January, some three and a half months earlier, and I was now rated Chief Petty Officer retrospective to that date.

What largesse! The back pay amounted to about £10, as a Chief Petty Officer I was now in receipt of ten shillings and sixpence per day.

Having had almost four years of war sea service, I expected to be shore based for a little longer than proved to be the case.

Had I remained a petty officer, I would have probably continued with the barrack working party, but there appeared to be an abundance of Chiefs, and apart from these with quiet numbers, there was very little work for them.

It became a routine of keeping out of the way until about 1030 and then spending the remainder of the day in the mess. There was no abundance of C.P.O. coxswains however, so, as far as I was concerned, this state of affairs lasted for only three months, after which I was once more drafted, on this occasion to HMS *Cowdray*, a Hunt Class destroyer.

HMS *Cowdray* 2nd September 1944 – 1st February 1945

I can honestly sq, that *Cowdray*, the last ship aboard which I was to serve, was also the only ship that I was glad to see the back of. To class the ship as a destroyer was itself a misnomer: the main armament of a destroyer was its torpedoes, but this was something with which the Hunt Class were not equipped, and so far as *Cowdray* was concerned, torpedo was almost a. dirty word so gunnery minded were the officers.

At a later date this class of ship became unofficially known as frigates, not quite so far off the mark – guns being the main armament, although they also carried depth charges.

I joined *Cowdray* in Chatham dockyard: my predecessor had gone sick and it was left to me to feel my own way around. It soon became apparent that my position had already been partly usurped; the Gunner's Mate, who had been standing in until my arrival, being unwilling to relinquish these powers and it did not help matters in that the officers continued to consult him on matters of procedure.

This then was the state of affairs when *Cowdray* sailed to continue her duties of escorting Channel convoys, nothing untoward happened until leaving Antwerp shortly after it's liberation, but first the visit to Antwerp itself.

An opportunity to go ashore saw us received with mixed feelings; many grateful for the liberation, but also the odd indifference, as with one innkeeper, asking for trouble in a way, saying he wasn't bothered whether it was the British or the Germans who bought his beer.

Perhaps he would have thought differently if one of the buzz bombs which Belgium was experiencing had had his number on it.

One thing that did become apparent was the bartering value of coffee, and if another trip ashore had been possible, I feel sure that very little coffee would have been left aboard *Cowdray*, but it was not to be, the ship sailing the next day.

Leaving Antwerp, a two-man submarine was attacked and brought to the surface, the crew abandoning, but salvage of the craft was not possible.

The skipper was a typical arrogant Nazi and would say nothing, but the second crewman, an engineer, plied liberally with rum, became quite loquacious (but I was never aware as to whether any worthwhile information was gathered from his interrogation or if it was just a waste of good navy rum.

A boiler cleaning at Grimsby gave the ship's company four days leave apiece: the last night of mine coinciding with a V2 rocket falling on a school some two hundred yards away from my home.

Being a cold night, and I having to leave at 0.00 next morning, instead of going to our respective beds, my wife, daughter and I snuggled up in a Put-U-Up situated in our lounge, a fortunate choice as it turned out, for had it not been so, my daughter would in all probability have been killed, or to say the least, badly maimed or disfigured.

I do not know whether I was awakened by the sound of an explosion or the ceiling falling on my head; the time was 0300.

Things were in a proper shambles – ceilings down, windows broken and doors blown off their hinges. Clearing up would take hours and I could not possibly return to my ship and leave it to my wife.

A phone call to the nearest police station set some kind of machinery in motion, and then, taking stock, I realised how lucky my daughter had been.

Her bed was one mass of arrow-like pieces of glass from the shattered window, the pieces not just laying on the bedclothes, but penetrating into the bedding. The pillow where her head would have been had ten of these arrow-like pieces protruding from it – How could they have missed her head, face and neck had she been sleeping there?

During the clearing up operation, a policeman called to tell me that I had been granted a forty-eight-hour extension of leave, not rejoining my ship at Grimsby, but going instead to HMS *Wildfire*, a shore establishment at Sheerness.

Having cleared up our own debris, my wife and I were able to go and see the extent of the damage where the rocket has actually fallen. The school was completely demolished. How fortunate it was that it fell at three o'clock in the morning, and not three in the afternoon, when it would have been full of children.

I was at *Wildfire* for three days before *Cowdray* sailed into Sheerness, and rejoining my ship it did not take long for me to realise that things were not as they should be, and that I was in fact *de trop*, a state of affairs which I would have to do something about.

What better then, than to emulate my predecessor by going sick.

Reporting to the M.O., I told him that I was being troubled with deafness; perfectly true, for my old trouble had returned, although it had not become so apparent as it had been aboard *Harvester* some four years earlier.

The result exceeded my expectations, being told by the captain that I was being discharged to *Pembroke* on medical grounds and, without relief.

I did of course, query this last, only to be told that as the Chief Bosun's Mate – a petty officer – had got his chief's rate through, *Cowdray's* complement was one in excess of this rating. Perfectly true of course, for, the complement was only one chief and he should have been a Chief Torpedo Coxswain for me.

What should have happened was that two reliefs should have been applied for, a petty officer for the Chief Bosun's Mate, and a Chief Torpedo Coxswain for me.

However, I was discharged without relief, which made it apparent that if I was *de trop,* another coxswain would be also.

I never did meet up with my predecessor, the other coxswain who had gone sick. I would have liked to, even if only to find out whether he had also felt unwanted.

So, *Cowdray* sailed without a coxswain: I don't know how long this state of affairs continued, but I do know that a quarterly state of complement had to be produced and that it was the coxswain's job to produce it.

Chapter 25

Pembroke to Civvy Street

HMS *Pembroke* 2nd February 1945 – 31st August 1947

Joining barracks for what was to be my last time, a notation to the effect that I had been discharged from my ship medically unfit, quickly brought about a thorough medical check; the outcome being that I was placed in the category *Shore and Harbour Service Only*.

This meant that there would be no more sea-going for me: Had it been during time of peace I would in all probability have been discharged from the service as physically unfit, for I still had two and a half years to complete before I was due for my pension.

As it was, I now had to settle down to being a *Barrack Stanchion,* this being the term applied to men who had been a long time in barracks, the inference being that if they left, the establishment would fall down.

There was still an abundance of chief petty not Coxswains, but with my medical category, my non-substantive rating was of no significance. With the abundance already mentioned, I suppose that I was fortunate to fall in for a quiet number – this being Chief in Charge of the Main Gate.

When I tell you that the job was worked in seven watches, you may realise how quiet a number it was, for it meant that two of us worked a twenty-four hour stint watch and watch, whilst the other five were free to go on leave; and, then there were the *perks*.

The job was on Lodging and Provision Allowance, which meant that no victualling or accommodation was provided, a. cash allowance being paid instead.

For services rendered, the Mess President turned a blind eye to the duty off. Watch chief sleeping in the mess and also partaking of breakfast.

The services rendered included those of allowing mess officials a free gangway at all times, and most important, keeping the mess informed whenever there were any Customs Officers in attendance at the main gate.

Such information would then be conveyed to the mess members, by the displaying, in the vestibule, of a large cartoon depicting a bird of prey swooping down onto his quarry.

Libertymen seeing this, and perhaps meaning to take out a little contraband, would then deem it wiser to wait until another day.

Just that one telephone call, not another word spoken, but every member of the Chief and Petty Officers Messes would know that there were Customs Officers about and there would be a possibility of a search.

With other perks it was a case of – *If you can't beat then, join them* – it being an understood thing that the duty petty officer cooks would provide meals and a few rabbits in return for their being allowed a free gangway.

Corruption? Yes! But as I have said earlier, the-Long Service Good Conduct Medal was awarded for fifteen years with undetected crime, and few who wore it could honestly say that they had never transgressed.

Why did I go along with it all? Remember the job was in seven watches and if I had been anti it would have meant battling against odds of six to one, and these were odds that I was not prepared to accept.

Besides, it was not rabbiting on a large scale for pecuniary gain; just a few perks to make life a little easier, the lodging and provision allowance helping to pay the rail fares home when they couldn't be fiddled'

A little dishonest – but if the stories were true – no more so than the practice of men in industry: men earning over £14 per week – a colossal wage at the time – but using part of their working day for making souvenirs.

Very little more space needs be given about this aspect of my life in the Royal Navy, although it might be of interest to mention a few of the visitors that from time to time brought their troubles to the Main Gate.

A girl seeking the father of her embryo child, a deserted wife, and another who did not know that she had been deserted until, calling at the barrack gates to see him, she had been told that he was on leave, and had been for a week.

Some instances pathetic, but others being on the humorous side, such as a homosexual looking for his friend – or could that too be pathetic? But one could hardly describe thus, the visit of a debt collector; hoping to dun a 'Wardroom Officer.

I was spending much more time at home than I was in barracks, and because of the travel involved, had perfected a foolproof fiddle which needed some outlay, but not nearly as much as the full fare would have done.

So life went on for two years and four months, the war had been over for two years and I had seen many demobbed men passing through the gate – But it was now to be my turn – for I was relieved from my duties in order to carry out the demobilisation routine.

I was not to get any further than the Medical Officer however. A cursory examination ended by him pronouncing me A1.

"No Sir!" I said. This rather took him aback.

"What do you mean No?"

"Well Sir", I continued; "For the past two years and four months, because of a defective hearing; I have been classified as shore and harbour duties only." – "How then can I be A1?"

Then the buck passing started – "Why isn't there anything about this on his papers?" he asked the Sick Berth Attendant. It didn't matter that the defective hearing had not been discovered during his inspection. In his opinion someone else was to blame.

The outcome was that I had to appear before a survey board, and another six weeks were to elapse before I was finally discharged as being Physically Unfit for Further Naval Service.

During these six weeks I was classified as a Chief Petty Officer Pensioner, drawing both pay and pension; but even so, I could hardly be classed a Baron; for the pension amounted to just twenty-seven shillings per week.

Before finally leaving Chatham Barracks I was to be involved in one last fiddle.

Several items had to be returned and a clearance chit stamped by the departments concerned before one was free to proceed through the gates a free man. For example, a gas mask had to be returned to the gas school, a visit had to be made to the loan clothing department in order to get a clearance from them, and – the one that concerned me – certain articles of uniform clothing had to be returned to the clothing store; these including two of my three blue serge uniform suits.

As it happened, I had only got two, this state of affairs having existed since some months earlier when my suitcase had been stolen from the chief petty officers' locker room.

In it had been a cloth suit, a serge suit and half a dozen white shirts, together with some photographs, and notes from various courses which I had been on.

After an investigation, I was given compensation, but only a limited amount. I was allowed the price of a new suitcase, three only white shirts, this being the regular uniform requirement – having lost an extra three was just my hard luck – and the clothing store price of two ready made blue serge suits.

The fact that I had lost a much more expensive No.1 cloth suit did cut any ice, for No. l dress had become optional during the war and had not yet been re-introduced as a compulsory item of kit. Because of this, and also because I had such a short term to serve, I had been making do with just two suits, and now came my visit to the clothing store, where a Leading Supply Assistant was waiting to receive me.

"Two hammocks Chief"

"Yes." I replied, handing them over. Several other items followed, all of which I was able to produce – then he asked,

"Two serge suits?"

"I only have one."

"Should hand in two Chief."

"Sorry Chief; you'll have to be charged for one." But before I could reply he continued –

"Perhaps I could forget it."

This made me realise that I was being subjected to a mild form of blackmail" so I went along with him.

"Will ten shillings do?" I asked offering him the money.

"Thanks Chief," he said; pocketing the note, and having received my stamped clearance chit – now completed – – there was nothing more for me to do but report to the pay and leave offices, where I received my pay and a liberty ticket enabling me to proceed on fourteen days demobilisation leave. I was also given a railway warrant to Portsmouth, where, on arrival, I was to be fitted out with civilian clothing before handing in my one remaining blue serge suit.

Only after this had been done could I call myself a free man. My discharge papers and balance of pay were sent on to me in due course, together with a War Service Gratuity of £99, this having been deposited for me in a newly opened Post Office Savings Bank account.

Due to the fact that I had been discharged as *Physically Unfit* my Long Service Pension was awarded to me as a Disability Pension, this meaning, that as well as becoming tax free, it was subject to an immediate increase of 20%, an age increase which was not normally payable until the pensioner had reached the age of sixty.

Epilogue

ASKING MYSELF whether under similar circumstances I would do the same again, the answer, with some reservations, must be yes.

Definitely the life for a single man. The *esprit de corps* which abounds on the lower deck could never be matched in civilian life, and in saying this I am speaking with experience of both ways of life, for I have now retired from my civilian occupation, having been longer out of the Royal Navy than I was in it.

I give but two instances to prove my point in this respect. The first concerns me when employed as Chief Petty Officer in charge of the Main Barrack gate. Due to some misunderstanding on my part, it was impossible for me to get back to Chatham in time to take over my watch, so I asked a neighbour if I could use his phone in order to ring the gate and explain what had happened, saying that I would be about an hour late.

Of course, I received the response that I expected; being told by my opposite number – "Not to worry, I'll carry on until you get here."

My neighbour had heard my end of the conversation, and having pieced things together, he was amazed. "Do you mean to say that he is going to carry on until you get there," he asked.

"Of course." I replied.

"Without reporting it."

"Yes"

"Then," said my neighbour, "You'll have a lot to learn when you get into Civvy Street, for if anything like that happened, you'll be shopped in no time at all." This brings me to the other example.

A shift worker on the boilers at a factory where I was employed as a Security Officer, had, whilst his mate was at tea break, unfortunately nodded off. When the mate returned;' seeing him: thus, instead of waking him he went and fetched the shift foreman, with the result that the hapless boiler man was sacked. Not much *esprit de corps* there, and in an emergency, who would you rather have behind you; the boilerman's mate, or my C.P.O. colleague?

It was after my marriage that things became a bit of a struggle; more so because, whenever the opportunity offered, I tried to have my wife living nearby: at my own expense of course; for married quarters for the navy in those days were unheard of.

Another thing – although it did not affect me personally – was that if a man decided to get married before he had reached the age of twenty five, he would not be entitled to the seven shillings per week separation allowance; this state of affairs continuing until the outbreak of war, something then having to be done for the younger men being called up and being already married.

Under different circumstances, meaning of course, the navy as it is today; the answer would be yes, every time.

I engaged under the 1919 rates of pay, and that was the rate paid during the whole period of my service, the only increments arising from length of service and advancement

My pension was also at the 1919 rate, and although this has been reviewed on several occasions, it does not come up to the amount paid to men who are retiring now: men who have probably never heard a single shot fired in anger.

Now, with their married quarters, a scale of pay which compares favourably with that of industry, *and* much shorter foreign commissions, life must have very few hardships for the men serving in the Royal Navy of today.

But for all that; it still pleases me to think that the navy in which I served was a navy that really did rule the waves, and also one in which the men in uniform far outnumbered the civil servants needed to run it; and in all honesty, it is my belief that neither of these is true of the present day navy.

Postscript

WHEN LEONARD and Winifred Harris celebrated their silver wedding on 8th September 1959, Len made reference to the fact that during their married life they had been apart for a total of twelve years because of his naval career. He had thought about leaving the Navy in the 1930s but decided to sign on again as there was little prospect of work in Civvy Street because of the then poor economic situation in Britain.

This turned out to be the best decision, as he would have been recalled to active service in 1939 due to his skills as coxswain. Thus he managed to complete twenty-four years of service and received a naval pension for the rest of his long life. It was made tax free because of his disability (gun deafness). So he was a naval pensioner for fifty-two years, more than twice the length of his service, although the pension was far insufficient to live on alone.

He wrote this book in the early 1970s shortly after retiring from Tesco. It was written from memory, without notes and only his service record for reference; clearly, he had good recall.

Many years later in 1988 one of his grandchildren Katy asked her Nanna what it was like being a sailor's wife during World War II as she was doing a history project for school. Winifred had until then spoken little about this period and she had no love for the Navy as it had taken her husband away from her for such long periods. The following letter from her adds enormously to Len's account of the war years.

At the outbreak of World War II

26-year-old housewife, 3-year-old daughter living in Gillingham Kent. Husband a Petty Officer in Chatham Barracks employed in training New Entries. Home three nights out of four.

After Neville Chamberlain's announcement, all leave was stopped, barracks personnel employed on mobilisation duties.

After four days, the leave restriction was lifted. Gillingham school children evacuated. Learning to cope with rationing.

30th September husband sent to Portsmouth on a ten-week course. Decided Gillingham was not the place to be. Gave up tenancy, stored furniture, went to live with mother in Cheshunt.

Period December 1939 – April 1940

Husband returned to Chatham Barracks. My daughter and I returned to Gillingham, took lodgings on a temporary basis. Period of the so-called phoney war, everything quiet. Some evacuees returned home, decided to set up home again, rented another house (fairly easy in those days) and moved back to be a family again. Took in lodgers, another naval couple.

Then husband drafted to commission a new destroyer being built at Barrow in Furness. Myself and daughter went to Gomshall near Guildford to help out at sister-in-law's difficult childbirth, earlier than expected (June 1940).

6th June husband arrives at sister-in-law's door at half past midnight by means of the last train to Guildford and a helpful taxi driver, details as follows. Ship was carrying out commissioning trials off Portland when she was despatched with all speed to assist in the evacuation of British troops from Dunkirk.

Operation completed, all personnel taking part were given 36 hours leave, the first six of which was spent in searching me out.

Husband returned to ship and later I returned to Gillingham to find my lodgers gone. Meanwhile husband's ship based at Liverpool – escorts for Atlantic convoys. Decided to join him at Liverpool, west coast being free of air raids. Stored furniture once again, gave up tenancy and departed for Liverpool and lodgings. Several other Naval wives followed suit, seeing husbands between convoys.

Air raids spread to the west coast, Liverpool bearing the brunt.

After about nine months husband drafted back to Chatham Barracks. The three of us went around saying our goodbyes during an air raid, daughter lost her handbag, no time to go back and look for it but saw a bomb drop where we would have been had we gone back. Returned to Gillingham, a shipmate still in Liverpool with his wife and son having loaned us his unoccupied house. Arranged for daughter to start school, an earlier arrangement made in Liverpool was of course cancelled.

Husband's stay in barracks only lasted three months, drafted to Belfast to pick up a ship for Freetown Sierra Leone. He was away for two years and nine months, although this was not known at the time. Daughter's school start in Gillingham had to be cancelled although she did eventually start in Cheshunt.

I worked in a factory making gun parts, but eventually set up home again in Islington to await my husband's return, at same time getting a job as a Post Office counter clerk.

Ships on which Leonard Harris served or was closely associated

1. Specifications

Should any readers be interested in technical details of the ships I served aboard or operated with, I give them here in chronological order of my being associated with them.

HMS *Tring*. One of fifty-three coal-burning minesweepers which were built under an emergency war programme between June 1917 and August 1919. Mean draught about 8 ft. Speed 16 knots. Armament one 4-inch bow gun. Complement 75. *Tring* was built by Simons of Renfrew.

HMS *Viscount*. One of twenty-nine 'V' class destroyers which were built under an emergency war programme. Displacement 1325 tons. Length overall 312 feet. Maximum draught 12 feet. Speed 35 knots. Six 21-inch torpedo tubes in two triple mountings. Four 4-inch guns, one 3-inch A.A. gun. Speed 35 knots. Complement 120.
Viscount was laid down in December 1916 at Thorneycroft's – Woolston. Launched December 1917 and completed March 1918.

HMS *Marlborough*. One of four battleships of this class. Laid down in 1912 and completed in 1914. Displacement 25,000 tons. Length overall 623 feet. Beam 90 feet. Mean draught 33 feet. Complement 1200 Speed 22 knots. Armament: ten 13.5-inch guns in five twin turrets – twelve 6-inch guns (six port battery and six starboard battery. (this class was the first to have 6-inch guns as secondary armament; previously only 4-inch had been used. – Two 4-inch anti-aircraft guns, four 3-pounders. 2 submerged 21-inch torpedo tubes. *Marlborough* was built at Devonport Naval Dockyard. Laid down in January 1912 and completed in June 1914.

HMS *Tetrarch* One of thirty-five Admiralty 'R' class destroyers laid down between August 1915 and July 1916. Displacement 1065 tons, length overall 275 feet. Maximum draught 12 feet. Speed 36 knots. Complement 98. Armament four 18-inch torpedo tubes in pairs, three 4-inch guns and one 2-pounder pom-pom. *Tetrarch* was built by Harland and Woolf – Govan was launched in April 1917 and completed in June 1917.

HMS *Furious*. Originally laid down by Armstrong Whitworth. in June 1915 as a heavy cruiser under the emergency war programme but was converted while building to an aircraft carrier. First with hangers for seaplanes, and later with a flush flight deck for fly on – fly off aircraft. Displacement 20,000 tons length overall 786 feet, Beam 90 feet, max draught 25 feet. Armament after final alterations ten 5.5-inch gun, six 4-inch A.A. guns and four 3-pounder guns. Speed 31 knots Complement 890.

HMS *Argus*. Laid down in 1914 by Beardmore, as the *S. S. Conte Rosso*. All work ceased at the outbreak of World War I. Was purchased in 1916 for conversion into Aircraft Carrier and renamed *Argus*. Displacement 14,450 tons, length overall 565 feet, beam 68 feet, draught 21 feet. Speed 20 knots. Armament two 4-inch guns, four 4-inch A.A. guns, four 3-pounders, Complement 400.

HMS *Ramillies* Five of these class 'R' battleships were built, being laid down between November 1913 .and January 1914. All were completed by the end of 1916 with the exception of *Ramillies*, who, because of an injury sustained at her launching, was not completed until Sept 1917. Length overall 620 feet, beam including bulge protection 102 feet, draught 29 feet, speed 22 knots. Complement 1195 displacement 29,350 tons. *Ramillies* was laid down by Beardmores of Dalmuir but was towed to Liverpool for completion by Cammell Lairds.

Armament eight 15-inch in four twin turrets, fourteen 6-inch guns (seven port battery, seven starboard battery), two 4-inch A.A. guns, four 3-pounders, 4 submerged 21-inch torpedo tubes.

HMS *Curlew* one of five cruisers ordered in 1916 under the emergency war programme, Displacement 4,190 tons, length overall 450 feet, beam 43 feet, draught 16 feet, complement 440. Armament five 6-inch guns, two 3-inch A.A. guns, two 2-pounder pom-pom, four 3-pounder guns, 8 above-water torpedo tubes in four double mountings, two to starboard and two to port. Speed 29 knots.

Curlew was laid down by Vickers at Barrow in Furness in August 1916 and completed in December 1917.

HMS *Cyclops*. Originally *S.S. Indrabarah* which was built in 1905 by Sir James Lang & Co at Sunderland. Displacement 11,300 tons, length 460 feet, beam 55 feet draught 21 feet, speed 13 knots, complement 314. Armament two 4-inch bow guns.

HMS *Daring*: One of eight 'D' class destroyers which were laid down in 1931 and completed in 1932/3. Displacement 1,375 tons. Length 322 feet Beam 33 feet Draught 8½. Speed 35 knots. Armament four 4.7-inch guns eight 21-inch torpedo tubes in two quadruple mountings, one 3-inch A.A. gun. Complement 145.

Daring was built by Thorneycroft and completed in November 1932.

HMS *Skipjack*. One of seventeen laid down between 1933 and 1937 to replace the coal burning minesweepers of World War I. Displacement 815 tons. Length overall 230 feet. Beam 33 feet. Draught 7½ feet. Speed 16½ knots. Armament one 4-inch bow gun and two 4-inch A.A. guns. Built by Clydebank Shipbuilders in 1934.

HMS *Emerald*. Was probably obsolete before the first turn of her screws, laid down in September 1918 as one of three ordered under the War emergency plan, but not completed until over seven years later in December 1925, by which time five of the more modern county class had been in process of building for over a year. Displacement 7,600 tons, length overall 570 feet, beam 54 feet, draught 17 feet. Armament six 6-inch guns, three 4-inch A.A. guns, four 3-pounder guns, two 2-pounder pom-poms and twelve 21-inch torpedo tubes in 4 triple mountings two to starboard and two to port. Complement 570 speed 32 knots.

Enterprise, a sister ship was also completed, taking about six months longer than did *Emerald*, but a third ship of the class, *Euphrates* was cancelled before any work could commence. Although *Emerald* was laid down by Armstrong Whitworth, she was eventually towed to Chatham Naval Dockyard for completion.

HMS *Eskimo*. Sixteen Tribal class destroyers were laid down in 1938. Displacement 1,870 tons Length 335 feet Beam 36½ feet. Draught 9 feet. Armament eight 4.7-inch guns (four twin high angle mountings), two oerlikons, four 21-inch torpedo tubes in one mounting. Speed 36 knots Complement 190. *Eskimo* was built by Vickers Armstrong and completed in December 1938.

HMS *Harvester*. One of six destroyers being built for the Brazilian Navy at the outbreak of World War II. Originally named *Japura*, this has changed to *Handy*, but in order to avoid confusion with *Hardy* – an 'H' class destroyer already in commission the name was changed for a second time to *Harvester*. Displacement 14,000 tons. Length 323 feet Beam 33 feet, draught 8½ feet. Speed 35 knots. Complement 192. Armaments four 21-inch torpedo tubes, four 4.7-inch guns, one 3-inch A.A. gun, two Oerlikons.

Harvester was built by Vickers Armstrong at Barrow in Furness and completed in April 1940.

HMS *Aster*. Fifty-six of these Flower class corvettes were built under the 1939 supplementary estimates programme, but later programmes almost trebled this figure. Displacement 925 tons, Length overall 205 feet. Beam 33 feet. Draught 14½ feet. Speed 18 knots. Armaments one 4-inch bow gun, one 2-pounder pom-pom, and four depth charge throwers. Complement 85.

HMS *Danae* Laid down by Armstrong Whitworth in December 1916, completed July 1918. Displacement 4,650 tons, Speed 29 knots, length overall 472 feet, beam 46 feet, draught 16½ feet. Armaments six 6-inch, three 4-inch HA, four 3-PDR, two 2-PDR Pom-poms. Torpedoes, twelve above in 21-inch tubes, in 4 triple mountings. Complement 462.

HMS *Cowdray*. With slight variations, about sixty Hunt Class destroyers were built between 1940 and 1942, but only a few of the later type were fitted with torpedo tubes. Cowdray was built in 1941 by Scotts of Greenock. Displacement 1050 tons 280 feet overall 31ft feet beam 7ft feet draught. Complement 146 Speed 27 knots Armament six four-inch A.A (three twin mountings) one 2-pounder pom-pom.

2. Their actions and final berth

HMS *Viscount*	Sunk two U boats in the North Atlantic U-661 and U-201
Sold for scrap in March 1945, eventually broken in 1947.
HMS *Tring*	Sold in 1927
HMS *Marlborough*	Fought in the Battle of Jutland in 1916. Fired 162 13.5in rounds. Hit by torpedo, 2 killed and 2 wounded and struggled to port under tow. Rejoined Grand Fleet after repairs. *Marlborough* evacuated surviving members of the Russian royal family, from the Crimea during the Russian Civil War. Decommissioned in 1932 and sold for scrap
HMS *Tetrarch*	Sold for scrapping in July 1934.
HMS *Ramillies*	Launched in 1916. *Ramillies* joined the 1st Battle Squadron of the Grand Fleet in May, 1917. In the disturbances between Turkey and Britain in 1920 *Ramillies* fired from her position in the Sea of Marmora at Turkish shore targets. In 1924, *Ramillies* joined the 2nd Battle Squadron of the British Atlantic Fleet. By 1926 she was with the Mediterranean Fleet.
During WW II took part in the bombardment of Bardia, August 1940 and the Battle of Cape Teudada. In May 1942 in the bombardment of Diego Saurez (Madagascar) she was torpedoed by Japanese midget submarine on the 30th May 1942. After

repairs she took part in the bombardment of German positions during D-Day as well as bombardment of Southern France She was scrapped at Cairn Ryan in April 1948.

HMS *Furious* — Originally a battle cruiser, *Furious* was fully reconstructed as an aircraft carrier in 1917. After this she led the Tondern raid in July 1918, sending her seven Sopwith Camel planes to bomb the Zeppelin sheds. Further reconstruction between 1922 and 1925 at Devonport Dockyard. In 1939 *Furious* was completely re-armed with twelve 4-inch QF guns in twin mountings and three 8-barrelled pompoms with a fourth added in 1941 and before the end of world war two a further fifteen 20mm Oerlikons were added. She survived the war with no major damage, serving in the home fleet 1939 to 1944 and the reserve 1944-45, but her condition deteriorated near the end of the war and by September 1944 she was taken out of service and finally scrapped in December 1946 at Inverkeithing.

HMS *Argus* — In the first few years of the Second World War, *Argus* saw service ferrying aircraft to Gibraltar and Malta to augment the defending aircraft during siege of Malta, and for Takoradi for onward staged flights to Egypt, 1941-1942. In June 1942 helped provide top cover for essential supply convoy heading for Malta. Upon entering the Mediterranean, the convoy came under almost constant attack from the Germans and Italians. The Sea Hurricanes and Fulmars from *Argus* did an outstanding job of defending the convoy.

Her operational duties included notably an Arctic convoy (early 1943) and involvement in the North African landings in November 1942. From mid-1943 she was again used only for training in home waters.

After being paid off in December 1944, she served as an accommodation ship 1945 and eventually sold on 5 December 1946. She was scrapped in 1947.

HMS *Curlew*	*Curlew* was used as a prototype for conversion to anti-aircraft cruisers. *Curlew* served in the home fleet 1939 – 1940. *Curlew* was sunk due to bombing from German aircraft near Ofot fjord Norway, 26th May 1940.
HMS *Cyclops*	*Cyclops* served during WWI and WW2, Between the war *Cyclops* served as a Submarine depot ship in the Mediterranean, and returned to Home Waters late in 1939, where she spent the war years until being scrapped at Newport July 1947.
HMS *Daring*	*Daring* was torpedoed by German U-Boat U23. 40 Miles east of Duncansby (North Scotland) on February 18th, 1940. The captain was killed, along with 156 crew. Only 5 others survived.

HMS *Skipjack* 1st June 1940 *Skipjack* was subjected to intensive bombing by a force of German bombers off La Panne (Belgium) and was sunk. *Skipjack* was assisting in the evacuation of British troops from Dunkirk. On board *HMS Skipjack* were between 250 and 300 soldiers just rescued from the beach. Survivors in the water were attacked by enemy aircraft. The majority of the troops were trapped in the hull. Nineteen crew and 275 troops were killed.

HMS *Emerald* For much of her time in service her top speed of 33 knots made her, along with her sister, *Enterprise*, the fastest ship in the Royal Navy.

When war began on 3rd September 1939 *Emerald* was directed to Scapa Flow. and ordered onto the "Northern Patrol", between the Faroe Islands and Iceland

In October 1939 *Emerald* sailed for Halifax, Nova Scotia with five tons of gold bullion from the Bank of England, bound for the United States to pay for war materials. Upon arrival Emerald was assigned to North Atlantic convoy escort duty. Since the *Emerald* had been designed and equipped for work in gentler climates this was very uncomfortable as well as dangerous duty. The Canadian Red Cross gave a large supply of warm clothes for the crew.

Later, *Emerald*, with other destroyers and cruisers acted as a screen to the British battleship *HMS Revenge* during a bombardment of Cherbourg.

Sold to be broken up for scrap at Troon on 23 July 1948.

HMS *Eskimo*   The winter of 1939/40 consisted of patrols and convoy duty. After a refit was completed in March 1940, *Eskimo* was ready to participate in the impending operations in Norwegian waters. During the Second Battle of Narvik, Eskimo had her bows blown off by a torpedo. She limped back to Norway for temporary repairs.

Surviving aerial bomb attacks, she was finally made ready for sea in May 1940. During the winter or 1940/41, the Flotilla was mainly engaged in the escort of the big ships of the Home Fleet. Later in the war *Eskimo* was damaged twice by fires, one accidental and one by dive-bombers.

Towards the end of the war she was sent to far eastern waters and after a refit returned to Europe.

Eskimo ended her days as an accommodation and headquarters ship for minesweepers, wreck-disposal vessels; salvage craft which were clearing the Thames and Medway estuaries. She was then laid up, first at Sheerness, then at Harwich and finally used as a target in the Gareloch. On 27th June 1949, *Eskimo* was sold for scrapping at Troon.

HMS *Harvester*	On 11th Mar, 1943, *Harvester*, escorting convoy HX-228, picked up 51 survivors from the William C. Gorgas, which had been sunk by U-757 The destroyer then returned to the convoy and sighted U-444. The U-boat dived but was forced to the surface by the following depth-charge attack and rammed by the destroyer at full speed. The destroyer was locked into the U-boat with a propeller shaft and both ships were unable to manoeuvre for a while. U-444 was able to creep away but was shortly afterwards sighted by the Free French corvette *Aconit*, unable to dive, the U-boat was rammed for the second time and sunk.
	Badly damaged, *Harvester* managed to get one engine running and tried to catch up the convoy, but around noon she broke down again. Helpless, she was hit by one torpedo from U-432 and a few minutes later by a second and sank almost immediately. The captain, 7 officers, 136 ratings and 39 survivors were lost. *Aconit* returned to the scene and with depth-charges, gunfire and ramming sank U-432. During the day, the French corvette picked up four survivors from U-444, 20 survivors from U-432 and 60 survivors from *Harvester*, including 12 survivors from the *William C*.
HMS *Zinnia*	Corvette lost on 23rd August 1941 while escorting convoy was torpedoed and sunk with all hands by the German submarine U-564 west of Portugal.

SHIPS ON WHICH LEONARD HARRIS SERVED OR WAS CLOSELY ASSOCIATED

HMS *Hollyhock* Corvette bombed and sunk by Japanese naval aircraft on 9th April 1942, east of Ceylon, along with the aircraft carrier *HMS Hermes*, Australian destroyer *Vampire* and two tankers.

HMS *Aster* Extract from biography of Lt. Cdr E. Hewitt RNR. Captain of corvette *Aster* from commissioning, through to the period that Leonard Harris was serving on this vessel.

In May 1941 Aster sailed for Freetown. In November 1941 Hewitt was instructed to take five ships to Cape Town for escort work there, but the situation changed with Japan's entry into the war (7th December 1941). On 1st January 1942 he was promoted to commander.

While in Cape Town C-in-C South Atlantic ordered Hewitt with one other escort to go out and search for submarines, which had been reported in the area. Hewitt said that one of the ships had her gun out of action and the other's ASDIC was broken down. However he was told that the *Queen Mary* was passing on a voyage from Suez to New York, and it was therefore imperative that they did their utmost to protect her. Neither ship expected to survive, but happily they did. In March 1942 he was ordered to take his escort group to the Far East. However with the fall of Singapore (15th February 1942) the escort group was diverted to Colombo, where they arrived just after the Easter Sunday (26th March 1942) raid was over.

While in Colombo Hewitt was sent to sea on an operation. The corvette *Hollyhock* was to remain in port, so Hewitt had some of her AA armament transferred to the *Aster*. In the middle of one night on the patrol the lookout reported a ship ahead. She was challenged. It was the cruiser *Cornwall* in company with sister ship *Dorsetshire*. On the afternoon 5th April 1942 the two cruisers were attacked and sunk by 53 Japanese dive bombers commanded by Lt. Cdr. Egusa. Luck was with Hewitt, and he returned safely to Colombo. Incredibly he must have steamed close to the Japanese fleet without him seeing them or them seeing him. Meanwhile *Hollyhock* had been sent to escort the aircraft carrier *Hermes*. In an attack by eighty Japanese dive bombers with fighter escort east of Ceylon on 9th April 1942, *Hermes* and *Hollyhock* were sunk.

HMS *Aster* survived WW2 and was scrapped 1948.

HMS Hollyhock

On 8th April 1942, the *Hollyhock* was ordered to leave Trincomalee, along with the minelayer HMS *Tiviot Bank*, R.F.A Pearl Leaf, the tanker British Sergeant and *R.F.A. Athelstane*. Nine Japanese aircraft from Admiral Nagumo's carrier fleet attacked *Hollyhock* and *Athelstane*. *Hollyhock* sunk within 5 minutes, with bombs going straight down her funnel. 53 lives were lost, the Captain, 2 officers and 50 ratings. Only 16 survived the attack, five of the 9 aircraft then turned their attentions to the *Athelstane*; she was also sunk, but all hands were saved.

HMS Danae Served in China during 1939-41, followed by the Eastern fleet from 1942-44 and ending with the home fleet from 1944-45
   Broken up 1948.

HMS Cowdray Bombed off Algiers in November 1942, repaired and recommissioned. HMS Cowdray was allocated to the Royal Hellenic Navy as *Admiral Hastings* from March 1944 until June 1944. Then returned to UK.
   Broken up at Gateshead 3rd September 1959.

L.A. Harris Medals

Palestine 1936-1939
Burma Star
Atlantic Star
1939-1945 Star
1939-1945 Medal
Long Service & good conduct

Shotley Barracks – harbour view.

Inside Shotley Barracks.

HMS Ganges Shotley main gate.

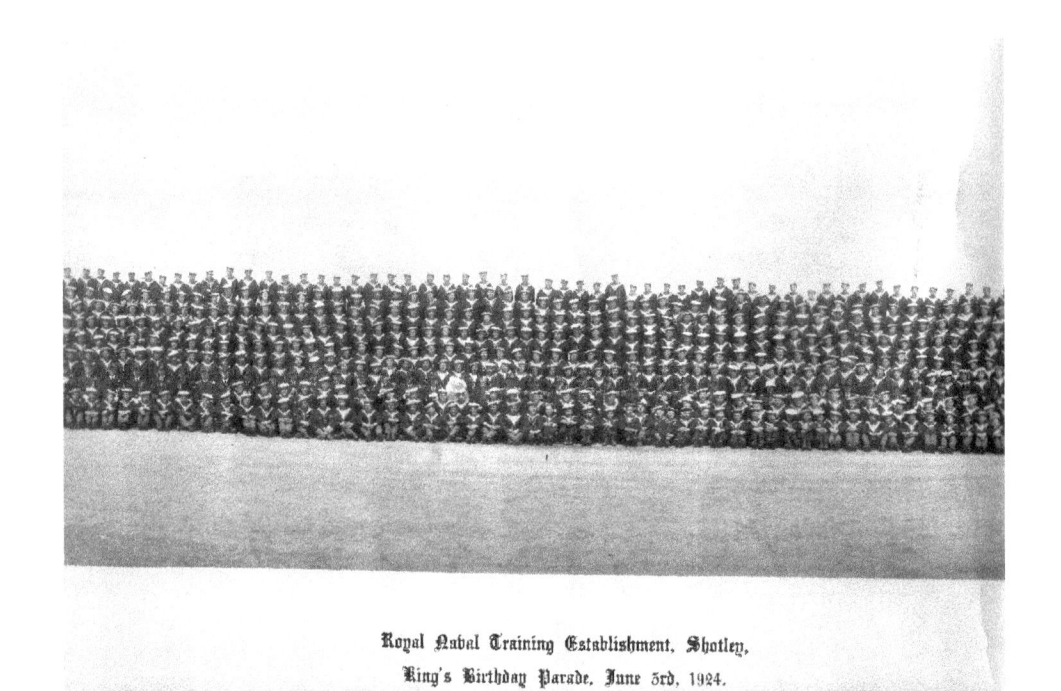

Royal Naval Training Establishment Shotley, 1924.

*Right: HMS Ganges Mast, Shotley Barracks 1924.
Leonard is on the upper cross spar leaning against the mast.*

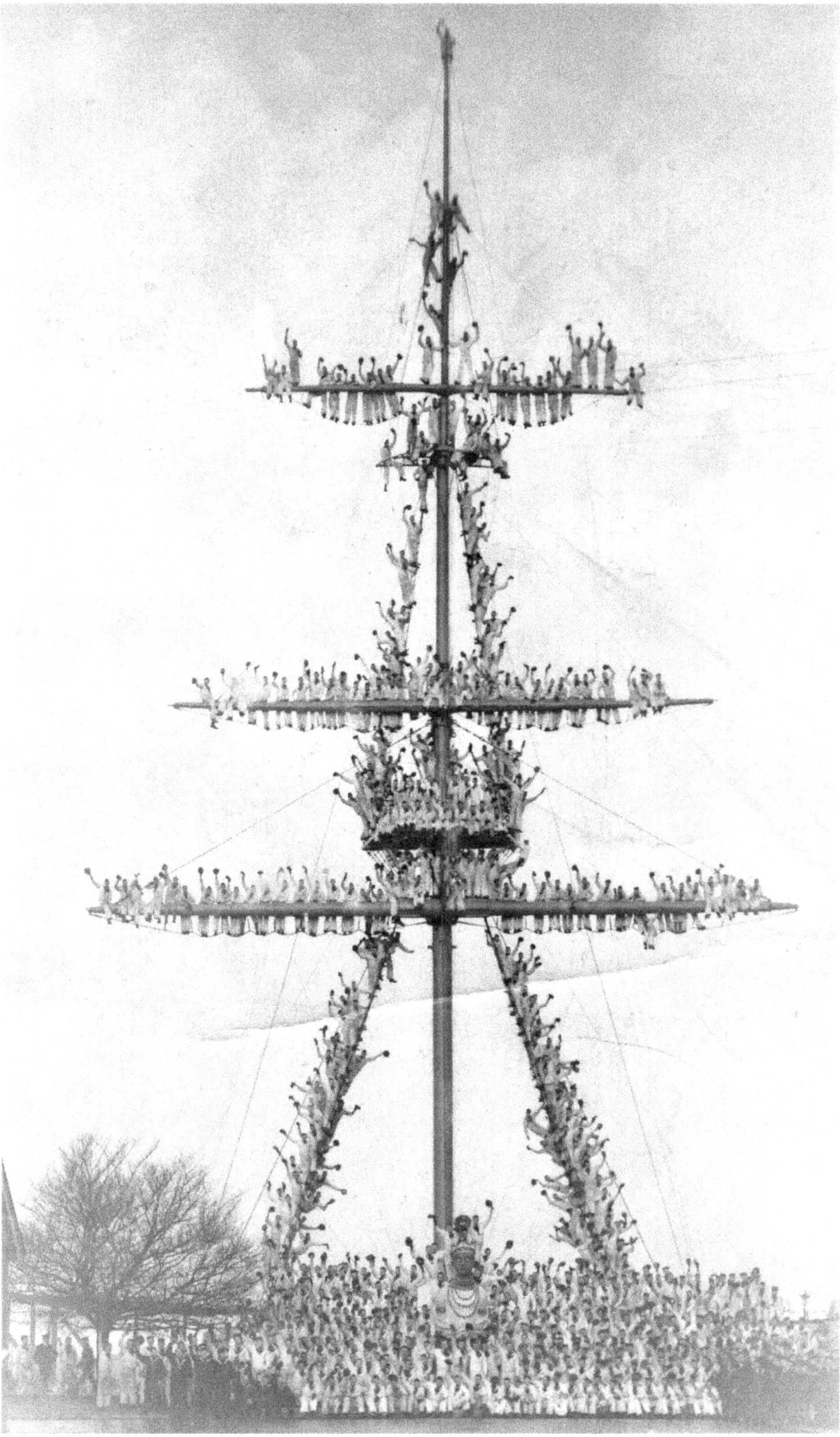

Leonard wearing HMS Ganges Cap 1924.

Ordinary Seaman 1925.

Black & White Bar Valetta, Malta 1925.

Holy stoning the deck of HMS Ramillies. Len second on left, 1928.

Canteen.

Sitting in the Whaler boat.

Ship's football team. Len is standing at the back, fourth from right.

As Leading Seaman in tropical uniform.

In the tropics.

Ship's painting duties.

Marriage as Leading Seaman to Winifred, 8 September 1934.

Captain's permission to grow beards!

Regatta.

Relaxing on shore, Len is standing on the right.

Marines and Sailors.

On board HMS Aster in the Indian Ocean.

Getting some shade!

Pat, Len and Win, 1938.

Petty Officer 1942.

Ingram Content Group UK Ltd.
Milton Keynes UK
UKHW021832300323
419432UK00007B/423